John Wesley Hardin

The Letters of

John Wesley Hardin

Courtesy
Special Collections
Albert B. Alkek Library
Southwest Texas State University
San Marcos, Texas

Transcribed and compiled by
Roy & Jo Ann Stamps

EAKIN PRESS Fort Worth, Texas

Published By Eakin Press
An Imprint of Wild Horse Media Group
P.O. Box 331779
Fort Worth, Texas 76163
1-817-344-7036
www.EakinPress.com

1 2 3 4 5 6 7 8 9
ISBN-10: 1571686223
ISBN-13: 978-1571686220

On the cover: Controversial photo of the notorious John Wesley Hardin. Stamps collection.

Note: Many of the words found in these letters are not found in the *Webster's American College Dictionary*, but can be found in the *Webster's New International Dictionary of the English Language*, The Merriam Series 1930

Library of Congress Cataloging-in-Publication Data

Hardin, John Wesley, 1853-1895.
[Correspondence. Selections]
The letters of John Wesley Hardin / [edited] by Roy Stamps and Jo Ann Stamps.
p. cm.
Includes bibliographical references and index.
ISBN 1-57168-622-3
1. Hardin, John Wesley, 1853-1895—Correspondence. 2. Outlaws—Texas—Correspondence. 3. Frontier and pioneer life—Texas—Sources. 4. Texas—History—1846-1950—Sources. I. Stamps, Roy. II. Stamps, Jo Ann. III. Title.
F391.H38A4 1999
976.4'061'092--dc21 99-
12738

CIP

To the descendants
of the Texans who suffered
during Reconstruction,
the tragic era
after the Civil War,
we dedicate this book.

Contents

These are the letters of John Wesley Hardin.
Nothing has been changed in transcribing them.
They are presented as they were written
more than one hundred years ago.
For authenticity, the misspelled words,
incorrect grammar, and so forth,
have not been changed.

Authors' Note

We live in Southern California and have done so most of our lives. Being avid readers, we came across a book on the Old West and while reading it discovered that Roy's grandfather was living in Ada, Oklahoma, when hired killer Jim Miller and his three cohorts were lynched. This fact bore investigation, so Grandfather was questioned. It was revealed that a Negro man had gone to the livery to feed the horses and had run into dangling legs. He ran back very excited, stating, "The whole town's hung out here." We also learned that Grandfather and the relatives left Oklahoma a year later, traveling to California by two different routes.

Jim Miller was related to the notorious outlaw John Wesley Hardin by marriage. Our trail took us straight to Hardin and these letters. Hardin turned out to be a very interesting fellow, and we began to realize that there must be more to his life than is portrayed in most books. While we feel sorry for his victims, still, we wanted to know, What kind of person was he? What did he have to say, and what made him run?

We have transcribed 281 personal letters written by John Wesley Hardin and the people who knew him and loved him best. In transcribing the letters, we have learned from them. You will, too. He loved Texas, this man who raised his children from a prison cell.

Hardin has become a legend in Texas. He was buried where he died, in El Paso. There, against the backdrop of Franklin Mountain, we found his grave. In our many research trips, we have heard Texans say that they had seen him out there, riding across their property, 'long about dusk.

ACKNOWLEDGMENTS

Our eternal thanks must go to Mr. Jerome H. Supple, president; Mr. Gerald W. Hill, vice president; and Mr. Richard A. Holland, head of special collections of Southwest Texas State University at San Marcos, Texas, for making the original letters written by John Wesley Hardin available to us. Without their consent, this work would not have been possible. Mr. Holland was endlessly at our beck and call, and then he asked that engaging question, "Are you going to publish them?"

We want to thank Fain Mc Daniel of Comanche Museum for being an endless source of information; also the wonderful museum staff there, as well as Gaston Boycan, we thank you.

Mr. Nelson Ross of Corsicana, Texas, contributed his valuable time, enabling us to retrace Hardin's steps, and he personally showed us the exact spot where Hardin taught school. Mr. Arthur Patrick Jr., of Richland, Texas, shared letters from his collection with us.

Margaret Waring at the Comanche Library, Mr. Donaly E. Brice of Texas State Library, Austin. Moya (Haynes) Cole of Bangs, Texas. Good luck on her endeavor. Chuck Parsons, for many telephone conversations and for literature sent us.

The end of Hardin's stormy life was beautifully reenacted on August 19, 1995. Members of the Paso del Norte Pistoleros reproduced and staged that fateful night when John Wesley Hardin was killed in an El Paso saloon. Bill Mansion, an El Paso police officer, played the part of Hardin. Writer Leon Metz gave an excellent narrative detailing how old John Selman had shot the gunfighter in the back of the head.

A special thanks goes to Bobby McNellis and Ranger, and the friendly people at El Paso Saddlery, who mysteriously found Hardin's tombstone dumped on their doorstep.

We appreciate the help of Gonzales City Hall and Gonzales Library. Many thanks to the reference staff at El Paso Library and El Paso Museum.

Last, but not least, Robin Campbell, who did all the lovely artwork for this book. We thank y'all.

A Brief Look At John Wesley Hardin

John Wesley Hardin, the son of a circuit-riding Methodist preacher, was born in 1853 in Texas. He spent his boyhood in her lush, green, live-oak forests. His passions in those days were guns, hunting, and the great outdoors. He became a crack shot by the age of nine.

Appointed Governor Edmund J. Davis was in power in Texas after the Civil War, and along with the dreaded State Police, he rode roughshod over the southern people.

John Wesley Hardin was always surrounded by violence, from the first brutal killing he witnessed at eight years of age, to his own violent death. In speed and skill with a gun, he had no equal. He was deadly; it is not certain how many men he killed, but it was somewhere between twenty and forty.

Hardin's trouble began at age fifteen, when he killed a man named Mage; he was an ex-slave, or freedman, as they were called. John and Mage had had an argument, and the next day while John was riding home alone through the woods, he came upon Mage. Mage blocked the road and threatened Hardin's life, saying that if he could but get hold of him he would kill him and throw his body in the creek. Mage had picked up a stout stick and proceeded to grab for John's horse's bridle. The frightened boy pulled out his .44 pistol and shot his horse free. Undaunted, Mage kept coming back for the bridle and rider until he was shot down.

Mage was not dead, however, so John Wesley headed for Uncle Clabe Houlshousen's house, then took Houlshousen to the site where Mage lay bleeding, angry, and calling Hardin a liar. "Mage still showed fight," Hardin later said. A high, fierce temper seized the boy. "If it had not been for my uncle, I would have shot him again," said Hardin. Mage died shortly thereafter. John's father

John Wesley Hardin in Abilene, Kansas. Insert shows the two Colt pistols that belonged to him at his death.

—Courtesy Robert G. McCubbin
Insert courtesy Kustom Quality, El Paso, Texas

told him he was sure to hang for killing a freedman in Reconstruction Texas and advised John to flee. So Hardin left for parts unknown; in doing so he became a fugitive.

By the time he was eighteen years old, Hardin had weathered many running gun battles and stand-up, face-to-face gunfights; he killed his last man on the streets of Comanche, Texas, at age twenty-one. Then he became the most wanted man in Texas, with a $4,000 reward on his head, dead or alive.

The Sutton-Taylor feud, which lasted for years, was raging in 1872. Hardin fought alongside his relatives, the Taylors. That same year, John met Jane Bowen and took her for his wife; she bore him three children.

Cattle were roaming loose in Texas after the Civil War. All anyone had to do was gather them up and take them to a railhead; good money could be made in doing so. In Abilene Kansas, on such a cattle drive, John Wesley Hardin had a celebrated encounter with Wild Bill Hickok. Yes, it was cattle that put John in Comanche on his twenty-first birthday. He, Jim Taylor, and Bud Dixson celebrated at six saloons. On that day, Deputy Sheriff Charles Webb came over from Brown County, bent on killing Hardin. According to a January 1, 1894, letter, he and Hardin talked, and Hardin invited Webb to have a "social cigar or drink." Then John turned his back to go into the saloon again. Amazed, Bud saw Webb draw his gun and hollered, "Look, out Jack!" Then came the deafening roar of a pistol; "Like a sneaking, cowardly assassin," Webb had fired at John's back. In the bloody melee that followed, one man lay dead—Charles Webb. Upon hearing gunshots, Sheriff John Carnes came on the scene.

"Who did this work?" he demanded.

"I did," said John as he handed his weapon to Carnes. But a howling mob had formed in the street and began chanting, "Let's hang Hardin, he's killed Charley Webb." Not wanting to fall into the hands of the mob, Wes fled and hid out at Round Mountain. Later, grievously stunned, John learned that while he was gone the mob had lynched his brother Jo and his cousins William Dixson and Tom Dixson. Hardin fled Texas, rendezvousing with Jane and the children.

The letters began in 1876 while he was living in Alabama and Florida under the name of Swain. Most of the letters are from

Photo by Roy and Jo Ann Stamps

Huntsville Penitentiary, where he spent fifteen years, eight months, and twelve days. While there, he studied law, and after his release he was admitted to the state bar.

He was shot to death in El Paso by Constable John Selman after an argument in which John Wesley Hardin summoned Selman to a gun battle by remarking that he was "coming out," and when he did, he would "come smoking."

LETTERS, PHASE 1

September 8, 1876–November 17, 1878

"They had me foul, yes very foul."

John Wesley Hardin felt that the killing of Deputy Charles Webb was an act of self-preservation. His letters reflect the mood and desperate position he has placed his wife and family in. As you read the letters, you will get an understanding of the time, and the different opinions about the justice he will get in Comanche, Texas.

—Courtesy Special Collections, Albert B. Alkek Library,
Southwest Texas State University, San Marcos, Texas

1. John Wesley Hardin to his wife, Jane

Euphalia Alabama Sept. 8th 1876

My Dear wife I Take Pleasure in writing you I am well at Present So my friend is, the Same, Jane there is no use to offer to tell you with Pen and ink How I love you and how bad I wish to Se you for all the Pens ink and paper together could not Express 1/4 one fourth not even one tenth So I will talk Business to you.. my Sweet darling Jinney remember me for ever your True JWH Jane I Suppose you are well at last I hope So take Care of your Self and think of me often you are in good hands. I am Looking a Situation your Board is paid mine is not your Board would not Be paid if you were here it takes money to pay Board— it onley takes Half So much to pay mine as it would yous and mine, together. do not be in a hurry, untill I find a Place, for you know how it is But as quick as I find a place Jane you and the Babes Shal Come come - do not think the time long dear But think of me and make the Children think of me when I am far away JWH Jane if I want money I Shal Telograph as I Told you which you know I will wan and want soon Jane give it to Mr J. T. S. my Best friend whom I love as a Brothe yes Who I know is a true man that is when I Telograph for it Jane I wrote to you at Thomasville Georgia that is to JTS.

this Let ter is to you all be careful

---

2. J. W. H. to a friend, John

Sept the 8the 1876
Eufalia Alabama

My very Dear friend I have Just finished writing to Jane therfore I Will write to you. my onley male friend in Florida. You hav Been a Friend to me yes a True Friend. John I Shal never for get you and your Sweet Family who I love as well as I do my self O/ that I can ever Be with you all again. Such pleasure I have Seen at your little farm yes your Hous of Sunday Evening when all was Still what a pleasure it was to be with you and you True family But John O/ the time is gone By But maby not for Ever John Think of me the Best Friend you ever had or will have aman that would Lie his life doun for you if nesisary John tell Bobby & Henry who I hop will live to be men that Should they Ever meet up with me When they come to travil this wid World over that that they will meet up with a man the will Stay By them in hours of distress a man that never Betrayed a human Being on earth But one that would give the Last

Surface embellishment with pen and ink.
—Courtesy Robin Campbell

drop of Blood for to defend a true man. John there is no use to try to talk you with Black and White at this time But will post pone. John Do take care of my Dear wife & children, donot Let them Stay in Jacksonville while the fevr panick is up When the panick is gone then Let her Board out the Bills Just as Soon as I get in to Business I will Send for her. do the Best you can in collectin an Remember me to your Sweet family John my friend Joins me in writing this Letter yor Friend untill death

Jn Smith J W H

AN ARREST ORDER WAS ISSUED FOR JOHN WESLEY HARDIN TO APPEAR AT MARCH 1877 TERM COURT.

---

3. *Joshua Bowen to Jane Hardin*

Zadlers Mill Texas May 6th 1877
Mrs Jane Swain:

Dear Niece I recieved your welcom letter of apri 28th I was more than glad to hear from you and to hear that you ware all well I had thought that I would never hear from you again this leavs my self well and all of the connection as far as I know. you wanted to know which one of Talers was Killed cince you left James Tayler was killed by the Suttin Party Billy Tayler was re captured a few days scince and is in Austin Jail all of the Clements is gone Except Joe he is here yet Jim and gip is up in the Frio Canyon Manning where abouts I am still living with him Nannie is married she married Tomy Tenneill they ware maried last Sept two of Bens Boys is grown and Edward is as larg as I am Mattie is Single yet Frank and Ann is nealy grown Puriety has four Children an the yungest a Boy I done as you told me I read your letter and tore it up and no one saw it giv my respects to Marian and his famly write soon and give me all the newes and how all is getting along

I will Close for the present from your Uncle **Joshua Bowen**

4a. *R. E. Barnett to "J. H. Swain" and Jane Hardin*

Brenham May 9th 1877—Mr J. H Swain

My Dear Nephew & Family

Yours of Apr 26 has been received We were indeed glad to hear from you all once more and to hear that you were getting a long so well We had not heard from you in so long a while we did not know where you were We wrote to you once or twice but got no answer to our letters do not know whither you got them or not There has been some sad troubles in the family since you were here among them the death of my brother J G. he died last august after a short but painful sickness I saw him once Since you were here I went to his house Jeff is still at home and is a very good boy I had a letter from Jeffs ma the other day they were all well herself and Jeff and Nannie and little J G is all there is of the family now Mattie was married last June did very well I suppose I saw the man she married when I was there he was a very good looking gentleman by the name of Smith. Jo C was here last winter he was in the hog droving business all the boys have moved off from out there except him and he is going to move if he has not already gone I have not heard from them since he was here I suppose you have heard that James T was Killed some time ago Billie T is now in jail a waiting his trial Times are dull here everybody seems to be for money many would like to make a rise if they knew where to begin The grasshopper made a raid through here last fall and this spring which made every thing look gloomy but they are about all gone now crops will be very late cotton is just being planted now by a great many farmers the boys have just finished theirs There is a great deal of murdering stealing and mobing going on in the state which is quite a bad state of affairs but I recon you take some of the Texas papers and get such general news as that. Elizabeths and Johns families are well or was the last time we heard from them John lives near Hempstead is farming has five children. Will is married he married the widow for who he was doing business for when you were here the other three are still with us I was at your aunt Nan S not long Since they were well She asked a bou you but I did not know much to tell her How did you enjoy the centennial we heard you went none of us had the pleasure of attending this one Mrs Jennie Swain has been sight sick but is getting well She has quite a hard time trying to make a living her husband drinks more than any thing else they have no children whiskey is the cause of many troubles in this life. I forgot to tell you that Gip C was married he has been married some time I do not know the name of the girl he married but it was a new comer She is pretty I suppose he and James live in the same section of country Man— lives in a different part I do not know exactly where I hope they are doing well Well I must close as M wants to write a page to Jane and Mollie may the God of mercies have mercy upon us all Remember the advice of your dear departed Father Our love to you all I am your uncle as ever. **R E. Barnett**

4b. Mattie to "J. H. Swain" and Jane Hardin

Direct to Lora Edney. Min PO Washington Co

Dear Cousin Jane

So it has been such a long time since I have heard from you I will try and write you a few lines you did not say a word in cousins letter but I have not forgot you if you have me I recon little mollie is quite a large girl by this time I wish I could see you all but I guess that is an impossibility at the present time I got one letter from Mattie B since I saw you She is not married yet or she was not last winter but I recon you get letters from her your self I have not seen your friend Mc Young in some time he is not married yet his sweetheart is though. I have been quite sick but am getting well now How long have you been living where you now are how do you like the country much better than Texas I recon. I would I know but there is places I would like better than Alabama I think how many children have you cousin any but little m has she forgot us all my paper is full and nothing said your **Cousin Mattie**

---

5. From "JWH Swain" to "Mrs. Jane Swain"

Milview Florida June the 6th 1877

Mrs Jane Swain Dear wife this Leaves me well Hoping that these few Lines will find you and famly well come here without a dollar I Have made Some money Since I come although I Did not get the money I Spoke of Jane I would Send you twenty dollars but the money I Have — is Scrip But I will Send you some money or Some things to Live on next week if I Live Jane do the Best you can and tell unkle N that I See an opening Jane you and the C will not See Hard times always I Hope. as for (my Self) I dont expect to Dye Satisfyed Jane I Have had a good trip as yet. Stop I here the Diner Bell ring So I will close till after D JWS Well Jane as I Have Just got up from the table after eating a very Harty Diner I will finish my Letter So here goes Jane be in Cheer old gal. you Know that it is a Hard win that Never seases: but do the Best you can Help a worn and weary Brother pulling Hard against the Stream tell Liza that I saw Her pa Bob & Jim McCrony there familys are all well Shep Says to tell Liza & Sallie that the Childrens Alis Ada & Lila Sings about there sister every day & also to tell Wash that he was doing well and that He thought He could if He would if he would come Back to Stick River that times were Beter Shep is Here now But will go Hone this evening give my Love to Josh Neal Caroline & Mary and also to uncle N & the Rest of the Family tell Josh that when I come Back to Be in trim for the Pearch if I Dont come Next week I will Be Shore to Send Ginee My Love to all and kiss the Children for me Yorers & John Duley

Your Lover truly **JWH Swain**

---

6. From "J. H. Swain" to Jane Hardin

J.S. CLARK & DAVID P. LEWIS,

Attorneys at Law

Marian Mc millan
I Hope will
consider Janes
circumstances and
Help Her all you cam

Please forward
imeDiately

Decatur, Ala. Aug the 25 1877

Give full names of all parties to suits. Non—residents must give security for costs.

My Dear wife and children this is the first time that I have had an opportunnity of writing you a Letter Since I was arrested in pensicolia. Jane they Had me foul yes very foul I was Sitting in the Smoking car Neal C & Poor (Jimmie M) By my Side with my arms Streached on the Seat Whe they come in. 4 men grabed me one by each arm and one by each Leg So the Strached me verry ——y and quick. But poor Jimie he Broke to run out of the cars and was Shot dead by some of the croud on the out Side. Jane I am in good Hands now they treat me Better than you have any Idea and asures me that I will not Be mobed and that when I get there that the Governer will Protect me from a mob and that I will have the Law Jane Bein cheer and donot take trouble to Heart But look to the Bright Side Jane I Have not Murded any Body Nor robed any one one But what I have done in Texas was to Save my Life Jane time will Bring me out. Jane I got a rit of Habas corpus yesterday But fail to get out my trial was set for tuesday but a requisition come for John. Wesley. Hardin Last Night So they Say & Swore that I was the man J.W. Hardin that killed Web of comanchie Texas So they Had to give me up Jane be cautious in writing me for they will examine your Letters before I See them — Direct your letters to Austin texas to JH Swain Jane they can Never Hang me nor Pnitenctiry me for live By Law times are not like they was when we Left Texas Mob Law is played out Jane I expect

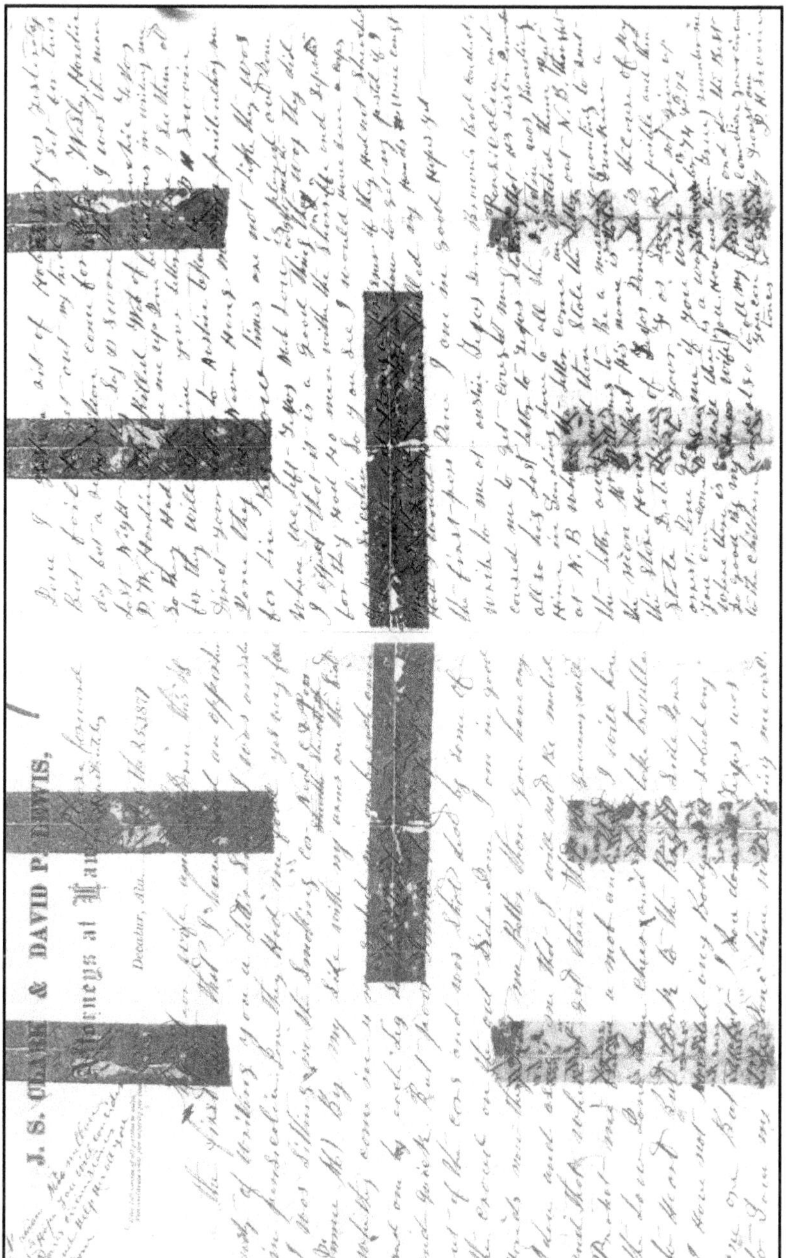

—Courtesy Special Collections, Albert B. Alkek Library, Southwest Texas State University, San Marcos, Texas

that it is a good thing they caught me the way they did for they Had 40 men withe the Sharriffe and Deputies of pensicolia So you See I would Have Been a corps now instead of Being a prisner if they Had not Streached me as they did Jane I had no Show to get my pistol if I had I would Have Been Killed my Hands were caugt the first pass Jane I am in Good Hopes yet

Write to me at austin Texas Jane Brown's Bad Conduct caused me to get caught me in Pensicolia and all so his Last Letter to Texas Stating that His Sister Joined Him in Sending Love to all the Detective was Boarding at N. B when the Letter came an watched them put the Letter away and then Stole the Letter out N. B. thought the man Mr Williams to Be a Merchant wanting to rent the Store Hous But His name is John Dunkin a State Detective of Texas. Jane B. is the cause of my arrest. Jane Go to your F as Soon as posible and then you can come to See me if you wish do not give up where there is a will there is a way Remember 1874 & 1872 So Good by my Dear wife (you. hay ever Been True) remember me to the children and also to all my friends and do the Best you can Tell you Connection your circunstances So good By Dearest one

J.H. Swain

JOHN WESLEY HARDIN WAS PLACED IN THE TRAVIS COUNTY JAIL IN AUSTIN, TEXAS.

SPECIAL OFFICER JACK DUNCAN RELATES THE HISTORY OF HARDIN'S CAPTURE IN FLORIDA BY HIMSELF, LIEUTENANT ARMSTRONG OF THE RANGERS, SHERIFF WHITNEY OF PENSACOLA, AND WHITNEY'S DEPUTY, A. J. PERDUE.

Dallas News

"—We got into Pensacola, saw the shariff and told him we wanted him to help us take a bad men. He was in for taking Hardin on the street, but we laid a plan to take him on the train.

The engineer was instructed not to start until the bell rang and then to keep going until he was rung down. Hardin and a party named Mann boarded the train and took seats in the smoker. Hardin took one seat and leaned back with his arms on the back of the seat. Mann took the seat just ahead of him. Sheriff Whitney volunteered to walk up behind Hardin and seize his hands while we handcuffed him. He did not know who Hardin was. We carried out the plan. Whitney came up behind him and grabbed his hands. He at once began to struggle to get his pistol, but Whitney was a strong man and could handle him that way. Jim Mann jumped up in his seat, pulled his pistol and was shot dead. He jumped out through the car window and dropped on the platform. Everybody in the car stampeded and went out of the windows and doors. Armstrong pulled the bell cord and the train stared out at full speed, and in the meantime we got the handcuffs on Hardin. He kicked and cursed and swore and didn't ever give up to us until we got to Memphis with him. We had to carry him into the smoker on the road home and hardly any body would stay in the car he was so abusive in his language." Aug. 24, 1895

—Courtesy *El Paso Times Daily Herald*

---

7. Mattie Hardin to Mrs. Jane Hardin

Sept 5th 1877 Elm's Dale Mrs-Jane Harden-

Dear Sister

With pleasure I embrace

This opportunity of writing to you I cant express my joy at hearing from you. nor my Sorrow that Wes is a gain a prisoner. I would-be glad indeed to See you and the-children as I See in the Gonzales Inquirer that you have more than one. This leaves us all- well hoping that it may be recieved and find you the Same. I am not married yet. Ann. and Frank-is both a bout grown. Ann. favors you very much Nancy is living near us She and William live on the place that Mrs Hupman lived on while you was here—they have three children the youndest is a girl named Jennie Dunk and Lizzie have moved to the mountains they have two children living one dead their babe is name William.Thomas they have been gone Six weeks we have not heard from them Since they left. Ma has had—2 children Since you left one boy name Beasly one girl name Beulah. She is 3 months old. Jane you must not grieve to much for Wes evry one that I hear Speak of him thinks he will come clear.—I saw aunt Margurett yesterday She is well-and the dear old creature evrybody loves her-that knows her I understand that Wes has employed 3 of the best

Lawyers in Austin. I am going to write to him this eve ning I Should be So glad to See him if I could See you I could tell you So many things that is to tedious to write Kiss your children for me and dont let Mollie forget me All join me—in love to you Lovingly your Sister Mattie. Bowen

It is Lizzes Second child that is dead Mrs. Anglin lives at the Same place—her little Mollie is gone to Louisiana to Stay a year—She has no child now with her-but little Dora. She sends her best love to you and your children & Says She would be mighty glad to See you Says dont take your trouble hard for-we all have trouble and must bear them the best we can— We have had a good crop year— there has been agreat deal of corn made this year Pa has-a very good crop — Frank and Ann & I have been picking cotton this year — This country is Settling up right fast uncle Josh and his boys and. Cousin Charlie Cammel live in a camp near our house they are building a house on uncle Joshes. place Nannie Cobb and Tommie Tennille have been married nearly a year Love to all Kisses to children

William Send his respects to you and Says if you need help he will do all he can for you.

---

8. Mattie Hardin to J. W. H.

Brenham Texas Sep th9th 1877 Mr J W Hardin

My Dear Cousin

Your letter was received last night which I was glad to get. glad to know that you had not forgot cousin mat I comenced a letter to you several days a go but did not finish it I was waiting to have some news as regards a lawyer for your case. I thought perhaps you were quite lonely in your present a bode but as you have so many callers I recon you do not get so lonely as one might suppose I am really glad to hear that some of your old friends and acquaintances have been to See you. I would like very much to see you my self but it seems impossible for me to have the opportunity of doing so

I hope you will not despair for it is thought that if you have a fair trial at Comanchie that you will come clear that is the opinion of the majority of the people but to be plain I do fear the mob for you unless you have the assurance from the Governor of protection but you said you had that

We received a letter from your ma a few days a go written the fifth she wrote that she intended to go to see you immediatly I will write to her again to day her post office is Bennett Station Red River County Mattie Smith your sister lives at that place your ma was at her house when she received my letter informing her of your present condition. Pa wrote to W B. Hardin of Polk as soon as he came home also to the same name of Hill county but has not heard from either yet Pa has used every effort with in his power to procure you a lawyer but has not succeeded yet and does not think he can he tried to get Hon. seth Shepard he offered him four hundred acres of Land but he said he did not want land but would go for one thousand dollars in cash and his expenses to be paid as for selling land for cash now that is impossible He tried several other lawyers but all to no purpose I wish the cars ran to Comamchie then they might be more readily obtained If you can get one at Austin you had better do so. Pa says he heard a man say the other day that you had a very strong friend, K— out west who says that you shall not lack for means he is a rich stock man and has money too now perhaps you had best to write to him immediately and get his assistance if he will render you any I think you will know who it is. Pa says let him know if a warrant has been sent for you yet from Comanchie or any where else I will write to cousin Jane and know what she is going to do I recon you hear from her often yourself I would like to see her and her three little children. I will send you the pictures you asked me to send they are all I have of them I sent the rest to her relations out west. Your Ma said that James Anderson ought to be at Comanchie if you have not sent for him it should be done. I suppose you have not for gotten a gentleman and lady frind you have here they seem to be your friends yet I saw her last sunday she seemed sorry to hear of your arrest Your other friend the young man that left with you I do not know where he is have not heard from him for some time Brother John is at Hempstead or near there he is confined very closely he is farming and has five children his two oldest boys are here have been here a week

Mr Burch was here yesterday he is in very bad health looks very badly none of the girls are married yet. Did you get the letter I wrote to you last may (I think it was that I wrote to you). I do wish I could see you and talk. I think I could ask many questions but you know that I am good at that., I will write to cousin Joe C to day we have

not heard from them in some time. the next time I write I hope we will have heard from some of the connexion. This is sunday morning I did not go to church to day stayed at home the weather is so very warm but cool weather is not far off and I am not sorry for it. I suppose you can write when ever you wish so I hope you will write often and let us hear how you are we all have anxious minds if not = plenty of money. but I hope you will know how it is. Pa and perhaps one of the boys will be at your trial where ever it may be
I must close for this time hoping to hear from you soon I remain

Your Cousin

Mattie Hardin

PS
the business portion of this put in at the request of R.E.H. Ma says put in a few words for her and you know she is always giving good advice She says do not let anyone *treat* you enough to make you say any thing that you should not say Any one sometimes would say somethings that they not think of if not under the influence of you know what I have written to your mother to day will hear from her in a few days if she answers immediately

Bell Hardin is in Erath Co Dublin or she was there when last heard from

Taste not Touch not &C

Your Cousin **M-H**

---

9. Elizabeth Hardin to J. W. H.

J.W. Hardin
In Care of the Sheriff
To John. W. Hardin
To the care the Sheriff

Red River Co. Sept 9th A.D. 1877

My Sweet Precious Johnnie.

I am here at Bennett Station 17, miles east of Paris. It is Sabbath morning I feel that I can not refrain from writing you a few lines it has been So long. years have passed away Since I could write one line to my dear absent boy. News came to me a few days ago that you was lodge in Auston Jail. O how it thrilled my heart. I had a hope that it was not true as it came in the papers the next morning I recived a letter from your Cousin Mattie Hardin confirming the news, it is all most more than I can bear. I Still look to my Heavenly father who has Sustained me in So many trying Scenes. my noble boy bear your afflictions and your confine ment like a man, and pray to the good Lord to give you friends. Johnnie if you can get a fair tryal of the commanihe dficulty I do not believe there is any Court in United States that will condemn you. many changes Since I saw you last. your dear Pa has passed away but his way was clear he tole me a few minutes before his death that the good Lord would take him right to heaven. O how hard to be left alone in this troublesome world. I have a very good friend four miles from here 300 and 60 acres. Jeff has been farming this year, ten acres in corn. 4 1/2 in Cotton the crop is cut Short on account of rain we have a nice lot of hogs, and plenty of nessesarys to live on

Mattie maried on the Second day of last March a year a go. a man by the name of Smith a very respectable man he has bought here and has put up a very respectable house the building as white as Snow he Says he is willing to assist you and if you have a tryal he will be there. Matt talks about you So much and Says we will all have to go to See you. She has no babies I. got a letter from your Sister Lizzie the other day She Spoke So kindly of you they live one mile north of Bonham. Jeff is for going to See you right away I tole him to wait untill we would get a letter from your uncle Bobb Nannie wants to See you So much She has grown a great deal Since you Saw her. She has been going to School all year. your Sweet little Br Barnett Gippson that you have never Seen talk about his buddie Johnie So much. your Sister Bell was in Doublin Ereth Co the Last accont at Castle lon's. Johnie if you want me to come to See you let me know amediatly and I will come. I think I could do you considerable good I kow that your uncle Bobb will do all he can to get you good counsil. Johnie I have the prospect of getting a considerable Estate from your Aunt Malinda Lee's Estate the Lawyers have instituted Suit all ready and I am expecting Something Soon. So you may expect your Ma to assist you in getting attorneys I do wish Jane and those Sweet little babes ware with me. may the good Lord bless and protect them Johnie I feel glad that you ware taken to Austin as they had arrested you. I have a high opinion of the authorities there I believe they will be true to you and afford you all the protection the Law will admit. my dear Son do not

despare. pray to your heavenly father for aid assistance that you may not fall intiraly in the hands of your enimies, and rest assured that your Ma is offering up petitions to the God of the universe in your behalf dayly and hourely. write amediatly if you are alowed
no more my Sweet child, adieue

Your Ma, Elizzabeth Hardin

---

10. From Alie B. Hardin to J. W. Hardin

th. Mt Calm Sept 9 1877

Dear Brother
I received yours of Aug the 30 yesterday I was sorry indeed to hear of your condition If I had money I would Start in the morrning to see you though I have not one dollar in the world I have not colected adollar from Commanche All I have had to live on was Eight hundred dollars I drew Inshurance money I will Send your letter on to sissie in to morrows mail All So write to your Ma her Post Office is Parris Lamar Co Texas they bought aplace thare and are doing well Mat is married She has bin married more than ayear She married a man by the name of Smith they are living near your Mother I think it would be imposible for sissie or Bent to come to see you sissies present condition would not admit of Bent leaving her. I think Mat and Mr Smith will come to see you. your Pa died last August with congestive chills John where is your familey how many Children have you. I am fearful you cant get Justis done you in Commanche. I dread you going there, Be in good Spirets John I think you can prove your Self cleare of the Killing of Weeb I heard Sherriff Carrens Dept Sherriff Wilson and many others Say you did not Kill him trusting you will answer this soon and tell me all about your Self and familey I remain your Sister

Alie B Hardin

Jodie is just like his Pa Sissies Post Office is Bonham Fannin C Texas

---

11. From Mattie Hardin to Mrs. Jane Hardin

R

R R

R

R 2 2 2-

Brenham Sept. 12th 1877

Mrs Jane Hardin

Dear Cousin

I once more make an attempt to write to you I have written two letters to you and have never got a line from you well I cant blame you for not writing then but I hope you will write now I received a letter from John a few days a go he told me to write to you and tell you he is all right he says tell you he is assured that he will not be mobbed I had expected you would have been in Texas before now Well you have quite a family now how old is the baby and what is its name John wrote to me that he had not heard from your Father but was expecting to hear from him Pa has been up to see cousin John he seemed in as good cheer as could be expected yet he could see that he was Sad Court Commences in Comanche the twenty fourth of the present month time is short

Have —

We received a letter a few days ago from Johns ma she wrote like she intended to go to see him immediately hers and Mattie Smith's P 0 is Bennett Station Red River county We are expecting a letter from there all the time Cousin John asked me for yours and mollies pictures. I sent them to him I sent all those you left with me to your kinfolks out west When do you expect to come to Texas I have not heard from Gonzales county in a long time I wrote to Joe Clements a few days ago I hope to hear from him soon Mr and Mrs S are well I saw her day before yesterday she has no children — I am in a hurry to send this to the office I must close for this time Kiss all the children for me and be sure and write as soon as you get this as we are anxious to hear from you Ma sends love to you Your Cousin

Mattie Hardin

---

12. From S E H to Mrs. Hardin

[UNDATED]

Mrs. Hardin

Your note recd I regret to hear of your unpleasant Situation I was never so scarce of money as now I send you $10.00 That perhaps will enable you to get to Austin You can find some one there who will take you down further When you get there Ben Hendricks will aid you Mr Cloud told me to tell you to call and stay with him Please do not mention my name in connexion with your troubles I am here where Wesleys name is unpopular and any aid I might be known to render you might unnecessarily make me enemies I would be glad to do more but am not able

Yours ore

S E H.

---

13. Mattie Smith to J. W. H.

Bennett. R.R. Co. Texas Sep. 15th.1877

Mr J. W. Hardin

Dear brother

It is with the kindest

of feelings that I have towards you that I try to address you. although it appears to me that I cannot Say one word that will interest you yet I know it is my duty to write you a few lines. I was glad to hear of you and your little family but Sorry to hear of your misfortune. But Johnnie you will overcome all your dificulty, if you will only trust and in faith to your heavenly Father. how — would like to See Sister Jane and those precious little ones. I suppose you have — Children how I love them for my dear Johnies Sake I have written to Jane told her all the news. and all I knew about you. tried to cheer and console her in her lonely condition. Mattie Hardin wrote the other — and told us where She was. We received a letter from Sister Lizzie She was verry much troubled and interested about you I know She would have written to you but She thought you could not receive letters I did not think you could for when we was at Comanche they would not let any letters pass or repass.

John Ma wrote to you the other day asking you must She visit you. She requested me to tell you she would go if you thought it best. She got thrown from a horse the other day was right badly hurt but not Seriously. I was there yesterday She was getting along verry well. We heard through Sisters letter that --- had returned to Mt. Calm we heard no new of interest. She Said little Jodie was larger than Dora. I suppose you heard of me marring Mr Smith is among the best men in the world he is --- rich but is Smart and industrious in good living circumstances. he Says he would like to see you the one he has heard So much talk about. well John I will close as the train will be here in a few minutes. Write Soon if possible I would Rather hear from you than any one Write Mr Smith Sends his respects to you good bye Dearest Brother

Your Sister

Mattie Smith

---

14. Marion to "Mrs. Jane Swain"

Pollard Ala Sept. 16 th 1877.

Mrs Jane Swain

Dear Cousin

Enclosed I send you letter. I opened yours thinking it was from John. & I was anxious to here from him I send you a pensacola paper in which you will See an article in regard to him All are well.
hoping this will reach you in due time & find you & the Children well

I remain your Cousin **Marion**

ON SEPTEMBER 19, 1877, HARDIN WAS TAKEN TO COMANCHE TO STAND TRIAL FOR THE KILLING OF DEPUTY SHERIFF CHARLES WEBB.

---

15. Lizzie Cobb to John Wesley Hardin.

[UNDATED]

Ma's Post office. they were all well when last we heard from them Ma is Getting along as well as could be expected. Jeff has Grown so much nearly Grown, I think he will Go to see you as soon as they Get your letter. We moved from Mt Calm here near two years ago. Sister bell got your letter there & directed it to me she said she would go to see you if she could would like to So much. Well Bro I suppose Court commences in Commanche next monday, I think if I could I would move my tryal from there as I do not think you will Get justice From all I have head I think you will come out safe if have justice done by you. I am so anxious to see you & would go to see you if possible, write where your family are I would be so

Glad to see them. I suppose you have written to Uncle Bob & Burnett. keep up your spirit & I think you will come out safe & do not for Get to Pray to the Good Lord to see you out for what is ask will be received if ask in faith. My Dear Brother I pray for you often & I believe my prayers will be answered.

Good bye Dear Brother Your's as long as life shall last & then through eternity

Your's Lizzie
Cobb

P.S. Write once a week if permitted, & I will forward it to Ma

Your's L. C.

Hardin arrived at Comanche on September 24, 1877, and appeared in shackles before the judge. He stood trial September 28 and was escorted back to Austin October 1.

---

16. "Doc J. An" to John Wesley Hardin

Pursley Post office **october the 13 1877**

Navarro Co Texas

Dear Cousin

John I take the opportunity to drop you a few lines to let you know that I have not fogot you you yet. John this leaves us all well and doing as well as could be expected John I saw a letter you wrote to aunt nan just read it John I am sorry all though I I expect you think I am mad with you but dont think so I am a fried to you and will be as long as I live John you must have me at ——— in Comanche shou ——— saw it all and knew th ——— John be quiet and ——— I think you will ——— yot John you w ——— trial from Com ——— tice there for John ——— out there. John you dont know what a close place they had me in they thought I was one of your men as they call them but come out allwright and left friends behind you know John they treated me verry well untill I left I Stayed there one week after they killed the boys and then I took tude and went home John that was the awfulest that ever passed me but could not say a word I left there broken harted John Jack Dixon is in illinois Jack is a man now. and a smart man to John any thing that I can do for you I will do it face open to the wourld John I am coming to see you. John your big fat aunt ——— will pray for you as long as she ——— had to pay a bout ——— out since I saw you ——— are through now ——— two ours with you ——— living with ma ——— close write to me ——— sin Doc. J. An John I will write to you again in a few days John be shore and wrte to me and tell all about your wife and where she is and what she doineng I know the man that arrested you he lives in dallas they had him chained down in comanche when I left for one of your gang as they called him I thought they would hang him I saw him in Dallas. about three months ago he asked me if I ever heard of you and said he wish you would kill all of commanche and said he would help you do it he is Jack Duncan

Jack Ducan Duncan Doc J Doc J An

Please give this letter to John, Wesley Hardin

17. Mattie Hardin to Jane Hardin

Brenham Texas Oct 14 th 1,77 Mrs Jane, Hardin

My Dear Cousin

Your letter was received some time since but I have neglected writing until now I have been waiting to hear how Johns trial came off Pa and Aaron went up there they have been home a few days John was tried and the jury brought in a verdict of murder in the second degree and the penalty twenty five years in the penitentiary but he has taken an appeal to the supreme court. he has been taken back to Austin we have not heard from him since he got back there I am going to write to him to day there were four lawyers employed for John Brown County came down to Comanche to the trial they would have liked to have had a chance to mob him but he was well guarded by the rangers and the officers of Comanche were against a mob Cousin I see many things in the papers that they say you have said but I do not believe them now is a time for his friends to say but little let news paper reporters a lone I got a letter from Johns ma yesterday she and family were well Sister and family have just gone from here her daughter mattie= is going to stay this week with us. What is your little babies name. I would like to see you all very much I expect little mollie has grown so much I would not know her

I do not hear from Gonzales much I do not know whether Joe Clements is out there or not I wrote to him but have not heard from him Write soon and let us know when you will be in Texas
Kiss all the children for me

I remain your Cousin Mattie Hardin

---

18. J. A. Lipscomb to John Wesley Hardin

[UNDATED]

I have written to your Father in Form about our fees & will take horses or anthing that I can use. I would like to represent you in your other cases. every man I have seen since & crossed the Comanchie County line wants you to be cleared & if we get the case reversed & think we will do it I have found some more evidence since I returned home we can show that Webb came to comanchie for the express purpose of arresting you without a warrant & that he said he was going to do it or Kill you. Write to me & let me know how you are getting along, Dont let any one write your life I want that Job myself. Dont show this part of my letter

Your truly **J A Lipscomb**

PS Uncle Bob & family are well J A L

---

19. Elizabeth Hardin to J. W. Hardin.

Mr Jo M **Red River Co, Oct. 26th, 1877**

My own precious Son
I received your kind letter a few days ago. So glad to hear from -y Johnnie but very Sorry to hear of you ware Suffering with your Side. I, do hope you are better. how I do want to See you. never did want to See any one half So much. We are all well. Jeff Nannie little Gippie and my Self here at Brights and Matt's came in a few moments ago Johnnie I was Some what Surprised to herar of the descision of your case but when I learned who was the Judge and the prossecuting attorny it is no thousan wonders to me that they did not Send you to the Penitentiary for life Flemings and Steavens ware the bitterest enemies poor Jodie had or you eather. Steavns is the one that tole your Pa that if they did not get you they would get Jo and perhapse him to John you never tole me who ware your wit-

Joseph Gipson Hardin, and his wife, Arabella (Adams) Hardin.
—Courtesy Comanche County Museum,
from the collection of Moya (Haynes) Cole

nesses at commanche I want to know if Jim Anderson and Dr Brockius was thare. I got a letter from your Cousin Mat Hard She tells me you have got a new hearing I. am So glad of do hope and trust that you may have a fare trial next time. I do believe you will. your trial at Commanche has made you friends the Public can See that they ware So prejudice that they could not do you Justice no doubt but their minds ware all ready made up before the trial, my Sweet boy be of good cheer I believe light will Shine on your path way yet, look to your Heavenly Father for that light he is the true and only Source he can deliver and he can Save my Sweet boy be prayful you was raised to pray, Johnnie do you think it advisable for me to go to See you, and if So when would you want me to come. I want to know when your trial will be. I thought perhapse then would be the best time to come I have a true Statement of the killing of Webb writen by your Pa. how we all ware treated and how your poor br was distroyed. he intended to have it bublished but died before he accomplished it he Said if he did not live to carry it out he hoped his friends would. Consult your lawyers and if they think it would .do you any good I will Send it to you or them. the Commanchies tried to make it appear that there was a combination to kill Webb, not So, there was a plot made to kill you the day Webb was killed by those that ware Styled your clan, Tom Dixson tole Cuninghan to raise a fuss with you and he Tom would kill you. your Pa gives the names of those that heard them ploting they all ware Commachies Jeff and my Self Stayed at Br J.W.T. Mckinzie's the other night all our talk was about you or nearly all he is a warm friend of yours. he Says poor John has been badly treated he Says he would be So glad to See you and if you remain there this fall he intendes to go to See you he tole me to tell you to be a good boy and pray that there is a chance for you yet that you may make a great and good man yet

your Ma Elizabeth Hardin

well Johnnie we all want to See you Jeff allinost gets wild on the Subject of visiting you if any one goes I think I am the one I believe I could be of some advantage to your lawyers, write Sweet Johnnie we are looking for Sissie on the train tomorrow night I will write in a few days again I am wrighting while all is asleep. good bye Sweet Johnnie.

Your Ma

TOM HALDEMAN WAS KILLED, AND THE MURDERER, BROWN BOWEN (JANE HARDIN'S BROTHER), ACCUSED JOHN WESLEY HARDIN OF THE CRIME.

---

20. William and Mat Bowen to Jane Hardin

Oct the 26th 18.77 Gonzales Co Texas

Dear sister

I seat my self to Write you a few lines in answer to yore kined letter that We have just Received I am glad to hear that you are Well but sorrow to hear of yore trobles I not heard from you in so long that I hardly no how to Write this leaves us all Well and hope this Wil find you and the children Well sins Wes a rived hear I hav been trying to get off to see him but never been able go yet but I hare from him oftem he has had a tryal on that Web Case and Was Sentenced to the Pentencera for 25 year but he has taken appeal to the higher court I cant say how he is going to come out Brown had his tryal on the Hademan case on the 18th of this month and Was to be hanged but has aplide for new tryal court is still in sesion and is not desided yet yore pa is now in town attending to it Wel Jane I beleive I hav giv you all the mews Jane you spoke of wanting Some money I am sorrow that I havent got some for you but I wil hav some soon and wil devide With you Willingly So nothing more present I Remain trew Brother untell deth

Wel sister I believe that William has giv you all the mews When I wrote you last Lizzie had moved a way but She has come back and is heare to might with us. She says giv hur love to you and the Children Jane I nevr hav been hapy Since you left heare you never said any thing a bout Coming out hear Write and let us no if you want to Come or not kiss litle moly for me Nancy says tell you that She has three Children as wel as you the last one is a girl hur mane is Purity Jane Lizzie has three Children two Living one ded one So nothing mor at present **yore Sister Mat Brown**

---

21. Elizabeth Hardin to J. W. H.

[UNDATED]

P.S.
My Dear Johnnie
I forgoten to tell you Jeff Nannie professed religion about two months ago Jeff talked like a preacher and little Nannie was the happiest little creature I ever Saw they Joined the Methodist church. Bright and Matt Sends their love and best wishes he Says the Supreme court will give you a fare an inprtial trial that the dessision at Commanche was cruel but do you good in the long runn write often. I do fell So thankful to the officers and rulers for their kind treatment to you at Auston and evry whare else. your uncle Bob and your noble nephew for their kindness and attention they have Shown you Be a good boy Br Mckinzie Says you are in the assendency good bye Sweet precious boy

Your Ma E. Hardin

---

22. M. Hardin to J. W. H.

Brenham Oct 29th 1877 **Mr Jno W.Hardin**

Dear Cousin
Your letter of the fifteenth of the present month was received some time since but I have been waiting to hear from you again as I wrote to you the day before ——— did I think we might write to each other every week I recon you get quite lonely in your present situation I have not heard from Jane. never received but the one letter from her have you heard from her and where is she I wrote to her about two weeks a go I expect she has perhaps got to Texas before now Pa saw Mr Lipscomb a few days since he said he was going to write to you and that he would send you all the exceptions as he thought he remembered them There was a young gentleman here to day who was in Brown County at the time of the difficulty he says that old Mr Han of Brown told him that Webb went to Comanche to arrest you and Taylor for the rewards as he was a broken grocery keeper and wished to make a rise and that he Mr Han went with him to help arrest you and that you had been told of it now you must try to remember who it was that told you he was going or had gone for

that purpose Pa says he thinks it would be good evidence for you if you get an appeal. We did not know what to think of your Jno L. Scott letter do you know who he is or who your friend of Kearnes is he seemed to write like he might be interested in you have you heard from him since Do you have as many callers as when you first arrived at Austin. I have not heard from your Ma since I wrote to you I guess you hear from her often She wrote several letters to me I would like to see her very much The boys have been very busy gathering their crop they will be through with their corn this week they are so lazy about writing that they wont write to any one so they make me do all the writing. Write soon as we are always anxious to hear from you

Your Cousin M. Hardin

---

23. Mattie Smith to J. W. H.

Bennett Nov 21st 1877. Mr John Wesley Hardin

Dear brother

I received your letter and was So glad to hear from you but So Sorry to hear of your Sufferings but I hope you are better by this time. We are all well. Mas family also ma wrote to you the other day has received no answer She is so anxious to hear from you. all her talk is about you. She would do a heap for you if it was in her power but you know we woman cant do much. Dear brother We heard of the cruel Sentence those Demons passed on you in Commanche. you do not know how our hearts beats in Sympathy towards you We was glad to hear that you had gotten a trial at the appellant court. I think you will undoubtedly get Justice then you have a great many friends here although they are not acquainted with you personly. they can See how biased they were towards you in your trial by reading the news papers. You Spoke of your trial comming off in April and you Said you would need Some assistance we will do all we can for you before then. I am glad you are kindly cared for if you have been treated wrong for if they are acquainted with you they know and good a heart as ever was John I will write for Jane to come to marrow. Mr Smith Says he will write and tell her how to come & give her all the directions necessary She can come in three days anyhow I hope She will come I want to See her So much and those precious little ones. if She comes then we will make arrangements to visit you. Sissie & Cobb Was down a week or two ago they talked a great deal about you and Said they had written to you but had received no answer well John Bennett is a right Smart busness place, is improving very fast Mr Smith is working at the carpenters trade & I have three boarders. Ma lives four miles from here She comes to See us once or twice a week they are getting along very well. Jeff works very hard he often talks about you and says he is going to See you this Winter if he lives. Nannie often talks of you & little Gippie was talking the other day before Some ladies the other day & Said he was going out west they asked him what he was going west for he replied to See bud Johnie. well Dear Brother I will close for this time. I will Write a gain Soon. Write often Johnmie only put your trust in the good Lord and he will bring you out all right in the future good bye precious Buddie

Your Sister Mattie Smith

---

24. Mattie Smith to Jane Hardin

Bennett Nov 25. 1877 Mrs Jane Hardin

Dear Sister

It is with a Sad heart that I try to write you a few lines. I received a letter from Brother John. the other day. he Said for me to write to you and tell you he was getting along very well. was at Austin Prison was well as comon I see he also wanted me to tell you to come here to my house and for us to fix a way for us to go to See him. I hope you will come we live about 90 miles west of Texarcanna on the Texas and Pacific Rail Road. I presume you have heard of brothers trial in Comanche and of the cruel and unjust Sentence. 25 years in the Penitentiary. but it was not unexpected to me as the people were So preduciced against him they did not have the heart to give him a fair trial they proved that Webb fired first but that did not make any difference they wanted him out of their way he has gotten an appeal his trial will come off in April next I think he will have a fair trial there. he has a great many friends here they Say that he did not get Justice. well Jane I Suppose you have long Since heard that I was married to a Mr Smith w have been married nearley two years he is one of the best men in the world We are living at Bennett a rail road town in sight of the Depot ma lives four miles from here She has a nice farm of about 160 acres. Jeff farms Nannie goes to School and little Gippie bosses around generally. Poor Pa he died a year ago last august. he died a very happy death I think trouble brought Disease on which caused his death. Now Sister I hope you will think it best and come all are anxious to See you you must write immediately and let us know John wants to hear from you very much. Mr Smith will get directions how to come the nearest way. I want to See your Sweet little children kiss mollie & John Wesley & Babbie for me. Write Soon and let us know

good Bye
Mattie Smith

---

25. M. Hardin to J. W. H.

Brenham Nov 26th 1877
Mr J.W. Hardin

My Dear Cousin
Your letter has been received we were glad to hear from you I also got one a week a go from you but I have been such a runabout that I have not had an opportunity of answering it. Last week was quite a gay one here the soldiers had a reunion and a big ball at night every one seemed to enjoy them selves finely I wish I could have gone to Austin to the fair and then I might have had an opportunity of seeing you but it seems impossible for me to get that far from home Pa received a letter from your ma a few days since she said that Cousin Lizzie Cobb had been to see her. She wrote that She was very much astonished to hear that your trial was over it was thought to be the best for you Pa says that according to law and evidence you should have been cleared and now we can only await the decision of supreeme court but you know that they may let prejudice rule but we hope that your case will be reversed &c Pa and Aaron saw Mr Scott of Marlin in town yesterday he seemed to be a man of many words but they know nothing more about him he said you had never answered his letter the friend of yours that he said had employed him was old man Choat of Karnes county he is not employed for you now he was only employed to go to Comanche

but sickness at home prevented him from going Perhaps if you corespond with Mr Choat he might assit you yet If Mr Choat your friend will employ him yet it will do no harm for you should have a lawyer at supreme Court you said in your other letter that you would send Renicks letter but we have not got it yet we would like to hear what he says. I got a letter from Jane a few days since she seemed to be anxious to see you I recon she is in much trouble. Are you any closer confined than you were before you went to Comanche I hope not for a close cell is bad enough Does any one go to see you now Write soon. all send love to you

your Cousin M. Hardin

---

26. Elizabeth Hardin to J. W. H.

[UNDATED]

Mr John W. Hardin

My Dear Precious Son

We are all here at Brights it is

Saturday night while all has retired to bed. I thought I would write you a few lines. I have been waiting to get an answer to my letter which I wrote to you a few week after you returned from Commanche. I have received no answer yet. Johnnie I was So astonished when I learned your trial was over at Commanche. O that awful desession it haunts me day and night but as -- when I learned who was the Judge and the prossecuting Attorney I new they could not give you Justice they ware they ware Such enemies of Jodie's and yours it was Stevens that tole your Pa that if they did not get you they would have Jo and the old man to perhaps my Sweet Johnnie I am So Sorry to hear of you Suffering So much from your wound I do hope you are better by this time I. do want to See you So much O that I could be with you I would try and Swoothe your troubled and aching heart. what a pleasure it would be if I could be with you and wait on you in your afflictions. my Sweet Son bear up in your afflctions and confinement. I trust a better day is dawning I wrote if you wanted me to go to See you I have not herd from you Sinc. Mattie got a letter from you a few days ago you Said you wanted us to write to Jane and for her to come to Matt's or my house. Mattie wrote to her amediatly and tole her to come and how to come. I would be so glad to See her and those Sweet little babes,

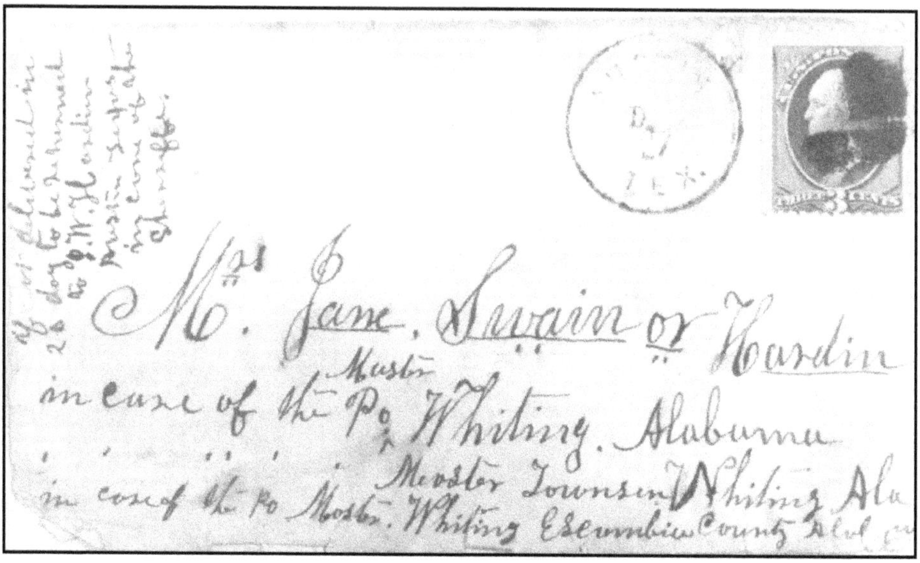

Envelope from Hardin Collection.

Johnnies loved ones. if She gets here Some of us will go with her to See you I have been waiting for you to Say what you wish me to do. I tole you if my last I thought it would be better for me to put off visiting you untill your trial and then I would go, if I had the means I would go now and then to I. want to See you So much I. have a true Statement of the killing of Webb writen by your Pa from an eye witness I think I it might be of considerble use to you and your Lawyers if you think they would let me know and I will Send them to you. I got a letter from your uncle Bobb the other day he is not in dispare about you. he says if the propper meanes are taken you will be all right yet. my Son you must not dispare the darkest hour is Just before day. Jeff Says he will See you this winter Nannie is going to School Gippie is a fine interesting boy. My Sweet boy you are on my mind all the time. I do not feel disgraced by you being whare you are. I know that you are inosent of the charg for which you ware punished, from the evidence and law you Should have been cleared but there was no Justice for you at Commanche.

Well John write to me and tell me all you can and I will write to you more often good bye Sweet Son

Elizabeth Hardin

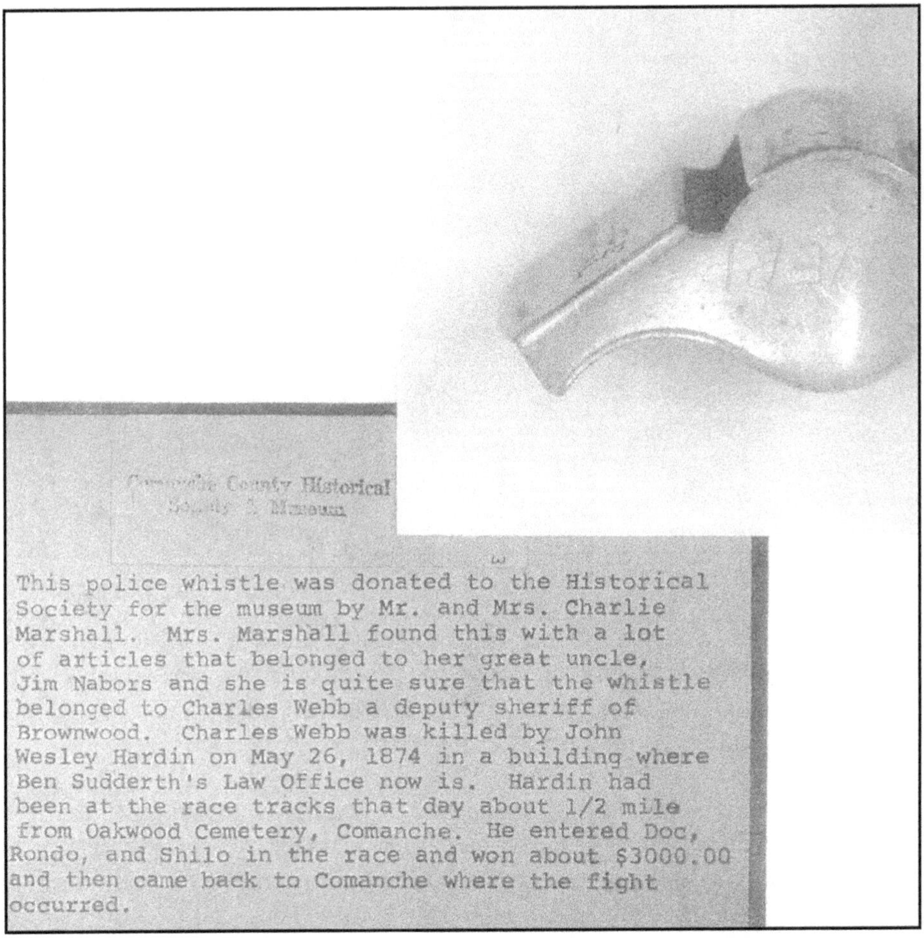

Police whistle belonging to Deputy Charles Webb.

27. A. C. Dikes to J. W. Hardin

Dec,, 3,, 1877 Eastland City Eastland Co

Mr,, J W Hardin:

Mr ever dear unfortunate Cousin I received you kind and welcome letter 2 weeks ago Mr Dikes has been gone to the range for over a month I have been looking for him every day for a week and so I thought I would answer it my self. I was very much overjoyed to get a letter from you I would like to see you so bad and talk with you of old times but I know I would not know you if I was to see yo the last time I seen you. you was not nothing but a Boy John. I synpathise with you very much for you seem very near to me John do you know that I nursed you when you was a babe it makes my heart ache to think of you and where you are I hope you will put your trust in God and you will get for giveneff for your sins and come out all right at last. and be a good religous man, I know you are not guilty for every thing you are accused of but howsome ever you will have to make the best of it you can, dont give up keep in good spirits as you can. John I have not got a dollar on the place are I would let you have it as free as ever took a drink of water when Mr Dikes comes he will send you some money John I suppose you know that your Father is dead you Pa and Ma and children stayed all night at our house when we lived at Ennis a bout 4 years ago that was the last time I seen them but have heard from them since John you know you had a good religous Father you ought to be religous to it is never to late as long as there is life god is merciful if you ask him in the right way he will bless you and take you home to heaven John you must right to your Mother you know she is the best friend you have got John I have seen a good deal of trouble since I saw you last If we never meet in this world I hope we. will meet in heaven wheare there is know trials and troubles there I expect to pray for you as long as I live John if you have one of your Photograph pleas send it I would like so much to have it to see how you look John I intend to pray for you as long as I live John I would be glad to get a letter from you any time write often and tell me how you are getting along, well I have no news to write so I mus close for this time hoping to hear from you soon so good bye my dear Cousin

A. C. Dikes

---

28. J. W. H. to Mrs. Jane Hardin

1St.

Dec the 5th 1877 Austin Travis county Texas

Mrs Jane. Hardin

My Darling and affecttionate Wif I. received your kind and most welcome Letter to day. Which give me much Satisfaction to Know that you had been able to get one letter from me and also to know that you & the family were all well. Jane this Leaves me well and injoy

James G. Hardin,
father of John Wesley Hardin.

Elizabeth Hardin,
mother of John Wesley Hardin.

better health than I have Since I came here. about 2 weeks ago I had a severe attact of my Side but received good Attention and did not Last Long. Jane I am wel cared for and Kindley treated have all the medica aid that maybe necissary for me to have. Jane I am in good
pag 2nd
Spirits as one could be under the
Same circumstances. one of my Lawyers have been to See me Since I Wrote to you he Says that for me to be in good Spirits that my case is Shore to be reversed & or remandede. Jane if So I am Shore to come clear yet. he Says that I Should of come clear at the commanchie trial, according to Evidence and Say that the courts of Appeals wil Say So. for the testimony was that there was no insulting Language or threats made by me and that the first insulting word was from web which as follows. No god dam you. puling his pistol

and firing at the Same time then I Defended my Self but not untill he fired the 1st Shot. J.W.H
page 3rd.
he also Says that the court errored in Several instances. I have received a letter from mat and one from Sister Lizzie who inquire much about you. mat Says that. She, Ma & Mr Smith mat husban wil or has all ready written to you and that they would Like for you to be with them much. and that you and Some of them would come to See me then. Jane write to them amediateley there postofice is Bennet Station red river county Texas. Jane my Dear you Do not know how often I think of you my Sweet & true wife, though many miles away. Jane Dearest do not Grieve for me for it wil do no good. but Look for a bright future which may yet come. I am able to bear my troubles and wil do it Like a man. Donot want one that is So Dear to me to grieve or be in Trouble. yours John W. Hardin to his wife.
Jane I have Sent your Letter to Brown he has returned it he Says that it is a good Letter. and that he is glad that one person has not yet forgot him he also Says that he wold Like to get a letter from uncle N or Some of the family that if he is going to Be hung on the 23 of this mo he Knows nothing about it Jane it is not So. Brown Says tell all to write and Sends his Love to all of the family and friends Jane Kiss the Children for me and tell them that I love them and for them not to forget me. Give My Love to C.M.N.J. & uncle N tell them that I have not yet forgotton them. Also to Jim Jane & F. Brown Sends his love to Mary & Litte N. Also. and Says he is in good health. Now my Dear wife I wil bring my Letter to a close by Sending Love to all expecting an answer Soon John W Hardin to his true wife Jane Hardin. good By Love til I hear from you again you are my Dearest
Please forward this to my wife Whiting or escambie county. alalbama please forward and not fail
Jane I heard from your pa Sunney Numan was here yesterday to See me he Says that your pa is fixing to Send after you he Says that I have not got an enemy down there Jane if he Sends for you you had better come by Mas or uncle bobs Brown Says Kiss the Sweet Little Children for him good by Dearest Remember me when this you Se

JWH

First Methodist Church of Richland, Texas

29. Elizabeth Hardin to Jane Hardin

Red River Co. Tex Decmber 14th, 1877

Mrs Jane Hardin) **Whiting Aala)**

My very dear daughter

I received your kind welcome letter. so very glad to hear from you and those sweet little ones although it filled my heart with sorrow and grief to hear and know that you ware so anxious to come to Texas and has not the means to come with. my dear daughter I am so sorry that I cant assist you. if I had the money I would send it to you amediatly you know our troubles at Commanche we ware robed of our dear Jodie and our sweet Johnie gone we knew not whare and our property stolen. and since that time I have had deep heart rending trouble I have stood by the bed side of my dear husband one that I loved above all others. wiped the cold dew drops from his marble brow. closed his eyes in death with my own hands. while Strangers ware sheding tears freely. no kindred relation was near except Nannie and my sweet little Gippie. death came found your Pa ready he tole me in his last monents. that the good Lord would take him right to heaven, my dear daughter a few more beating winds and Storms I to may be wafted home to meet loved ones that has washed their robes and made them white in the blood of the lamb. Jane I want to know what kind of buisness Johnie he engaed in and what was his circumstances he never has tole me. though I have never asked him. poor boy I am so Sorry for him. Sometimes I feel like I can not beare any more. I received two letters from him the day that I got yours. he was in better health then he had bee for some time. he say that his keepers are kind and his treatment is good as yet. he wants me to write to you for you to come to my house and you and myself visit him. I would be so glad if you could come. I have pleanty to live on we have our own meet and corn potatoes Melasses and you and those Sweet little babes Should Share with me. Johnnie wants me to visit him if you cant. I expect to start to see him the first or Second week in January. Jeff will go with me he Say he wishes he had the money he would go after Sister Jane. O it is So hard to think that we are not able to assist you. the only way that we have to make money is by Jeff running the wagon and that is a very slow way poor little fellow he is left to tug and toil in this wourld with out the help or instruction of a Father. Jane if you can not raise the means. to come on I would call upon Strangers. cant your Pa help you I do want to see you So much kiss your babes for me. tell little Mollie to come to See gran Ma and I will make her tea to drink. Jane write amediatly. Johnnie tole me to tell you to bear your troubles the very best you can. perhaps there may be a brighter future. Jane if I see that we can assist you any this winter we will gladly do so. cheer up you are too young to dispare good by dear child. your Ma Elizabeth Hardin P.S. I hear from your uncle Bob often he is helping Johnie all he can you wanted to know if Mattie is married. She is. She Married a Mr Smith a very nice cleaver man he thinks there is no one like Mattie and I think a great deal of him they live four miles from me. Bennitt Station Mr Cobb and Lizzie was down to see me a few weeks ago they live at Bonham Fannin County

EH

---

30. Mattie Bowen to Mrs. Jane Hardin

Mrs Jane Hardin Gonzales Texas Dec 20th 1877

Dear sister I take the pleasure to write you few lines to let you know that we are all well at present and truly hope when this meets you it will you and Children the best of health my self and William answered you letter but have never herd from you since William &

Duncan McGee Says that if you want to come out here they will Send after you Pa & Uncle Ben & William will be out there in January with Some Horses and you can come with them Suney Newman has Just been up to Austin and Seen Wes and Brown. they are fine Spirits times is dull here at prest Money is Scarse but plenty of Corn and meat Give my best respects to Uncle Neill and famly and tell them to write to me write Soon as you get this and let me know how you are getting along the family there love and. respects to you **from your loving Sister Mattie Bowen**

---

31. Mattie Smith to Jane Hardin.

Bennett Texas Dec 29,1877 Mrs Jane Hardin

Dear Sister

I Seat my Self to write you a few lines in answer to yours of the 20. I was So glad to hear from you and yar little children. we are all well ma and the children have just gone home. they spent christmas with us we had a right lively time at Bennett christmas eve had a christmas tree. and then the next night the young folks Stormed us and danced. I had plenty nice cake & pies to hand around. well Jane we received a letter not long Since from. John he wants ma to come to See him. She wants to start by the middle of January. he wanted you to go with her. She is going in a waggon it is about tree hundred (300) miles Jeff is going to take her now Jane if you can come write immediately for Jeff will have to Start So he can get back in time to make a crop ma answered your Some time ago. John Said he was in better health than he had been in Some time well I have no news to write and I am in a hurry to mail it Kiss the children for me answer this immediately Mr Smith Sends his regards to you

Your Sister Mattie Smith

---

32. Elizabeth Hardin to Jane Hardin

Red River. Co Jan 15th. 1878 Mr J.W. Hardin Auston. Tex

My very dear son.

I am here at Bright's I. thought I would write you a few lins. I have been laying my plans to visit you for some time but have not been able to get off as yet. the weather has been so severe and I wanted our meet cured before I would leave. So my dear child do not dispir your Ma is going to see you shure if providence smiles. O how I do want to see you my dear boy. all the day long I am thinking of my dear sweet Johnnie. you seem dearer to me then any thing on earth for I know your troubles and oppressions. my dear boy bear up. I hope a bright future is awaiting you. I do trust that you may have a fare and inpatial trial next time. I received a letter from dear Jane your sweet wife not long since she sayed that she had the promise of some money the first of this month if she gets it C-C will soon be here on her way to Auston if She comes we will go together I intend to start by the first of March a the furthrest and then I will stay untill your trial if the good Lord will p ———. as you- Pa said to poor Jodie when they hurried him off from us to the guard house. put your trust in the good Lord my son O Johnnie O bee prayful. "God is our refuge". write to me often I am so glad to get a line from you we all talk and think of you so much. Often I dream of being with you. but when I awake I find it all a dream I receivied a letter from R.E.H on the 4th inst. Jeff and Gipie is well sends love to you my sweet boy how I do want to see you. I will write soon again, good bye Sweet Johnie (E. Hardin to J. W. Hardin)

GABE SLAUGHTER WAS KILLED BY BILLY TAYLOR ABOARD THE CLINTON STEAMBOAT, AS PART OF THE SUTTON-TAYLOR FEUD.

---

33. J. W. H. to Jane Hardin

Jan the 29 the 1878 Austin Texas Mrs Jane Hardin
My Dear an affectionate Wife I received your Kind and affectionate letter to Day dated Jan the 20 Which Give me much Satisfaction to here from one that has ever been to me the Dearest of all . allthoug we are now many miles apart . and bondage charms our wings . but Dearest and Truest one I hope it wil not allways be So . But remember me Deares . you write as though you did not Get my last two letters . at Least you Said that the Last one you received was on the 7the of Dec 1877 this My (Darling one) is the 3rd one that I have Writen you Since that time and hope that you may Get this one . but Dearest Donot think that

2nd
I ever shal forget to answer a Letter from you my Darling wife for you (Dearest one) I wil ever remember allthoug there may yet be many changes . I wil not forget the My Darling wife Jane this Leaves me well at presen. and in as Good Spirits as could be expected . Jane my Lawyers think that my case wil be remanded . if So I am all right Billey Taylor was convicted for Killing Slaghter on the Clinton to the Penitenitiary for 10 yr his case has been remanded .So I hope Billey wil yet Get out he is in the Galveston Jail. When you come home if you Should come by Galveston if conveniant Go to See him . he Says he would be Glad to See his cousin Jane . Mannin Clements has been here in Jail with me 6 weeks
3rd
to a day. he Started to day for Gonzales accompanied by the Shariff in Charge of Killing Patten Patterson in 72 . Jane he Goes down there on a writ of habeas corpus for Bond . I think he wil Be out Soon on Bond he is Just the Same as when you Last Saw him .he Sends his Love to you and the Children. Mollie C wrote me one Letter She inquired much about you and allso Sends Love to you and the Children . Man Says if you are not here by the time he Gets out that he wil ether Go or Send after you . I think he is Sure to Get out Soon . Jane ma Says that She wil try and have you to come to her House and that you and her wil visit me by the 1st of March at the furthest So Dearest Good Bye for this time J.W.H to His Wife Jane Hardin
4th
Jane my Dear wife do not grieve nor take trouble to Hart remember that wher there is a will there is a way and that the darkest hours are Just before day Give my love to all of the family and Kiss those Sweet children of mine for me my Dearest one and do not Let them forget me I know that Callie is bound to Be a fine Sweet Babe Oh how Dear you all are to me though now far away But yet I wil remember the. Brown your Brother Joins me in Sending Love to all SoGood By my Deares truest & Grieving Wife I hope you wil not all-ways Be in that Contry John.W.Hardin to his Dear Wife Jane Hardin Escambia co. Whiting Alabama Good By
Please forward this in haste
Please forward to Jane Swain or Hardin Whiting ala

34. J. W. H. to Jane Hardin

[UNDATED]

Jane I Dont believe I told you But I am well vs common Jane I wil Say a few more words and then Stop for this time I Done what you asked me as soon as I got through reading your letter which was to Answer well while writing Brown has Been Playing the fidle Jinne Calowow Drunkards lamentation and many other favorite tunes in His cell Brow is Here we talk to gather every day but cannot See one another I have Seen him Several times he Says that he is fatter than He ever was. they found him guilty of murder in the 1st degree for killing tom Halderman he has Stood tryal and is Here for Safe Keeping he has also Appealed His case Brown Sends his love to all and Says kiss the Children for him and also Sends His Love to Mary and little Neal Brown Says for you all to write Sends his love to umcle Neil and Famly He says to tell marry that he is enjoying good Health and in good Spirits and that He would like to Here from them all any time tell uncle N to write me a letter- Good by to All Kiss the children for me and be Sure to Send me your picture (Jane the Judge of camanchie Was Fleming and the prosicuting Attorney was His pardner J D Stephens)

From J.W. Hardin to his Distressed wife J. Hardin

Jentelmem please forward this Letter in Haste to Jane Swain or Hardin Whiting Alab

Ma postofice is Bennette Read river County Texas

" " " Bennette Red river Co Texas

---

35. J. H. Clements to J. W. H.

P.J. PONTON. W.S. FLY.

Prompt and special attention given to

BUYING AND SELLING LANDS ON COMMISSION

PAYING TAXES FOR NON-RESIDENTS.

—And—

INVESTIGATING LAND TITLES IN ANY PORTION OF TEXAS

PONTON & FLY,

LAW OFFICE,

LAND AND COLLECTING AGENCY.

Gonzales, Texas, Jan 31 1878

All lands placed in our hands for sale
will be liberally advertised at our expense
J.W. Hardin Austin Tex
Dear friend
I write this to inform you that Manning arrived here in yesterday evening safe and well after having a very agreeable trip And we all feel under many obligations to Sheriff Corwin and Mr Turner for the kindness and indulgence allowed him which we will never forget His trial on "Habeas Corpus" will not be tried before 21 February as Judge Lewis will be necessarily absent holding Court until that time—Manning is in good Spirits and does not fear anything if a fair and impartial trial is granted to him - He sends his kindest regards to Brown Bowen as well as yourself—and any others who may feel interested to inquire after him

Your Friend

J. H. Clements

JANE HAS DEPARTED FOR TEXAS.

---

36. M. Clements to David Baker

Gonzales Feb 15 1878

frind David B.
I Received your kind and welcome letter and will answer Dave i have no news worth writing I am in the Cage with 15 others I get plenty to Eat and treated as well as a prisenor is Expected Dave I hope your case will Come back all Right and all soe if I get a trial next thursday I will Come and see you boys if i get out tell dell Doublin to hold up his his head —pe dies hard all looks faverble in my Case and I will Come out all Right if I can get a fair trial Soe dave write me as soon as you get this note give my Respects to all the Boys Dave tell W. to Belt them up when the need it so i will Close I Remain as Ever yur frind Answer soon as you get this from a frind

M. Clements

To, D, -, Baker

---

37. Unknown writer to J. W. H.

1st. P **Feb 15 1878** **Mr JWH** **Austin Texas/**
Dear Cousin I Received your welcome letter this morning and will Hasten to answer this leaves me well and hope will find you enjoying good health Well I have no news to write only their has two Cases here that went to the applet. Court. Nelson ——— Hodg for atenped Murder ——— & ———& James - Carnes for the theft of a horse affermed 5 years. Wesly I was glad to here from you and Brown and to here Ben & Josh had been to see you. write me the news why did Brown not write me at the Same time you did. James & gip has gone out on ——— have not seen them since ——— wrote will be here at my trial Wesly their is nothing worth Relating here i have the ca—r— you know I all ways have here you ——— Every thing is Faverbly well Wesly i was proud to here the Express had come tell chilldrs not to let you or the other will eat my cake Keep it for me tell all the Boys i would like to See them out on the green right side

---

38. Elizabeth Hardin to J. W. H.

Red River Co. Feb. 15th, 1878 Mr J.W.Hardin Auston Texas
My very dear and Son
I write from home this morning we are all well except Nannie and little Gippie has the Hooping cough I received your letter some time ago I thought I would wait a few days perhapse I would hear from Jane and the other day we got such a kind sweet letter from her. though I am so disappointed she says her father is going after her. that he will return by your uncle Bob's I was so in hopes of seeing her and those sweet little babes at my own house I have so much to tell her. O John I do want to see you so much there has been so many changes and heart rendings scenes since we last parted. I do want to talk with you so much I feel that it would be a great sourse of pleasure to me to meet with you any whare though it ware in the prison house. for I know that you was put there unjustly. if they had gone by law and evidence you would not been whare you now are. But my dear son do not dispair I do hope you may have a fair an impartial trial next time that the Judge will not be wayed by preju-

dice. if I had the chooseing the place for your trial I would perfur Auston before any place else in the State. you say that your keepers are kind O I do feel so thankful to them for their kindness to my dear oppressed boy. my dear som be prayful I believe you do pray a boy that was raised as you was can not forget to pray. it is prayr that unlocks the gates of Heaven, if it was not for prayr. my heart would fant and dye. my dear son your Pa lived a prayrful life and died a praying. now my dear Johnnie I intend to be at your trial, write often it does me so much good to get a line from you I read it over and over again the children all wants to see you. we talk about you so much. Mattie is expecting to be confined at any time now I received a letter from (R.E.H.) the fourth of Jan. I sent it to your uncle Bob for Jane as Jeff is in a hurry to go to the Station I must close.

O let us meet in heaven
O let us meet in heaven
in heaven alone no sorrow known
and there no parting there

Your Ma Elizabeth Hardin

---

39. Lizzie Cobb to John W. Hardin

Feb. 17, 1878 **Bonham**
Mr John W Hardin **Feb 17. 88**

Dear Brother,

I received your Kind letter Some two weeks ago. I must acknowledge I have been to negligent about an swering your last letter but will do better here after. I hear from you occasionally through ma's letters. I am always glad to read a line from my Dear Brother. I received a letter from Ma yesterday they were all well, I also received a letter from Sister Bell at Mt Calm She was well, She was inquiring So particular about about you She was afraid you would not get justice at your next trial as She did not Know it was moved to Austin, for She thought it would be better for you if you could move it to another place. I wrote to her this morning it was moved to Austin. Ma Says She thinks She will be at your trial, write how many Lawyers you have, write if you hear from Aunt Nan & uncle Barnett. Well Bro I hardly Know what else to write. Only I am looking forward for the happ days you will See if you get out of your trouble which I am in hopes you will. I read your trial in Several papers it was So unjust & illegal, I think you will have justice done toward you this time. The public Sentiment of the people are very sympathetic toward you Thought you were done So wrong in your trial in Commanche write immediately yours as ever

Lizzie Cobb

PS I will Send you our pictures as Soon as we have them taken. Direct your letters to Lizzie Cobb box 93

---

40. Elizabeth Hardin to J. W. Hardin

Mr J.W. Hardin from his Ma E Hardin

Red River Co. Texas Feb 26th.1878

Mr. J.W. Hardin Auston Tex

My very dear Son

I received your kind Sweet letter some time ago and hasten to answer it. have not received an answer yet. hope I will Soon. Johnnie it does me so much good to get a line from you and from one I love so dearly. John I have got good news for you. Jane and your Sweet little babes arrived at Bennett Station last friday morning on the nine O clock Bright and Mattie so glad to see her. Nannie was all redy at the Station. next morning Bright brought Jane Nannie and the little ones to my house. O I can not express the Joy and pleasure her arrival afforded me though my cup was mingled with Sorrow Sandness. the recolections of the past rushed through my mind, like the rushing of many waters. we Spent that eavning in talking about you. that night Jane Jeff and myself Spent nearly the whole night talking reading letters and Sometimes laughing and Sometimes crying. John Jane is the most devoted wife I ever Saw She bears her troubles well her hole Soul is Set on you She is a great woman your Sweet little ones talks about you so much. and Says they are going to see Pa Pa. they are Such Sweet interesting children I love them So dearly. Jane is in fine Spirits of Seeing you soon Jeff and myself wants to go with her if we possably can about the midle of March we will write to you again and let you know more about us coming. Jane said she recivied a letter from you the day before she left she thought she would wit untill she would get to my house and then she would write to you. yestarday we ware both Just going to write you, and Mr Smith sent for me in a hurry Matt was sick and this morning about day light she was delivered of a fine daughter weighed nine lbs Mattie and the babe are doing well. Jane tole me to write to you for her while here as it would be a day or too before she would have an opportunity of sending you a letter. John you are all this wourld to her she is so true to you. John you must keep in good Spirits I trust we will see you soon. Son I do thi— that there will be a brighter day for yet, you know that your former dificulty with the negro, and the negro police and mobs that has been crying for your blood except the last difeculty that is the Well diffculty and he fired the first shot. now son if you can get a fare trial which I think you can at Auston you will be bound to come clear. I got a letter from Br Robert a few days ago he was quite sick though better. John write to your uncle Barnett to attend your trial if he is able I believe he would attend. I have been looking for an answer from you for some time. write and Jane and myself will often. O how I do want to see my darling sweet boy. why John I am proud to tell strangers that I am the Mother of John Wesley Hardin though you are published as the notorious J.W Hardin a thief and a murder and all this yet, I know that you are an honest man and those that know you best say that you are honest honerble and high minded Sisie says tell you she writes to you

Good by sweet Son you Ma **E Hardin**

---

41. Mary Campbell to Jane Hardin

Santa Rosa Fla March the 9th. 1878 Miss J. Hardin Dear Cousin I received your letter Last night and was glad to hear you got home safe and all rite this leaves us all well hoping it will reach you and children the same there is nothing new since you left we have not heard from John nor Brown since you left hard time here yet but we are glad you have got where you can do better and hope you will have good Luck Carline says for you to write to her for she wants to hear from you as often as she can Josh and PaPa sends their respects to you and the children and says for you to write to them and we want you to write to some of us when you get back from Austin and see John & Brown and let us know how they are getting along we want to hear from them so I will close write as soon as you get this that is all only I Remain your Cousin

Mary C. Campbell

---

42. Lizzie Cobb to J. W. H.

Bonham Tex March 11th, 1878 Mr John W Hardin

Dear Brother.

It has been some time since I received a letter from you. I wrote to you a week or more ago but, but received no answer yet & I am always glad to hear from you & I will write to you again as I am afraid you did not get my last letter . Do write of ten to me, I am so anxious to hear from you, Mr Blair of Bonham debtuty Sheriff) was to see us a few days ago said he was to see you & intended to bring a letter from you to us, but he was detained of some thing in Austin & could not go back to get your letter. he says you are in good Spirits & are well cared for. Well Johnie live in hope & pray to God to bring you out of you troubles for God is our Father & our friend & also (he) is love. I received a letter from Ma a few days ago they were all well Jane & your children were at her house Jane was so anxious to see you I hope before this time she has been to see you. Oh how I wish I could see her & the little ones, how I love them for your sake. Mattie has a little Girl named Lillie Smith about two weeks old. I hear from Sister Bell often she is so proud you have your trial moved from Comanche. Well Johnie I hardly know what else to write only to wait patiently & I think & hope at leas you will come out alwright in your next trial, you are Gaining friends all the time, the people Generally simpathies so much with you, think your trial in Comanche was so unjust. Write immediately & tell if Jane has been to see you Good bye Dear Brother

Yours as ever **Lizzie Cobb**

---

43. J. W. H. to Jane and Elizabeth Hardin

March the 14the 1878 Austin Texas Mrs Jane Hardin

My Dear wife

I received a letter a few days ago also one today dated the 9the would of wrote Sooner but have been very unwell have had the mumps for 17teen days am better this morning but Still Like a heap of being well. but hope to Be all right in a few days my case is Set for the 13teenth of may nearley one month off but the appellit court is now in Session here and I am in high hopes of having my case reversed if So I consider myself all right, at Least my chances wil be Good to Be a free man once more.

W. B. Hardin & John Godfrey of Hill County Say they wil Stand by me as long as there is a hare on my head. and have Sent me Some money to pay Att fees. & Say they wil do more Soon. they wrote to me first to know the least amount of money could be got along with at present. they are my Cousins ma can tell you all about them John Godfrey married Marthie Waddle Barnetts Sister

Jane Dear Brown has Gone to Gonzales to receive Sentence as court is in Session he wrote a long letter before he left here to the Governor Stating before his high God that he brown Bowen was to Be hung for another mans crime that he did not kill Tom Halderman and had nothing to do with it that John Wesley Hardin done it But did not avail any thing. he allso wrote one to the Statesmam a newspaper here in austin which Said his letter was to long for publication and Just abstracted a Shorte note of it Stating that before his God he did not Kill Thomas Halderman and that he was to Be Hung for another mans crime & that he did not have any thing to do with it that John Hardin done it So you can See the Game he tried to Give me & Neal Bowen Last court Got an indictment against me in curo for murder in 72 this is the Game They have give me you can bet that they are my friends Jane Dear I answered browns piece in the Statesman & Did with reluctance but Self preservation is the 1st Laws of nature Jane Dear you know I have allways been a friend to N Bowen & have rendered him many favors whch you are well aware He is your Father but I tell you Dear he has even tried to Lay Browns

----

Jane My Dear what I have told you is not hearsay but what I know to be So & Dear if it had not Been for Browns & your Pas letters I would have been a free man today but nevertheless they cannot hurt me now it was Browns Letter that detected me in Florida and if he Brrown had of taken my plan to do he would of been free but alas he did not allthough I made every thing plain to him but he would not Listen went his on way

Ma do you remember Georg & Beisly Campbell of Sumpter Sallie their Sister is here she is my friend but no one knows it you Bet She is Sollid allthou a prostitute but my Friend a poor Girl on the town Do not mention her name in your Letters to me but use Some thing else Jane Dear I wrote this to Send out at the door but wil Send it out on the Sly and of course donot expect an answer onley Such as I wish the Jailors to Se Jane Dear Brown would of Been a free man to day But I could do nothing with him he told all the Lies & Truths he could on me to the Jailors evry time I put confidences in him he betrayed me So you See I could not help him nor myself either. If he new or thought any one was trying to get out of Jail he would tell it he would not get away nor Let any one else But Dear as for myself Donot fear. for my friends wil Stand by me in the end and Say it is onley a mater of time Dear I consider my chances good but you may think the time Long and it may So but I hope not you can bet I am in high hopes of yet Being with you and wil Say to you that I bear my Troubles well & never think that I am gave up as long as there is Life for I am not if my case is reversed I wil arrange So you can come & See me which I think it wil be but cant tell Dear I have wrote more than I Should of writen under the Circumstances but nevertheless all goes **John**

---

44. J.W.H. to family, with enclosed letter from John C. Godfrey and W. B. Hardin to J. W. H.

M Clements (PO) is SanSaba County
Richland Springs I look for him Soon

Woodbury Hill Co., Texas
March the 15th 1878
Mr John. W. Hardin
Auston Texas

Dear Sir my Self & W. B. Hardin take the liberty of droping you a few lines as. Barnett got a letter from Aaron. B. Hardin to day Stating your Counsell at Waco had rote to you to raise Some money for him to carrey on your case. How mutch will it take and how little can you make out with we are prettey hard prest but on a Strain could raise a little let us heare from you Imediateley all is well your cousins as Ever

John. C. Godfrey &
W.B. Hardin

Dear Mother Sisters & Brothers Love to you all write to me often I write to you all whenever I have paper & envellopes Dear mother Do all you can to Soothe Jane my Dearest troubles & tell her that we cannot help what others do keep her in Good Cheer Kiss all of the family for your Son and tell them that I think of them often ma I write to you ever chance do not think hard But write and take care of my oppressed family Love to all good by Dear ones

John W Hardin

---

45. J. W. H. to Jane and Elizabeth Hardin

March the 17 the 1878
Austin Texas

Mrs Jane Hardin

My Dear and Loving wife

I now Seat my Self to write you a few lines to Let you know how I am getting along at present and allso answer your Kind and most welcome Let which was received by me a few days ago and read with Great pleasure. my Dear I have been Sick with the mumps for 17 days passed but at present am a Great deal Better and am improving in health fast. I am allso treated very kindley by my Keepers who are very attentive to me and brought in the Doctor Several times while I was Sick. Dear I received a letter from S H Rennick of Waco yesterday he has had my case Set for the l3the of may he wil Be here on the 11th to get ready for trial he Says that he is confident of a reversal if So I am all right and my chances are Good to Be a free man once more you Bet I am in High hopes Dearest one write me often you donot know how Glad I am to receive a line from you my Dear Wife John. W. Hardin

Dear I look for manin C here Soon he went to Gonzales on the 28the of last month to Stand trial for killing Pate Paterson he wil assit me all he can but is rathe cramped at present John Godfrey & Barnett, Hardin of Hill county are willing to assist me and Have Sent me Some money to pay Att and Say they wil Stand by me as long as ther is a hare on my head you Bet I am in High Spirits. Dear I wil come to a close by tilling you to Kiss all the Children for me tell M

& John to be Good to Callie there little Sister Love to All Adieu my Dear and affectionate Wife J. W. Hardin

My Dear Mother I have wrote Jane the news but wil write you a line or two ma I have not got a letter from uncle Bob in Some time would like to heare from him do you keep up corespondence with him or not tell him I wish to here from him Besides you can tell him I have writen him Several Letters and as yet received no answer Dear Ma write often you donot know how much comfort it is for me to Get a letter from you Tell mat to write I believe She has Been Sick or Something else Love to all Kis Jane & the Babes for me my Dear mother hoping to here from you Soon & often your Son John. W. Hardin. this was done in Haste and have had no paper for Sonetime

---

46. J. W. H. to Jane Hardin

March the 26the <u>1878</u> Austin Texas

Mrs Jane Hardin My Dear Wife I have Just received and read your kind & welcome Letter and read with pleasure Glad to here from you once more and to Know that you were all well Jane Dearest do not Grieve or Bother yourself about me of course it is hard for us to Be appart but I trust it wil not Be So allways. you Do not know how I long to See your Swet and Smilling face once more. one who has ever been true to Me. and has Gone through So many trying Scens. this Leaves me well and in Good Spirits of course I am opressed and am Sorry to See things as it realey is Brown is convicted and case afirmed & wil have to pay the death pennelty the way it Stands now. No relief onley from the Govner he had M.C Arrested for the Pate Paterson murder but Mannin is out all right now on Bond onley $500.00 he has Been to See me once and is to Be here Soon he is our Friend yet and wil do all he can for us. But you can rest assured that (N.B) & Brown are not. but have done all they can against me. I am Sorry for Browns condition but yet it is onley Justice & right & right wil rule. he has tried to Lay his foul & disgracefull crimes on me. but they dont go worth a cent. Jane I have Just explained a few things to you but do not let them Bother you nor Give them one thought. Court comences here the 1St monday in april donot think my case wil be heard of for 6 week yet my Lawyers Say that I am all right cant tell time wil but you can Just Bet the devils cant hang me and as long as there is life there is hopes. I realy think that my case wil be remanded but can not tell for ceartain you can bet I Stand true to my corse and wil never give a man away no not even to Gain my own Liberty and it is a pleasure to me to know that I have a few friends who has not nor wil not go back on me even in my trying Scens. but I hope yet to meat you my Dearest one my Shoulders are broad and hope to Be able to Land nay But Safe

Jane Dearest write Soon & often it is a great pleasure for me to here from you my dear wife

J.W. HARDIN

---

47. Elizabeth Hardin to J. W. H.

Red River Co. March 30th. 1878 Mr. J.W. Hardin Auston, Tex

My own Dear Son

I write you a few lines this morning to let you know that we are all wewll. when you wrote me last. you said that you was not as well as you had been. I do trust that you are quite well now. dear Johnie no tungue can tell how much I do want to see you I can not get the money to go to see you I have been doing my very best not even enough to go by private conveyance I have been looking forward and making my arangements to go. at one time I was preparing my clothing and evry thing look fair. and finaly I could not raise means enough. it all most broke my heart and does yet to think that I can not see my own dear son. who is so much oppressed I. do hope your case may be renanded and you be all right yet. my son you know from the evidence at Commanche you should have come clear, if you remain there this summer I think shurly there will be some way for me to visit you I. have writen to our kin of Houston and Liberty and your uncle Barnetts of Polk. asking them to do something for you I tole them you needed assistance in order to procure able counsil. if your case is properly attended to I do think you will get a new hearing and if so I do not believe you will be condemed. I do trust you will be a free man yet John you say your keepers are kind I do feel so thankful to them all. Jane and the children are well She is so anxious to see you She is a true wife She

Says She wishes She could get a letter evry day from you your sweet little children are so sweet they talk about you so much you said you ware glad that Jane and the little ones are here so am I. do not be uneasy about them while they are with me for I will do for them Just the same as I would for you. She is very anxious to go west. She wants to See you So much and. I think if She could visit you She would be perfectly willing to return here. write to me Sweet Johnie it does me So much good to get a letter from you and I will write to you. my Sweet Son I do want to See you more then any one on earth. Jeff has gone to farming as he could not or we could not visit you. Nannie is Sick Gippie is a fine boy they all talk about you and wish they could See thir budie Johnie write write.
Now my dear Son do be prayrful I know that you believe in prayr pray that you may yet be Successful that your enemies may become your friends and that your Soul my be washed and made white the blood of the Lamb remember what a prayrful Life your Pa lived and your Ma is Still Praying for her Sweet boy. when you read this remember your Ma

O let us meet in heaven
In Heaven alone no Sorrow
Known and there no parting there

Your Ma. E. Hardin

---

48. From W. B Hardin to J. W. H.

Hill County Aprile the 6:78

Dear cousin After my love to you I will Say we are all well John I got your leter a fiew minits ago datied march 25 John I Startied, 40.$ dolars to you in a redgirstera leter on the 2 day of this month which I hope you have got John hoald up your head iff you can get anew trile you will beat a your case let me know what you are dew Renick tell him to put your case thrue I am Dam wiling to do all I can and ready at iney time to do alitle I want you to Anser this as Soon as you get it and keep me poastied and John I will Stand by you as long as there is a hare on your head keep in good Spearits The people are turning on your Side fast I got aleter from unkle Bob doant forget to let me hear from you oftin and keep me poastied I will cloas for I am in the poast ofis hoald up your head if you —y hard I want to no Renick fieas your Cousin **W B Hardin**

---

49. John C. Godfrey to J. W. H.

Woodbury Hill Co,, Texas April the 7th AD 1878
Mr John. W. Hardin

Dear Cousin I avail my Self of this oppertunity of droping you a few lines this leaves my Self & family all well Barnett was down yesterday all well except there Babey it was not well. John in regard I will Say this to you Barnett & my Self Sente you $40.00/100 forty dollars in Registered letter on the 2nd of this (Inst) would of Sente you more but on Such Shorte notice that was the best we could do at that time I had the promice of 27 dollars to be handed me yesterday but the young men that had borrowed my money Skiped out to Arkansas last friday morning and I have lost that had I of got it I would of gladley Send it by to days mail John we have had to Shorte a notice Still If you cannot get aney help from aney other quarter and money will Still Be a benefit to you let us heare Imediatley. from you and we will work day and night till we heare from you and Mabey we can do a little more for you by that time I have just paid out $675 00/100 for land Since Christmas your cousin Mat is willing to assist you in the darkest hour of your troble it is now neare 11 oc and raining we neede it very mutch hoping Soon to heare from you Soon Has Dr Shegogg helped you aney or can he or will he lives at Enis. Elis co,, Texas What has uncle Barnett done

I am Sir your cousin as Ever
John. C. Godfrey

P.S. What time do you think your case will be called for a hearing Please State J.C.G

J.W. Hardin Austin Texas
in care of Sheriff Corwin

---

50. S. H. Renick to J .W. H.

—OFFICE OF—

S.H.RENICK
Attorney and Counselor at Law.
Waco, Texas, Apr 16 1878 John Wesley Hardin Esq
Dear Sir:your favor of the 9th to hand. I am glad to hear from you. I am aware that your Case is set for the 13th of May That was done at my request and for my accommodation. I will be there. do all you can to be ready. I will be in Austin on the 11th and get ready for the argument. I am confident of a reversal.
Yours as Ever **S H Renick**

---

51. Mattie Bowen to Jane Hardin.

A Prile the 19th 1878 Mrs Jane Harden
Dear Sister I seat my self to Write you a few lines to let you no that We are all Well at this time hopeing this wil find you the same I was in Auston on the 15th of this month I saw Wes he was Well and in fine Spirits he Said he was Sattisfide he would get a new tryal and come out all right he requested me to Write to you and let you no how he was getting a long he told me that you rote that you had Writtin three letters and got no answer Jane I hav rote you one or two and William rote two since We heard from you Jane I hav sad news to write on Friday Night after I left Auston I got Home When me and Jo got their We found Browns corps their he was hung on friday the 17th and his Body Was sent Home and Bearid hear at Home Jane I Want you to Write as soon as you get this letter you dont no how glad We Would to heare from you Wel I wil Close for this time So Nothing more
I Remain yore Kind Sister until death **Mattie Bowen**

---

52. J .W. H. to Jane Hardin

April the 29 the 1878 Austin Texas Mrs Jane Hardin
My Dear & loving Wife it is with pleasure that I now Seat myself to write you a few Lines. allthough it has been Some time Since I have received a letter from you my Dear. But nevertheless I wil write you whenever oportunity wil admit knowing that you are ever anxious to heare from me. and my Dear wife I assure you that to here from you at any time is a pleasure to me. and hope even yet admitten our

Circumstances that we may be blessed yet with a hapy life together. and enjoy the pleasures of this world as once before. notwithstanding the many Difficulties which are now inbeded in our path. but I hope those obstacles wil be moved. Dearest & Truest one Time wil Tell. Dearest one I did not think we would both ever live on this earth and be apart as long as we have Been but My Dear wife Circumstances allters casses in this ugly world of Faces.
My case is Set for the 13 teenth of may S.H. rennick of Waco wil be here on the 11th . . . to prepare for business he Says that he is confident of a reversal. I am in high Spirits, for I think if the Judges wil onley have nerve & honor to Stand by law & Justice that my case wil be reversed, if so I consider my chances Good to remove the dark cloud which now covers my injoyment on this earth if my case is remanded it wil be a pleasure to me. to even lie in Jail and await trial, and Show the world that John W. Hardin is not the man as has been represented Dear one Do the best you can. Donot let afliction trouble your mind allthoug they may Seeme Severe be pleasant and try to make all arround you happy Dear my health is improving at present have had th mumps for one month But am all right at present one & have been treated Kindley by my attentive Keepers I wil Close by Sending Love to ma & all the Family & kis those dear children for me my Loving wif Adieu John. W. Hardin. (PS) Dear Ma write me a letter and remember my Dear Little Family for me Sisters and Brothers wil Be glad to here from you all any time Barnet Hardin & John godfrey wil do all they can for me Say they wil Stand by me as long as there is a hair on my head. I hope to here from you Soon Donot wait for answer but I wil write now and then you Son **John W Hardin**

---

53. J. W. H. to Jane Hardin

DENNIS CORWIN SHERIFF — OFFICE OF — JNO—KIR-, .DEPUTY.

[Sheriff of Travis County,]
(IN COURT-HOUSE,)

Austin,Texas, May the 18th 1878 Mrs Jane Hardin

My Dear & Loving wife
It is with pleasure that I now Seat myself to write to you once more. Jane Dearest & trues it is true I am more than oppressed but Dear

one I cant help But be Cheerful and live in hopes of better days yet to come. and even yet consider my chances good My case was argured on the 15the but no descision as yet But cannot think the Judges can do anything but reverse my case although I have been convicted by news paper reports and by the Lies of cowardley murders & assasins to predjidice the minds of the people and courts of the State of Texas against me but dear one I can bare it all. Let my fate be what it may. but dear my case wil be dcided Soon & whether reversed or affirmed be Cheerfull. as for my own & personal Trouble it does not bother me. but dear one I consider that I have more to live for than most any one could be aware of. as for myself my mind has been made up long ago. which I hope Dear you are well aware Jane Donot Grieve or Trouble you mind but be Cheerful my Dear wife your troubles has and is Great and I do wish I could bear them for you Jane Deares I think of you and those Dear Babes often while in my uncomfortable Situation for dear one I Know you think of me and I do hope we can yet enjoy life together as once before & ever remember that I am you Loving Husband and who would willingley bear your Troubles if possible Jane Dear your Pa & Sister mat was to See me on the 15th mat is as ever your Pa also. of course it is reasonable to Supose that you Pa has done all he could to Save Poor Brown but to no advantage he is troubled all but to death he could do nothing Jane Dearest I think as much of your pa and Family as ever and blame him for nothing allthough I have been badly treated. but dear: one your account & Sister Mats I forgive/ your Pa & Mat Sends there love to you and the family.. Jane Dear one your Pa wanted to know if there was a State ment I could make that could Save brown I told him no not honerable and I hoped he wished me not to make a false one in fact I said a True Statement wil do him no good & a false one I cannot make but told him I would do the Best I could as he insisted as the govner would not allow him even 30 days So I retired to my cell. So they come back the next morning and asked the Jailor for the Statement the Jailor informed me that they were there I made no reply So in about 10 minutes I received the following note.

(Brother John you told me you would make a true Statement) (about my Brother oh god why Dident you oh my god my Poor) (Brother has to Be Hung oh my god do Something for him on) (my acount Signed M. E. Bowen.)

So I answered her note Dear Sister my wil is good. but Let every tub Stand on its own bottom you Say for your sake. for your sake I would do anything honerable and I Know you would not ask me to do any thing dishonerable I cannot be made a Scape goat off and a true Statement wil do your brother no good and a false one I cannot make. but Sister I have a Statement all ready a true one in fact and wil give to you or your Pa then you can do as you please with it I am your Sympathizing ing Brother John W. Hardin.

Jane Dearest I cannot help But Let you Know what is going on. but Mat nor your pa called for the true Statement Dear I forgive poor Brown for his false and unfounded reports and may god forgive him. even after the cap was taken of of him he Said he was inocent but Said Jon. W. H done it and than fell 7 ft lived 7 Seconds witnessed by 4500 people May his poor Soul be in place and Hope that god forgive his Sins. Dear & loving one remember me and Kiss those darling babes for me once more and ever remnember that I am your loving & True Husband John. W. Hardin

Jane Dear write often I am in good health at present

Ma a few words write me often I wil write you soon again Love to all try and console my Dear wife and remember your Son JWH wil Do the Best he can allthough it may Seem poor You Son John W Hardin

Ma I wil write you Soon you must write often tell Jeff to be honest and Truthfull whatever he does and Hope he wil yet be an honer to our name Kiss all the Children for me adieu

John. W. Hardin

I Send you Some prees from the galvest— news let me know if you receive

---

54. From M. Clements to J. W. H.

May 29 the 1878 Mr J.W. Hardin

Dear Cousin I have Just Received your letter of date may the.8.th & mailed may the 10th I Was glad to hear from you.. and to Know that you was Well.. it found me and Familie in averige healthe.. and glad to hear from you.. and to know that you are still No.erd With the Living. well Wess I doe not know hardly what to write to you that would interest you. only James Harison staid Several days with me

Black Tom Caffall and Brown Bowen.
—Courtesy Special Collections, Albert B. Alkek Library, Southwest Texas State University, San Marcos, Texas

I guess you have not forgoten him. he is a sport that was with you at Cuero the time you took in — he told me to tell you he had not forgotan you.. and would write to you Soon he has been on the Run for Two years.. but is all, WRight now well I received a letter from J.L. Scott he wrote me that he would be at your trials I think he is a man of his word. I all soe Received a letter from John C.godfrey & Barnett, Hardin they told me they would meet me at your next trial. all soe. you bet Wess I will be their if all works wright.. well Wess you ben Judge for your self. how I am situated I have to be in Cureo by the 10th of june to Court will Come By as I goe down if I can and if i dont Come By I will Come By as I Come Back.. it is not because I doe not want to see you that makes me not come oftner it is other circumstences not necsary to mention on pappr. Well Wess I Will write to you Every time I have spare time and Come to See you too.. But you ought to know what Ive had to Contend with. without my Saying any thing about it you Can bet I had my hands full at all times But you Can Rest asured I
ve not forgottin you and never you be uneasz about that if I doe not write often it is because cercumstances wont permet will W write to me as soon as you get this after the first of June I will be on the Road to Dewitt . to Court I will Write to you as soon as I get their Well I done away with my thousand dollar — Case at gonzoles . you bet.. I had dared them Fellows down their. . Wess the gonzoles Boys Showed up & up you bet. W. you need not doubt Bill . Philips I doe think he is all Right he proved it to me any how. . in a way I can not mention for the want of Room — N.B. & Joe sunday seemed to have a good dive of Cash . they Showed up when down at gonzoles . 2 rools of green Back to amt of ($500.) the men was Reliable men and it is the opinion down their it is part of the Reward N.B. got from Duncan — it is my opinion it is soe Well Write as soon as you get this Letter let me hear from you W. I have writen to Jane But no answer and me and Mollie will write again at once so I will Close write as soon as you get this give Jane and all the Boys my Regards Soe I Remain as ever your Cousin untill death **M. Clements. To J W.Hardin**

Cusin John Pa. is Writing for me, &, manen. We are well & Would be glad to see you cusin John to Rassel With Litle J W H Jrs. I Will Rasel & Box With him next fall I would be glad to see you you must write to me me,&, Sallie I have got your name sake yet But Mr

Harison said we had better send him to the Hot spring Will write soon We Remain as even your Cusins **Clements Manen & Sallie**
P.S. oh dem Bugs is soe Bad I can not write give all our love to Jane & children Mollie & manen
P.S. Mollie will an others —

---

55. Elizabeth Hardin to J. W. H.

Red River Co May 30 1878 Mr J. W. Hardin) Auston Texas)
My own precious Son
It has been some time Since we have recived a letter from you. I wrote you last and I have been waiting with So much anxiety to hear from you you Said that your trial was to be on the 13 of this month we have had no letters from you and we See nothing in the papers So I suppose your case has not been investigated as yet. I do hope your case may be remanded and if So my Son whare will your trial be at. Comanche or whare I am anxious to know. Jane recived a letter from her Sister She Said that that She was in Auston with her ——— 15 of this month ——— that She Saw ——— She Said that you was in fine Spirits and wished her to write to Jane She did not tell what their buisness ware at Austin I immagine that they ware there Seeing what they could do aganst you perhapse I am wrong. he has been doing So much or trying to. that is the reason why I am So ready to believe Such things. Son I am So uneasy and anxiouely expecting to hear from you. it appears as though I cant wait. I do hope that when I hear I will hear good news. Jane and the children are well your little babe is So Sweet She can walk a few Steps and calls Jeff. Jane is going to write to you in a few day poor thing I am So Sorry for her though She bears her troubles well under the circumstances She is going to Brights in a few days to Spend a week or two. Jeff is farming has a fine prospect of a good crop of corn and Cotton Some of our farm is rented out Nannie is Still going to School at Bennett Your little Br Barnett Gip is a fine inteligent little boy he talks about his buddie Johnnie So much. I do wish you could See him. well Son I do not know what to Say. for tongue can not express my desire to See you. my love is unbounded has no end. Son I look back to your childhood days and even a few years ago when you ware with me and loved ones that that has passed away.

the recolections of those happy days have left green Spots in my memory forever Johnie I do hope we will yet meet again, write me a long letter it has been So long Since your Mama recived a Sepperate letter. though I am glad to get a line from you at any time. Son I am afraid this letter will not interest you. for my mind feels So blank

good bye my Sweet Johnie

Your Ma Elizabeth Hardin

---

56. M. Clements to Jane Hardin

Sansaba, Texas. June 1st, 1878 Mrs, Jane, Hardin, Dear cousin, it is With pleasure I seat my self to Write you afew lines this Leaves all well at present, hoping when it Reaches you It, may find you and the children well- Jane I Receivd a letter from Wes to day it Was Wrote be fore his trial, he Was Well then I have not heard from him since his case went before the court of appeals. I have Writen to him and the last letter was May the 10th I think he was in good spirits I have heard Rumors Some says he got a new trial others say it went against him I hope not But let it be as it may Jane we will have to doe the Best we can I am willing to help him but am not able to doe any thing untill he gets a new trial then I can and will doe all I can for him. but Jane I guess you have heard the perticlers of my troubles I am out on Bond and dont think will have any trouble in beating the case but it has broke me up it has cost me all Ready ($.800.) Eight hundred dollars. and money is Scarce With me I cannot see why the parties treated me this way when it was no advantage to them and other wise wer an injury Will Jane Wes Wrote me to send you money to Come and see him Jane I have not got the mony and I have to start to DeWitt County to court In the morning will be their untill about the 20th of June if you get this in ten days after date direct your letter Cuero. PO DeWitt County Txas, and if it is older than that direct your letters to San saba, County, Rich Land Springs po. To M. Clements and I will get it Write as soon as you get this Well Jane I was arested in December the 19th and stayed With Wes and Brown untill Jan 29th then I went to gonzales and stayed in jail their untill Feb 21th before I Could get a trial then give Bond for the killing one Paten, Patterson my Bond was ($500)

Five hundred, dollars Jane I have been to gonzales Twice since I was arested and stope and Saw Wes booth times times is hard With me but when I get out of court I can make a living and help my friends as same as I Ever did But Jane write to me and when I get Back from Cuero I will try and come and see you dont dispair Hold up under your troubles. I no it is hard but can not be helped. it is not in my power to help it or I would freely due soe/ Well give my love to Aunt Elizabeth and all the children tell them to write to me so I well close hoping to hear from you soon. I well Write again when I goe down below so Mollie Manen & Sallie joins me in sending our love to you and the children and all of the conection, Mollie says write to her she would write to you in this letter but is busy fixing for me to goe to court soe good By. your cousin untill death

M, Clements

P.s. Write soon as you get this give my love to all Will Write to Wes at once MC.

---

57. J. W. H. to Jane Hardin

its June the 2nd
instead of may the 26th **June the 2nd 1878**

Austin Texas **Mrs Jane Hardin**

My Dear and loving wife another week has passed and no letter yet from you or Ma. . allthough I have been very patiently looking to here from you once more. But have looked in vain. . Dear I Supose that the letters must get misplaced before they reach austin for I believe that I would get them if they Should come to Austin. . most especially if they come in charge or care of the Sharriffe. Jane Dear you Donot Know how anxious I am to here from you and loved ones at home , I think of the old fashon cot Ive left it for amany a year the last words I got God bless you from my mother & father So dear. oh. Dear write me a letter from home. . for I Know there is loved ones at home who wil love me where ere I roam. . its loneley and oppressed: I Sit in my lonely cell an Dear I think: of you & brighter days yet to come.. and often wish that I could See your Smileing face once more. . oh the past: I cant help but Cherrish for I know you wil ever remember me.. but dear donot think I am down hearted because I am oppressed. for Dearest you know that I cannot help but be merry.. allthoug you may well know my heart is oppressed. . Dear as I have written you before my case has been arguered on the 15 of may but no descission as yet. Cant help but think that they are bound to reverse it. which I am in hopes they wil for I well know that I have Been convicted by illegal power cloked with legal authority. but dear whether they do or not I wil do the Best I can. and you can rest assured that I expect to carry my load like a man although it may be heavey and for my Self I am able to cary a Good load if necissary and dear I wish that it were So I could take your burden my Dear true and loving Wife : Kiss the Children for there (Pa) once more) Love to all Good by wil write again Soon if it is Gods wil you True Husband

John.W.Hardin

(PS) Ma a few words I am treated kindly by my keepers and am in Good hopes & health at present hoping to here from you Soon ma remember my Dear ones at home and Kiss my Brothers & Sisters all for me and my Dear Wife allso remeber me to all of the F and write me a letter from home

Your affectionate Son & H till death

John W Hardin to His wife & Mother

---

58. Mollie E. Hardin to J. W. H.

Woodbury Texas June 7th. 1878

Dear Cousin

I seat my self with plesure to write to you, for the first time. We ar all well at at present. Pa received a letter from you, a few days ago and, was glad to here from you John I am Sorry to here about you a going to that dredful place but it cant be hapt If I coulad do any thing in — I would do it if I had the money and, it would cl—r you I would send it in hast to you, but Pa has done all he could do. o & Ma has had bad luck she lost her Baby it has bin dead a but a month its nane was Joe Hardin the one net to the Baby is nane John. he— died on the 2 day of June if he had lived untill the 10 he would bin ayear old. he was sick along time be fore he died he is better off than any of us. John I wish I could see you once more. If you can have your picture taken send it to me yfor I want it. o you would no me I dont expect but it has bin along time sence — you saw me I have written to letters to day besids this one you must excuse my bad writeing for I am in ahery. The Children sends there respect to you. I will close for this time by saying write soon. & Answer this if you can.

—I remain untill death **Mollie. E. Hardin.**

---

59. J. W. H. to Jane Hardin

June the 11the 1878 John. W HARDIN Austin Texas

Mrs Jane Hardin

My Dear & loving wife I have Just received your kind and welcome letter. which I read with pleasure oh how much pleasure it is for me to receive a line from you for I well know that there is no words which can express your love and feeling for me. allthough I am the Notorious (John W Hardin). yet I know that your love is beyond any language therfore Dearest & truest Jane I donot expect you to even try use language with the pen. and Dearest one I know that you do not doubt me. But Dearest we are appart. and it Seems that the Strong hand of man is against us. besides the publick opinion, which I have Been convicted & Sustained by the courts of appeals. on the acctount of the enormity crimes of John W. Hardin and associates. this is the Language of the Judg who affirmed my Sentence besides I understand that he was rathy at the Jury or mob of Commanchie, because they did not find a virdict of murder in the 1St degree. So you See the current is against. me besides. I have cost the State of Texas two much monie, to be allowed my Liberties whether right or rong. we can even go back to Ancient History where the assembled Jews Let Loose the Guilty Barrabas. and crucified inocent Christ. So you See what publict opinion does for man or men & even what it done for Christ My Dear wife for what ever you Do be cheerfull and take every thing for the Best for there is nothing So Bad but could be worse as for my own punishment Dear I assure you I receive it with Gratitude & pleasure and think under the circumstances which I have had to labor allthoug very unfair that I have done exceedingly well. Dear. on yours my Children Sisters Brothers & my Devotet mother I would think death a blessing Sent if it would onley remove your Giefe & Sorrow. Oh Dear Donot think that Such wil allways be the case for truth & Justice wil prevail, and Dear if you & others wil onley be

Cheerfull & Patient all wil be well in the end. for persevrience and indostry truth never was known to fail. it is true there comfort is biter, but Dear there fruits, are Sweet. Deares cheer up, and if I could onley know that you and dear ones wil bear your Troubles. an not give way to them you can rest easey as to my own punishment for Dear if you wil only take my rule I wil be as hapy as a king and take it all for my part as if it were a (reward) for my (Service) rendered to the Honest & Good people of the State of Texas) Dear in other words from the Best information that I can Get is that your Pa would of Swore my life away in cuerro for the murder of one morgan allthoug He talk very diferent to me even before the Jailor he Said that I did it in Silf defence and that the man follered me up and that he never would Swore a lye against me that I was his child that he did consider me as one but you can bet he did not take the Statement He was trying to Sacrifice me & Save Brown you Bet he was Jus right and I Blame him for nothing he is your pa he Spoke very Kindly about you but he was badly Bothered mat is the Same I thought of you Dear your Love

John W Hardin

Jane Dear Bil Phillips is a true man and our Friend we correspond to each other Write to him as a Sister Dearest one I wil write you a long letter in a few day Love to all and dont Grieve Deares kis ma Sisters & Brothers & Dear Children mine

Jane Dearest write once a week I wil if not oftener I an well and am treated well visitors til I cant rest tell mat I wil write to her one of these days allso Send my love to Sissy Be Sure Deares Good by hop we may yet meet

Mat Said She would write Jane Dear answer your Sisters letter.

---

60. J. W. H. to Jane Hardin

Austin Texas June the 15th 78 Mrs Jane Hardin

Dear Wife I have Just received yours of the 13 ins and you cannot imagine how much comfort it was to me to received a line from you my Dear & true wife and dear how much more Satisfaction it was for me to know that you my Dearest would Say you would try. Oh ow proud I am to know that you my Dearest had not forgot that once familliar word Try. Oh Shuch a consolation it was to me dear dont ever feel oppress . pride in your Troubles all I hope wil Be for the Best & you can rest easey there is no Body Scaired but the driver Jane yes Dearest Some may Say you are disgraced but Darling those who Know me on the out Side wil never Say So for they wel Know that what I have done has been done honerable and above Board and only to Save my own Life Jane Dearest you can console your Sweet Self. with this consolation if no more that your Husband John W Hardin has and allways wil have nerve to accomplish any act when honerable that mortal man could accomplish at Least he has got the nerve to try and whend dishonerable allway ready to Say no or Do it yourself and Dear when I loose this principle I donot wish to Live any longer Dear please cheer up and write me a Lively letter as for my part alone I can & wil Stand it with pleasure & Dear you Know that I would consider Death a blesing Sent if it would only Soothe your Broken heart & Loved ones at Home Dear Darling ma never Gave me any Bad advice & I Know that She never wil Give you any So Be Sure and notice my Dear mothers advice Be very careful in the traing of our Children whil young ma plan is a good one be Sure & never allow one to tell a a lye Jane Dearest Dont be melancolly or Said but Dear be as you useto Be you Donot Know how cheerfull I am . I wil remain here untill about the 10 the of Sept then be taken to commanchie for Sentence to be passed thence to Hunstville I am assured a good Guard dont be uneasy Dear I Dont think that Capt Lynch wil ever get me.. the commanchie citizens treated me So very Kindly while I was there they know I am convicted for a crime which Done to save my own Life and I have considerable. incouragement there besides other places not worth while to mention I was talking to Some of the most influential Citizens of this county & they Say for me to Say to you that I have Some friends here who Do Sympathize with me Dear I have So many visitors even yet occasionly the fair set come to See me allso Jane Dear I am treated as Kind as circumstances wil admit as to the mob at commanchie they were Supose to be mostly from Brown county Dear I am yet alive and dont intend to die Like a fool if can help it I consider I have to much to Live for Dear I look for mannin here Soon Billy Taylor is out all right come clear of Killing Sutton & admited bond on the ballance M & Billy are at Cuerro attending court billey Beat one case there allso So you See how it is no tilling the future the Survivors of or at least most of them the Jack helm party are Bound to Hang no Hanging on our Side Dear look at it right my friends Say they can & wil help me at the right time Be easey Dear onley a little time. Jane as to you coming to See me I wil try & See conserning that next month I think more than Likeley but write often I wil Write once a week as long as allowed Jane Dear I am proud the change of our Sweet Little Babes name was acepted Kiss the Children Mollie John W H & Jane My Little gippe & nanne excp for nane Donot Let them forget me Besides Kiss Jeef & Ma & dont Slight Mr Smith & matie & her Sweet Little Babe tell mat I cannot write to all nomore than I do But wil write to Her & Mr Smith Soon I have treated Sister Lizzie mean in regard to writing write to her for me adieu My Dear Wife hoping to Here from you Soon Love to all your Husband John. W. Hardin

June the 15 teenth

Dear Little Sister I read your Sweet Little Letter Oh how interesting it was to me it was Splendid Nanne your older Sisters have had a much better chance than you but Little Sister you write a Splendid Letter and if you wil only persevere & Study your Book from the Language of your letter you wil excell them Both . Sister take the advantage of your time and imploy yourself to your Book be kind to your School mates & obedient to your School mistress Dear Sister take good care of your Sweet Little nieces & nephew manine take your mas advice also Kiss your Sister Jane for me tell Little Gippe he wil live to be a man after while but to Be Sure & mind His Ma
Your Brother John W Hardin
Jane I Send my love to all excuse for paper is Slim

---

61. J. W. H. to Jane Hardin

— Have no——— to write at present wil write Soon again
Love to all Adieu Dear– one

June the 23nd 1878 Austin Texas Mrs Jane Hardin
My Dear wife
I received yours Dated the 20ith & —o's the 21st inst. Dearest Jane you do —t Know how consoleing your -—ters are to me and how much bet – –at when I can here from you my Dear Darling wife and loved ones at Home Jane Dear I wrote to ma last night this Leaves me well all but pains & weakness from my old wounds which at this

time Dear are very Servere but Hope they wil not last long Jane ——— that I am prefectly ——— and am treated very Kindly by my Keepers am allowed a cell all by my Self this Hot weather which is much Better than being crouded with company Wel Dearest I was So Glad to heare that you are Getting along So well at present Dear I Do hope you wil not take trouble to Heart your Letter was So interresting oh how I love to heare of the Sweet Little Babes of ours Jane Dearest you can Be lively an– Dessolat Just reckolect time wi— —prove all things, truth & Justice wil prevail Jane Dearest be Satis— at present all I hope wil Be for the Best Dear I had a nice treat to ice Cream to day by lieutenant Rundels who taken me to comanchi I th— of our visits to the ice cream Salon in New orleans Jacksonville & C oh Dear I ——— wil not ——— remember me to the Children Love to all Jane Dearest the past how Sweet it memories the future may yet Be as the past Love write me a lively letter all about the Children Give Mr Smith & Mat My love & tell them to write
Your True Husband **John W Hardin**
one J. T. Smith of Jacksonville is Dead — I wil write Soon again wil have ——— ——— in a few days

---

62. J. W. H. to Jane Hardin

June the 27the 1878 Austin Texas Mrs Jane Hardin
My Dear Darling Wife I have Just received yours of the 23inst which I asure you was read with Great pleasure & Comfort Dear this Leaves me well & in good health and Spirits as one could be under the Same circumstances I am treated very kindly by my Keepers and realey need for nothing my friends come to See me and encorage me all they can Jim Dorst from Gonzales was here yesterday he is one of my old friends that is allowed to live free manny & Billy Taylor are at cuerro court Jim Says they have Beat all casses that has come up against them as yet and wil Beat all of there cases I think they wil you know how proud I am to heare of my friends coming out all right. Jane Dear I ate a piece of watermelon to day for the 1St have Had Ripe peaches for 2 weeks Dear I have no nuse of interest to write Last week I was very unwell But Seem to Be all right now Jane Dearest I wil See if I cant arrange So you can Se me Before long and you can inmagine from time past & gone by how

proud I wil Be to See you my Dear & truest Friend & Darling wife remember me to all of the Family you Donot know how well pleased I was to get a letter from Brother Bright his letter was So consoling besides he Spoke of you & Dear ones So kindly Love to all Your true Husband **John W Hardin**

(PS) Ma I reckonized your few lines

Dear Ma No nuse at present I hope you all will try and enjoy your-seves all wil Be I hope for the Best Ma take good care of John W H & Gippe & Dont Slight My mark nor Sweet Little Jane M from your Son John W Hardin

——— J C Landrum was to See me a few days ago

Dear I wil write to you Again Soon if no Bad Luck Adieu John W. Hardin

Jane Dear tell Bright to excuse I wil Write him a letter Soon

---

63. Mattie Bown and W. C. P. to Jane Hardin

Gonzales Co Texas June the 29 th 18.78

Dear Sister

I Seat my Self to Write you a few lines in answer to yore letter that I Received two Weekes a go Which found us all Well and this leavs us the same hoping it Wil find you and children Well Jane you Wanted me to giv you all the news in jeneral I hardly no What to say What to say you hav heard What they don for Wes Wes Wrote William a letter Whi— he got on the 15 th of this month he said he had Wrote to you that his sentence Was confirmed Which I no Distresing for you to hear Jane I wish We was to gather So I could help you Shair yore trobles tho Jane it looks like I hav my shear Wel Jane you must chur up and look a head for better times Jane We hav fine crops hear and a good Range and that is a bout all Wel I wil close for this time by asking you to Write soon and often yores Sister. Mat. Bowen PS Wel Sister I Wil drop you a few lines to let you mo that I havent for got you and yore little babes yet. Jane I promist to go and See you this fall Which if life last you may look for me and then I can tell you all the new

yorse as ever **W.C.P**

---

64. J. W. H. to Mrs. Jane Hardin

July the 4 the 1878 Mrs Jane Hardin Austin Texas
My Dear & Loving wife. It is with pleasure that I am now allowed throug the mercies of the all ruling power to write you a few lines. Which leaves me enjoying good health at present. and as cheerful as one could Be under the present circumstances. Dear Jane. M. Clements has been here ever Since the 1st day of July has been to See me 3 times was here this evening and Left for home allso. he has Been awaw from home about one month Down at cuerro at court. come out all right Down there & Says your people are all well. Dear M. is Just as he allways was Just the Same old mannin no diference he told me to give you and Family His love Besides he Says we have many friends yet in Gonzales & DeWit and talks very encouraging Seems to think that I wil not have to Stay at Huntsville as long as one might Suppose he thinks all wil yet Be for the Best. Darling wife I hope So and I think a little time wil help things & make a considerable Change Dear I think of you So often and think of our travails & adventures we have Seen together the pleasure & comfort we have Been to one another dear and ask if it wil ere be So again Darling I hope So and I Do hope that you wil Just Live in hopes as I have told you for I Do believe Dear I can Live out yet and be a free man once more Dearest you Donot Know how much pleasure it is for me to even think of you while in my uncomfortable position for Darling I know you think of me in return Dearest I hope & think it wil Be So you can See me before I Go to commanchie for you Know I long to See your Sweet Smiles once more allthoug I am Barred from freedom But Dear remember that as for my part I can an wil act my part like a man and wil do the Best I can. and do wish that it was So I could Bear your Troubles an would think them Light Dearest I am treated Kindly by my Keepers and have many visitors as yet & pass the time of as merry as possible cant be any other way Dear I Do hope you wil Be cheerfull remember me to all of the family & Kiss the children for me my Darling wife & Tll Mr Smith & mattie that I appreciate there Kindness Besides his letter was So comforting to me because he Spoke So kindly of you My Dear Tell Ma I wil write her Soon Jane Dearest I think it wil Be So you can come to See me after while before I go to commanchie Tell John W & Gippe to be Good Boys & mind there Ma & Grandma ant to not Slap Little Jane M Tell

Mollie that She is papaws little Texas girl. sister N I answered your Letter So be Studious and Be Sure & Take your mas advice Jeff Dear Brother I hope you wil Shun evil company Dear Jane I hope I wil here from you Soon by by for this time my Darling wife

John. W. Hardin

(PS) I answered Brother Brights letter But wil write Soon again Tell ma to excuse me this time that I intend to write her a long letter So no more at present **John. W. Hardin**

---

65. J. W. H. to Jane Hardin

[UNDATED]

Wel Dearest I found one envellope therfore I wil write a little more Dearest I wrote you I Had received a letter from (mc) So write to Him at once at San Saba tell Him your circumstances and if you Should Need any thing He wil oblige you Jane Dearest I think there wil Be a Bill past to commute time for convicts for good conduct at Least I Hope So then I think convicts or at Least Some of them wil Learn how to tell the truth Better or at least I Hope So for the truth is Bad enough without exageration So I Hope it may Have a good effect Now write me How the children are getting along Tell me How Molley is getting alon at School So Give my Love to all and ever remember your Husband John. W. Hardin untill Death

Well Little Sister Nannie a few words write me How the children are getting along for I Know you wil tell me all about them tell me if molley can Spell or not allso all about JW & J.G. How they get along and if they ever Fight or quarrel or not How Little M. is I Dreamp of Kissing Her & Jane the other night. I Hope I wil Some of these Days. Be a good girl Learn your Book mind your ma & School mistress Be Kind to your Brothers & Sisters. Love to all your Brother

John W Hardin

Jane Dearest I wil next time write you about a Lady who came into the Shop yesterday and asked to Speak to me and what was Said for the want of Space Defer

---

66. Nannie Hardin to J. W. H.

1878 July the 9 Red River Co — Mr J W Hardin

My Dear Sweet and loving brother I thought I would write you a few lines this morning while it is raining very hard well Johnnie school is out I an not going now last wednesday a week ago we had our Examination I went through half of my geography and never missed a word and went through my grannar without missing a word I was to the 130 page in my davies Arrithnetic Sister Jinnie and Matchel went to See us be examine then on thursday night we had our Exhibition I enjoyed my Self very well thoug Sweet Johnie I thougt of you so often to think that you could not be here to injoy your Self the Same as I did well Johnnie I will try and tell you sonething about the Sweet children they get along So well everwhere they go little Jinnie Martina trys to follow then She can walk any where She wants to in the house and She can clinb out of the Steps and walk around in the yard and clinb up in the chairs. oh She is so sweet a little while ago I called Mollie and Gippie in the house and I ask then what I must tell you and thy Said for me to Send you a Kiss both of then cane up and Kiss me for you. Well Johnni- I beleive I have writer about all of the news well good by Swe— John—

fron your Sister Nanne H

P S Johnnie Sister Jinnie has writer to you Sweet Johnnie I want you to Send me a piece of your hair Johnnie you must writ to me as Soon as you get this lettle Johnnie good by **Nannie Hardin**

---

67. J. W. H. to Jane Hardin

July the 14th 1878 Austin. Texas Mrs Jane Hardin

My Dear and loving wife It is with pleasure that I now Seat my Self to answer your Kind & most welcome Letter Dated July the 11 the which found me injoying Good Health and in as Good Spirits as one could be in my condition Dear no one can immagine the pleasure it is for me to Get a letter from you one who has ever been So true and Kind to me even in the most adverse condition. But God has Brought us thus far Safely through what it has looked to man as an imposibility and it is to Be hoped that he wil even yet land us Safeley ashore. Jane Dearest you must not Get impatient. but Hope for the Best even if the worst comes. Jane Dear M.C Spoke So very Kindley about you But you Know what maning allways thought of you. Besides He Said He would fix So you could See me before I

Go to Commanchie if posible Jane Dearest one I received a letter from William Phillips He Spoke So very Kindly about you and regretted that he was not able to assist you He Said Nancy was Sick with fever but not dangerous. never Spoke of any the rest of the family but Said Some of my Good friends Sleep Sound when they Heard my case Had Been affirmed Dearest Jane I am So Glad to here the chldren Get along So well besides to know that our Sweet Little Jane M is So peert and interesting tell Mollie that She is papa's Little Texas Girl besides She Has travailed and ask J W if the Gofer Scratches on his Back are Gone and if that Bone in his Leg hurts him much. Jane Dearest I Know they are interesting and hope that careful attention is and wil be paid to them. I am treated Kindley Dear and as for myself and the trouble I have to Go through I Dont Dread nor even bother me. but Dear when I think of Dear ones being in trouble it rather Get away with me but I do Hope they wil take all for the Best and live with Patience. allthoug Patience is bitter. Yet how Sweet it fruits are. Dear remember me to Mr Smith & Matt & all of the family besides Kiss the children for me once more My Dear and loving wife So I wil Bring my Letter to a close hoping to here from you Soon

So Adieu My Darling Wife **John. W. Hardin**

---

68. J. W. H. to Jane Hardin and Elizabeth Hardin

Austin Texas Aug the 2 1878

M.C. Has Just Been to See me wil not Leave for Several days yet Sens his love and Says. to take my Advice he Says He wil write to you to day again Dont Fret Dear but make up with ma Kiss those Babes for me my loving and True wife So I remain you true husban and are for you above all others

John W Hardin

Austin Texas Aug the 2nd

(Answer favorable if you can) (and y can) Dear ma you & Janes troubles are foolishness Dont hold any Spite at Jane consider my interest looks like Some one allways unintentionly is Doing me harm ma for every thing you Do make up with Jane if posible tell her She is your child and not to think hard of you to come & go home with you Just tell her She must go with you and Stay there that you are

Sorry Such hapend & you wil never think of it any more ma you Know She is metal or I never would of had her She is to true Ma try and Get Jane Quiet Some way you Surely can her troubles are great So I remain your Son tell her what is her interest is yours now I wish to here of her being at mas So love to all **John W Hardin**

Jane Dearest Dont think I care what you Say Allthough its righ I belong to you and no one else Dont get mad at ma get mad at me I am —

Jane is Little John W H much Sick I though I had Seen trouble but it has Jus begun
Ma be Sure & Give this Letter to my darling wife

Dearest Jane if you get it Show to ma at once

---

69. J. W. H. to Jane Hardin

Aug the 2nd 1878 Austin Jail Texas Mrs Jane Hardin
My Dear Loving & Grieving wife it is with Said heart I now write But with pure motive Mannin is here and wrote to you yesterday he Says to Be Cheerfull you know him he Says you Shall come to See me before I Go to Commanchie and his House is your Home Jus as long as you wish and Say, tell cousin Jane not to fret that he wil do all he can for her & Says I wil Be all right Sooner than any one can imagine cant explain till I See you my Dear wife. Jane Dear I am Sorry of yours and Ma's trouble can you forgive ma if So do it it is Mother & wife and I am Satisfied you Both are to Blame, But reck-olect never can I Blame you for nothing and whenever it comes to the point you are my favorite, above all others. But dear ma is for-giving She Says She wil forgive you and be glad to have the chance. Sureley ma wil treat you Kindly if you wil Just consider as I think you Should. You wil make up with ma for She loves you So She Says So do it for my Sake until you can See me

Jane ma was mistaken when She though you a Bluff She knows it now So She regrets I never Knew you to have a word with any Lady Before. but Jane Dear I allways Knew that your Temper would not Suffer to much from any one but Dear controll it. for my

Sake. Dont get out with ma. if I thought you would Sufer your Self imposed on by any one I never would write to you again. that you Know I admire. but Dear consider. and Dear Dont think I Blame you. for I never wil Blame you. and am for you aliways My true and Loving wife But Dear for my Sake if you can make up with ma do So and Let By gones Be By gones ma I hope wil Be more Considerate from this on and She wil Know you Better Loving Jane Do So if you can honorable but Dear if it is Dishonest Dont Do it forgive forgive my Ma if you can Jane Dearest I have writen to Several of my friend you wil be cared for. Dont Doubt. But my Dearest you Know Purity her Husband Says God dam you if you come there he would Kick you out of the yard a friend of mine told him and Joe Sunday God dam them if you was ever mistreated By them and if they did not Stop talking about you that he would Cut there throats from ear to ear and made them eat what they had Said against you and Said John W H. is in But God dam your Souls I am out and when ever you think that I dont Stand in His Shoes you are Left allso told them that you was a credit to all of them and if ever any one imposed on you that he was loose allthough he was under Bond. You Bet your Friends are now ready to help you Just as quick as they can Jane Dear Dont Sell your Jewerley we wil have money yet. Dear Give my love to the family that you are with tell them there Kindness Shal never Be forgotton by me and that if I live they wil Be rewarded. Jane nothing Bothers me but the trouble you my Darling True are Seeing whom I Know to Be as pure as Snow Jane Dearest Do forgive ma take my advice We Ihope wil not be apart allways Besides I have went over this road Before and I See my way Clear Shore Dont Doubt it does look Like you all could live in piece I am Safe) I wil write you Some thing funny Poor children litle John Sick. Jane have you got me foul you Bet I am Safe Dearest Say what ever you please

Jane the Best we can do is all we can do. Answer at once. I think it is a dam Shame on all excuse I am mad for th 1St time in one year

JWH

Jane Dearest you are at Liberty to Say what you please as to me foul or not you Bet I Know your pure Heart Jane never was I troubled before (am I bound to destruction at your hands) Let me Know

Answer Answer

70. M. Clements to Jane Hardin

August 3rd 1878 Mrs Jane Hardin

Dear Cousin

I. seat my self to Write you this Friday Evening hoping this Will find you and the children in good health. Jane i will write at Wes. Request in regard to you and Aunt Elizabeths Troubles Jane dont pull out With her if you can posible get arond it for J. W. good fix up Evry thing it Will make against him I have been here 4 days See Wes Evry day my Boy Manen Came down to See. Cousin John and was proud to See him Jane i will fix for you to see Wes be fore he goes to Commanchie you can depend on it now you and Aunt Elizebeth get a long and content your self it is hard but could be worse give my love to all the coniction Except —a cousins Love I will work for JW as long as their is any hope and thier is hopes as long as life you bet

Soe good By

(2nd)

Write as soon as you get this Letter direct your Letters san saba Co Rich Land springs PO. and to me what you need and you bet, I'll help you all though i am poor But will help him and you all i can _ dont write any troubles of yours to J. W. it will doe no good only fret him and I think he is a good chance to come out all Right Rest Easy and dont you take trouble to heart I Remmain as Ever your Cousin

until death M. Clements

To Jane Hardin

---

71. Elizabeth Hardin to J. W. H.

Bennett Red River Co. Aug 16th, 1878

Mr J. W. Hardin) Auston, Texas)

My very dear Son

nearly two weeks has passed and no letter from you, my dear Sweet boy what has come over the Spirit of your dream, why keep your dear troubled Ma in Suspense, it affords me more pleasure to get a line from you then anyone on the earth, perhapse you think you have a reasonable excuse. I have been a true and faithful Mother to you and your dear ones, and if you could but know what I have had to bear for two months past especialy last month I know you would

Emanuel (Mannen) Clements
—Courtesy Western History Collection, University of Oklahoma

be bound to Say ma you have taken to much and if you could a had your way you would of Said I will not let Ma be imposed on in any Such a manner. Well Johnie Jane left last monday night week ago on the train for Auston expecting to arive there a ——— morning I hope her and your dear babes arrived Safe. her friend Snell do not believe She intended to go to Auston as She talked So largely. I think She Shurly went as She appeared in a good humer with us all and promised Matt and me She would write the day She arived arived thare and not a line yet now Johnie if She has changed I can not help it when She left She Said She would rather live with your people then any one. and She Said She would come back She Said if you had mony to Send for her you could Send her Back. So you can See how we all parted with the kindest of feelings. I was So Sorry to part with Jane and her dear little children. I was taken Sick the night She left and was very bad off nearly a week. Johnie I think it very doutful whether I will be farly represented to you or not. O:I am So anxious to See you I often wonder if I ever will See you again, and then think yes Some time. Johnie do not dispair the darkest hour is Just before day truth and Justice will prevail. Johnie my troubles are So great and the last trouble in my family the trouble that I have tole you of has hurt my feelings behond telling though it is past and gone and I am mad at no one Johnie I try to live a christian life it is very hard to do right when we have So many crosses but the Bible tells us they that bear the cross Shall ware the crown. and we Shall never be tempted above that which we are able to bear. Johnie I do not expect to live a great while. but I feel that there is a home in that Sun bright climb for me whare Sorrow never comes. Johnie write me a long letter and I will write once a week. Mattie has been very sick though up now write. Gippie Sends you a Kiss Jeff and Nannie Sends much love to you and wanders why you do not write there is a great deal of Sickness in this Country good byee Sweet child for this time **your Ma E. Hardin**

---

72. Mattie Bowen to Jane Hardin

Zedlers Mill Texas August 19th / 78 Mrs Jane Hardin
Dear sister
I take the pleasure to answer your letter which I recieved Satur day

I was glad to hear from you and to hear that was well that is more than I can say Pa & ma and 4 of the Children is doun with the Fever but is some better with little more Medisin they will be alright Jane it imposable for me to come to see you at present give West my respects Liza was here yesterday She was well and her Children She sends her love to you we hav got fined Crop of Corne & Cotton this year tell moly & Bet Freeman to me tell Molly when ever she gets me alittl Ca pict Out I will come And see her Frank says that she is not going to sleep at the foot for her sweet Hart is not biger than toad Frog Net says she wishes that she could see little Molly all of the rest of the Connection is well so I will close for the present so I will close for the for present
from your loving sister

Mattie Bowen

---

73. M. Clements to Jane Hardin

Can not See to Write Much Will be their By the 7th sept

Aug 27th 1878 Texas, Mrs Jane. Hardin.
——— is With pleasure ———f to Write to you. ———ot home at last. Jane ———een Very sore — Was ——— after i left town they ——— not Well yet i am ———gogles an Would of wrote ——— not see. Well i found ——— & hope you and the ——— are Enjoying good ———o news to Write——— Will be at Austin ——— & 7th Mollie Will ——— if She can get off ——— children So i ——— J W H to hold up ——— he Will come out ——— So i Will ——— Eyis is to bad ——— —llie & the children———g our Love & best ——— own Cousin ——— M.Clements To ——— & Jane Hardin

---

74. J. W. H. to Jane Hardin

Mrs Jane Hardin Austin Citty Present

Aug the 28the 1878 Mrs Jane Hardin Austin Jail
Dear wife this leaves me well and in Good Spirits Mr Steward was here to See me to day & he incourages me no little. which I wil tell

you when I See you my Darling Wife hoping to See you Soon I remain your Husban **John. W. Hardin** True

---

75. Elizabeth Hardin to J. W. H.

Red River Co. Aug 30th, 1878 Mr J. W. Hardin)
Auston Texas)

My very dear Johnie
I went in to the Station yestarday when I arived there I received yours and Jane's letters, writen one on the 18th the other on the 19th I was So rejoiced to hear from you and very glad to get a line from dear Jane, as it is the first line that we have received from you in more then three weeks. I did not answer your letter last eavning as I had left Nannie and Gippie and had to return the Same evning. came back home found Gippie Sick and not— I am in Such a hurry that I cant write half enough to eather of you. as Nannie is going to the Station for Medicine perhapse Matt will come home with her. we are getting along as usual. Jeff is working at the Station this week. he Says he is going out west this fall he is one of the best boys to work I ever Saw he is getting $one dol a day Johnie Write me and, let me know when you will leave there. you Said that you was in fine Sprits and believ you will be a free man I. do hope So and I have always believed that truth and Justic would pervail and there is So many truths that can be established that I am bound to think that there will be a change I do not think the Gov will not allow an inocent man to Suffer So long. Johnie I have So many papers that I know that would interesting you So much and that droped letter that your Pa got at Comanche. I will Send to you and one that they Sent to him after we left thare while we ware at Mt Calm So you may See what they intended to do with him. I intended to have them published but have not as yet. your Pa had writen a long document consrning you and all the dificultys at Comanche, with the intention of having it published. death came to Soon. Johnie I am So Sorry I did not get to visit you I intended to let you See all of those papers. I think I will have use for them yet I want the proper time to arrive if you live I think you will See them. yet Johnie I have never Seen or herd of as one Sided game played ever Since your troubles comensed. write me a long letter and and tell me how to direct my

letters when you go to Huntsvile if you go thare. O my dear Son how it piercies my heart to think of it. but Son do not give up but live in hopse if you die in dispair. that has been my motto always. have been hope on hope ever and never dispair. I am So glad Jane enjoyes herself So much and I am more then glad to hear that your keepers are So kind to her and those Sweet babes of yours in allowing them to visit you So often and are So kind to you. I know they must be great and noble men. and I know it is a great pleasure to you to See you dear family although you See them in prison. my dear Son if I could but meet with you I care not whare in the dismal cell or in the crouded halls of fame I would be proud to call you my Son. for this day you ought to be a free man. the children all talk about you So much. little Gippie nearly evry morning awakes and Says Ma I dreamed of buddie Johnie Write me a long letter O it does me So much good to get a letter writen by my own dear Son Whome I love So dearly. my Sweet Son I must close as Nannie has returned with the Medicine and I am writing to you it is about twelve O clock at night and I have to give medicine evry three hous I hope little Gippie wil Soon be well I will write Soon again good night my Sweet Son

E. Hardin

.P.S.

Johnie you must Send those letters back take a copy of them I want them I have Showed them to a great many and your dear Pa has Showed them to a great many they all Sayed it was Such a cowardly peace of writing—what about your cake I sent you

---

76. Elizabeth Hardin to J. W. Hardin

Mrs Jinnie Hardin) Auston Texas) [UNDATED]

Dear daughter

It is quite late but I must write you a few lines any how I commensed wrighting to Johnie to day but had to postpone untill tonight as Nannie had to go to the Station She went in after noon and returned in good time. is She not travling fast. Well Jane I have had Such a lonesome time Since you left it was So lonely that I could Scarsley Stay on the place and evry thing that I could See and evry place I would go I could think of you and my Sweet little ones. O how I do want to See you and them I dream of being with you So much, I am Siting up alone Giving little Gippie Medicine. you can immagine how lonely I feel although there is a pleasure attatched to my lonelyness for I am wrighting to absent loved ones I went to Matts yestarday they ware all well little Lillion as Sweet as ever but more interesting I have recivied two letters from Sissie Since you left She Sent her love to you and the children She is so troubled about her brother J. W. She has no heart to write to him

Mr Cobb cant walk yet as soon as he gets able they air coming to see us Mr Cobb writes So kind about John and Says if the proper means are used that John will come out all right yet Jane write me a long letter and tell me if Johnie got your picture tell Mollie I misses her about parching Coffe gran Ma will write to her Some time tell J. W grand Ma wants to See him I hope he is well Kiss little Jane M. for me and all the children for me Nannie is allmost crazy to See you and the children Adieu **E Hardin**

---

77. J. W. H. to Jane Hardin

Mrs Jane Hardin Austin Citty

Aug the 31st 1878 Austin Jail Mrs Jane Hardin

Dear wife

Please Do not for get to Get me Some envellopes this evning Hoping this wil find you and the Babes well I received a letter from Sister mat this morning all well nothing more at present but a Sack of Tabaco yours with respect I remain yours as ever your Husband Adieu untill I See you. **John W Hardin**

---

78. J. W. H. to Jane Hardin

Mrs. Jane Hardin Austin Citty Present

Sept the 11the 1878 Austin Jail Mrs Jane Hardin

My Dear wife if you can conveniantly come up this evning please Do So you & M See Mr Hendricks So you can come to Some Definite understanding tell Mannin if he can come up this evning to please do

So. I wil also be glad to See Mollie & the children So dear Jane I hope I will See you this evning love to all I remain your Loving Husband

John W. Hardin

---

79. J. W. H. to Jane Hardin

Sept the 16 1878 Austin Texas

Dear Wife Mr Corwin Says he wil assist you in going Home with mony So Se him Mr Corwin the Sherriff So good by Dear Your true Husband

John W Hardin

---

80. J. W. H. to Jane Hardin

Sep the 17 teenth Rons. Springs Mrs Jane Hardin

Dear wife

this leaves me well my guard is good men and I aprehend no danger My treatment Kind & I dont consider that I wil be in any danger atoll. Mr Corwin Told me he would & could Assist you to money to go home on Mr corwin the Sherriff wil Do Just what he told me Love to All I think I wil be back to Austin by the 2nd oct write to me at once to Comanchie So I remain your husband Love to all

John W Hardin

John Wesley Hardin was taken to Comanche for sentencing for the Webb killing. From there he was taken to Huntsville Penitentiary.

---

81. J. W. H. to Jane Hardin

Sept the 24the 1878 SanSaba Texas Mrs Jane Hardin

My Dear wife this Leaves me well and under the Circumstances Have Had a good time as yet for I have Been in camps with the rangers ever Since I left austin and Have faired as they have in other words have have had a good time. I think we wil Get to comanchie by Friday evening or Saturday morning as it is only necissary for me to be there long enoug to get my Sentence I aprehend no danger as I wil have a true & good guard Dear I hope I wil hear from you at Comanchie I think we Wil leave comanchie for austin or Some other railroad town on or about the 29 inst but Hope we wil come by austin but I cant Say for certain if So we wil get to Austin by the 5the or 6th of October Jane Dearest Mr Corwin Said if you needed any assistance He would assist you Give my best wishes to Mr Corwin & Nichols Should you See them allso to Joe & other ——— Friends Kiss the Children good by. Dearest if you Should not here from me again until the 6the write to John W Hardin Huntsville in care of Goree Superintenant But I wil write as Soon as I get to Comanchie but Dear I do not think I wil be Sent back by austin cant tell for certain until I get to Comanchie but I hope I wil When you go Home Give my love to all. but I hope I wil See you again before long cant tell So I remain your true & loving Husband

John. W. Hardin

if I am not in austin by the 7th do not: wait any longer

Love to all JWH

if you Should See Manin Love to him & Family tell him to write me This is writen in camp excuse Dear Jane

JWH

---

82. J. W. H. to Jane Hardin

Tyler Oct the 4th Mrs Jane Hardin

Dear wife. this Leaves me well at present & hope it may find you injoying the Same I Sent you my Satchell by express to Benit in care of Brother Bright both coats were in it Give my love to all at Home I think the comanchie People are changing in my favor more than ever was expected all looks favorable for a better future Lieut Renols with 6 of his men are Still with me Frank Wilson allso I saw many Friends at ft worth yesterday be Sure and write to mannin tell m that I Give tom a good talk and all is Just as it once was Tom is all right Jane Dearest I hope and believe that I can Manage So you can come to See me once an ocasionley So keep in Cheer Kiss the Children Give my Love to ma & all tell Her to write & write often Jane Dearest I hope I wil here from you Soon Direct to John W Hardin Huntsville Pennitenitary in care of the Superintendant goree I wil write as often as allowed if you Should See Sherriff corwin or mr Nechols give them my best respects allso Send love to Joe & my Kind wishes to Mr Kindrick So good By I hope to Here from you Soon be Sure & write to m give him my love allso. I Send you and all of the Family my Love So good By Dearest no more at Present Your Husband **John W Hardin**

Let me here from you at once excuse Bad writing For the cars are & have been Runing

I Send you a piece out of the ft worth Democrat Let me Kmow if you receive it Dearest good by

---

83. J. W. H. to Jane Hardin

[UNDATED]

Jane Dearest as for my treatment Here I am treated Kindley and believe that I wil have no Trouble in Geting along Here as I believe this prison is carried on by men who his Just Honerable & even Benevolent in other words if a man wil onley Do right he wil be Treated right of course if he Does rong He mus bear the consequences Dear it is as you know my intention to try to do right Let who wil do rong therfore I Do not think that I wil Have any trouble in Living peacable & agreeable here with all that may be around me Dear Do not Be uneasey about me for I asure you that there is more Done here for a man than one can imagine if he gets Sick He Has attention which I believe is good at Least it is Said to Be. Dear I Had a Splendid time with the rangers for we went by Sansaba where they were camped and Staid 7 days in camps with the rangers there treatment to me was the very best for they done all in there power for my conveniences and tried to make me as comfortable as possible you can tell ma that they are a different Set of rangers to what Wallers men were besides I believe that they would of Stood by me untill the last hour in the day So Did the mobb Dearest I received the Scraps and I asure you that they were thankfully received besides to think that you my Dear wife had Sent them to me Dear tell ma to excuse this time but you can give Her the Jeneral news Tell Brother Bright & Mattie that I wil be glad to Here from them any time but to not Be in a Hury But to take there time for Better once than never But tell them I Do intend to write them one of these Days not to Be in a Hurry Tell Jeff that I Hope & Pray that He wil shun the company of all Dishonerable and if ever any Dishonerable act is preposed Have nerve to Say no that is what makes a man is to Say no do it your Self Tell Nan to write when ever She chooses that Johnne loves to get a line from his Little Sister Kiss all of the family for m You True Husban

John W Hardin in a Hurry Adieu

---

84. Elizabeth Hardin to Jane Hardin

Bennett Station Red River Co. Oct 10th, 1878

Mrs Janenie Hardin) Austion Texas,)

My dear Daughter and Sweet children

It has been more then a month Since I herd a word from you. I Saw in the papers that Johnie parted with you in Austin on the 16 tenth of Sept and that was the last news untill the other day I received two letters from John he Said you was in Austin the last account. that you expected he would return by the way of Austin but he was disapointed he went by the way of Ft worth, poor boy I Suffered So much uneasiness about him, he expected you was at my house and wrote you a letter. Said if you was not here **Hardin** in a Hurry Adieu

to write to you at once and tell you to come as Soon as you could and Send you his letter he Sent his Satchel to you in care of W. B. Smith it has not come yet. well Jane I thought you would write and let me know all the particulars conserning Johnie and not a line have I got from,, you know that I would be So glad to here from you and those dear little loved ones it appears So long Since I Saw you the childre' all wants to see Sister Jane and the Children. Nannie Says tell Mollie that She would have writen to her but did not know whare to write little Gippie Says when Sister Jane comes back that we will have a little baby that can walk and no boddy can take it away. well Jane we have all been looking for you. and Still looking now Jane if it is your wish to live with me all wright, it appears as though Johnie does not want you to live any whare else. whether you come or not write to me and of course you Shall hear from me. Mattie is Sick has been in bad health for Some time little Lilly is So Sweet and interesting She has two teeth. Jeff has cribed his corn about one hundred and 25 bushels, will finish picking our cotton to day School will commence at Bethel next monday, Jeff has been doing finely, I believe he has got over the west fever well Jane I will Send you Johnie's letter write to me. Matt Says howda, Bright Says

Huntsville Penitentiary as it appears today.
—Photo by Roy and Jo Ann Stamps

he needs a house keeper. Kiss the children for me and tell them Grand Ma loves them So good bye for the preasant. I wrote to Johnie yestar— **Your Ma E. Hardin**

---

85. J. W. H. to Jane Hardin

Oct the 20ith 1878 Huntsville Texas Mrs Jane Hardin My Dear & loving wife Having Just received & read your Letter Datted Oct the 17teenth Which I asure you Dear filled my Heart with Happiness to receive a line from you my Dearest of all one who has ever been true on Know an foreign Land besides one that has ever mantained my Cause and one that Has ever clung to me in time of Trials Troubles & adversities Dearest of all you Do not Know How anxious I am for Sunday to come for that is our mail Day once a week for I then expect to Here from you my Dearest & other Loving Friends Dearest I received a letter from Major Vandegriff of austin 2nd

He Said you Had Started Home. Dear I hope you are Home Safe ere before this time and that your trip was not wearisome and that you and the children enjoyed your Selves while at austin Besides Dearest I Know that it was a Great Source of Pleasure to be with you and my Dear children at austin allthough a prisner but Still I enjoyed you company & presence & Deares. I hope you injoyed yourSelf and that you are now Satisfied much Better than Before you com to See me and Dear I Do believe you Can & wil live in Hopes of Better days though it takes nerve that few wimen possesses yet I Know Dearest that your nerve is Strong Just that way & Dear I Do Hope that we wil be allowed our Liberty once more as for what

3rd

my own troubles bothers me I consider them nothing but Dearest yours (Oh) that I could only Bear all. then I would feel perfectley Contented yet Dearest it is out of my power and all I can do is by Kind & Hopefull words which I Hope and trust are not Fiction for Dear I Believe them to be truth Dear I Know you left many Friends at austin and dear I do Hope that you wil find ma's Family all well and that you all may Live in peac & Happiness to each other and all that may be around you Deares I want you to Know that even the Comanchie Judge Himself told me that at Some future time He would interfere in my behalf besides he Said that He Knew that I had Been Sined against more than I had Sined others that I never thought Jim Homesley Mart Flemings Said that there would be no trouble to reduce my Sentence to 5 yrs even in comanchie County that all the people wished to Know was that I would Live at piece with them and Said that my word would be Good I told them that it was my intention to Live a quiet & peacfull citizen Should I ever be allowed & that Should the people of comanchie ever Do anything for me that I hoped that they would never regret it but I told them that if it was not due me that I did not want it they Said it was due me and that I Should Have the Benefit of it in the end. Dearest Jane I am proud to Know you Speak of visiting me in a few months you Know I Dream I think and even pray for you my beloved one of all. Tell Mollie to mind Her Ma & Grand ma Tell JWH to Be a good Boy and Tell Little Jane to Kiss mama for papa remember me to all Kiss all of the children for me Love to all tell ma I wil write her next Sunday your Love your Husband John W. Hardin

Be Sure & write in the midle of the week

allways adress to John W. H in care of T,J, Goree Huntsville

---

86. M. Clements to Jane Hardin.

—OFFICE OF—
Walton, Green & Hill,
WM. M.WALTON,)
JOHN A. GREEN,) Attorneys at Law,
ROBT. J. HILL,)
N. S. WALTON.)

Austin, Texas, <u>Oct</u> <u>21</u> 1878 Mrs Jane Hardin)

Dear Cousin I seat my self to write you this morning. hoping to Reach you By letter & find you & the children all well. Well Jane I had my trial Friday the 18 of this month and the Jury never left the Box had no Trouble at all in beating the case. found many friends this time at Gonzales. Jane James. Joe. & Gip. Was all at my trial and Was in good health & Spirits & sends their Love to you & the children & the Rest of the Connection all soe. William Phillips was at my trial & came up this far with me With the Expectation of seeing you and the children & Will goe on up home with me. Will. Jane col. Stendergraf the Lawyer which Boarded at our Hotel is— Writing a letter for me to. Wes. H.ardin for me while I write to you Jane take good care of the children & your self and let me hear from you ofteen Give my Love to Aunt, E. Hardin & all the Connection tell them i Will not forget them Write to Wes how i came out Give him my Love and tell him i Will not forget him Jane i Will start home So do write me at home Bill Phillips Joins in sending his love to you & the children good By at present write often & tell all to i Remain your Cousin until death **M. Clements**

---

87. John S. Van de Graoff to J. W. H.

—OFFICE OF—
Walton, Green & Hill,
WM. M.WALTON,)
JOHN A. GREEN,) Attorneys at Law,
ROBT. J. HILL,)
N. S. WALTON.)

Austin, Texas, Oct 22 1878 John W. Hardin Esq. Huntsville
Manny Clemments has just returned from Gonzales, and at his suggestion I drop you these lines. He was tried and acquitted, the jury not leaving the box. He reports everything quiet in Gonzales County, and no news of interest . your brother—in—law William Philips came on with Clemments as far as Austin. All your friends are well and manifest great interest in your behalf. Mr Clemments will go on to San Saba tomorrow. He sends regards &C.
I wrote you the other day that your wife and Children had gone to your Mother's. &C &C.

Thine Truly, **John S, Van de Graoff**

---

88. J. W. H. to Jane Hardin

Oct. 27the 1878 Huntsville Texas Excuse this paper
Mrs Jane Hardin
My Dear & Loving wife
It is by the mercies of the all ruling power that I now endeavor to write you a few lines allthough I have nothing of importance to communicate you but Simple write to you as I Know you are more than anxious to here from me at any time and I assure you that I am allways anxious to here from you my loving wife nevertheless I am in Bonds But Dear I Do Hope & feel that the time wil come when these Bonds will Be broke by legal power and that we may enjoy life as in time past and that the world wil Know that I never taken that which I could not give only where my life was in eminent danger and Dear wife believe me I thuog that I Had a perfect rigt to Save my Life allthoug the result at present is Hard But yet I Do not Believe that Such wil allways be the case Dearest as to my Health it is good as to Speak but my Side & Body Seems to Be affected yet with pain which I Hope you understand thoug at present not of a very Serious nature yet by no means are the pains a pleasure to me for Dear I Know that in the end they wil Drag me to my untimely Shore But Dearest that is one debt we all have to pay Soon or latter So there is no use for one to try to Shun for when Death claims its own Let it Be the King of Kings they must obey Dearest I am treated well as yet by my Keepers and I Believe them incapiable of misusing a man who is unfortunate enough to fall im there Hands Besides we have visitor who come to See the curiosities of the penn at present it

Seems that there curiosity is Jeneraly in the wheeling Shop all are doing well Here and are not worked only by reason the food is Good Substantial and good enough for Laboring man Dear Kiss the Children for me and remember me to one & all it Has been 2 weeks Since I got a letter from ma and have not received any from you Since you left austin So Dearest Love to all

John W. Hardin to Jane Hardin his wife

Ma I hope you wil ——— all ——— in my interest as it is at present all with you write to parties at comanchie F. Wilson told me He wrote you So Adieu **J.W.H.**

---

89. Nannie Hardin to J. W. H.

[UNDATED]

Bennett. Station Tex 8the 1878

My Dear Sweet Johnie

I thouht I would write you a few lines for the first tine in life I an here at Matchel's. sister Jinney cane hre the other day to stay a week or so with Matcel She — has got three the sweetest's little Children I most ever sween Callie can walk most any where she wants to little Mollie and Johnie talks about their papa so much Mollie and I went a berry hunting yesterday and got a gallon and ahalf Johnie I am a going to chool here at bennett to a lady nane miss pinkie Noris she is a Graduate I an studing Histry Dictionary grannar and arithnetic the school will be out 20the of the month they are going to have Exaninenat- and an exibishion we are getting our peaces now we had any a pa— the — of last month

Johnie to day is sunday this we their ise singing at this place Johnie Matcel's has got such a sweet little girl it can set a lone Jeff is farning he has got 4 acres in cotton and 8 in corn. he has lade his corn by. Johnie I an 12 years old I would have written long ago but I could not write much and I was a shane to I wrot so bad when I get older mabe I can write better little gippie talks about his buddy Johnnie so much he says he is going to see his Johnie sonetin well Johnie I mus close has I have mothing more of inportance to wite Johnie you write to me as soon as you get ths

well goob my sweet preshous Johnie

fron you Sister **Nannie Hardin**

P.S. Dear Johnie this is wenday I though I would write to you a lit-

tle more in my letter as I did not get to send it off your lettle cane to hand last Momday. the one you wrote to mama O Johnie you do not know how sad and sorrow I was to hear of your lettle read dear sweet Johnie. I can not express my feelingi you wrote for us to fe cheerful for your sake Johnie we will try thoug it is very hard under the Circustance Johnie Ma and gippie cane hear last we O Johnie you do not how sorrow Ma was to hear the sad news She took it So hard — well Johnie I mus close so Ma can write to you Johnie you must wite to me
good by Sweet Johnie **Nannie Hardin**

---

90. J. W. H. to Jane Hardin and Nannie Hardin

[UNDATED]

Nov the 17teen— Mrs Jane Hardin

Dear wife
Having Just received & read your letter Dated Nov the 16teenth which I assure you was received & read by me with pleasure Glad to Here from you all & to Know that you were all well Besides I was proud to Know that Sissie was to See you all give Her my Love & tell Her what I told you at austin tell J W & Gip not to impose on Mollie But to be Kind to mollie Because She is the oldest & of the female Sex Besides I Know they will not impose on Little Jinnie to noble for that Be Good children & mind your ma & grand ma

Dear you Said that you never received any letters from me in the Last 2 weeks wel Dearest I have written ever Sunday But one Since I come Here to you my Loving wife my Health is good as General Speaking and am Getting along as well & Better than one could Suppose. of course Being away from loved ones is all that Bothered me remember me to all of the family So adieu my Loving wife

John. W. Hardin

Well Dear Sister
N. Paper is Scarce
Nannie a few words you letter was received & read by me with pleasure So Dear Little Sister I Hope you wil write often and I wil Ans as I can but Sister Dont think that I intend to treat you mean if you never get a letter from me But write often Kiss all for y Brother

John W. Hardin

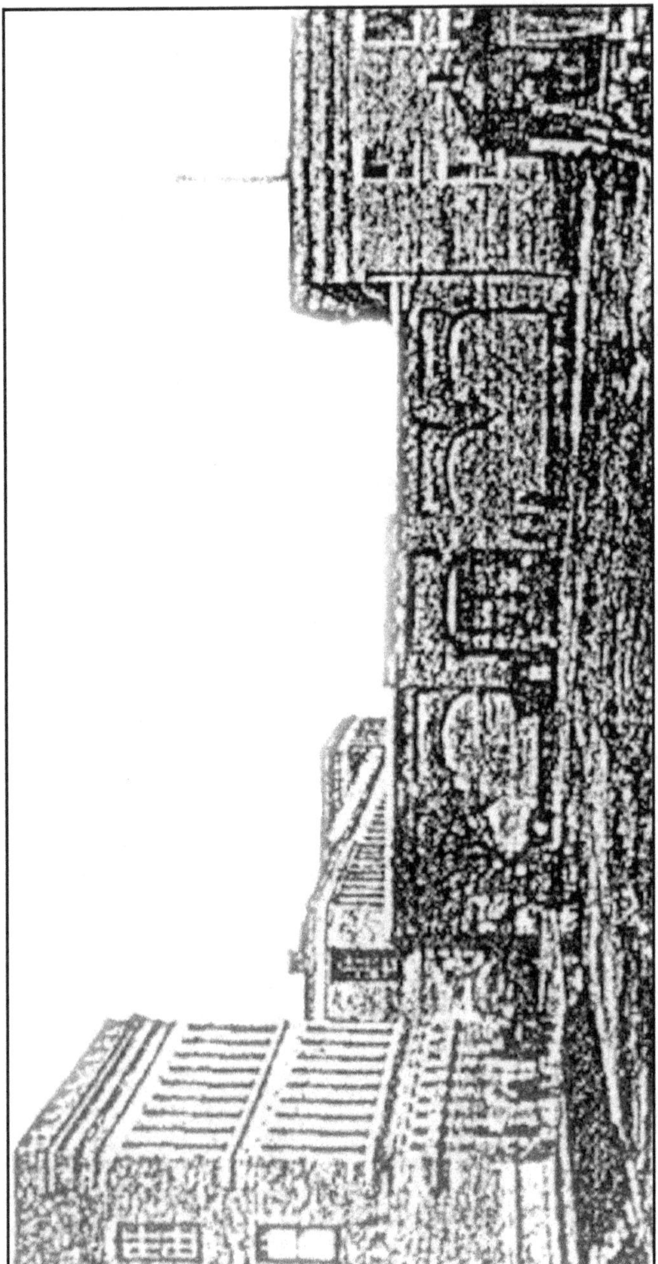

Outer gate to Hunsville Penitentiary around 1895 before wall was built.
—Printed with permission of Texas Department of Criminal Justice, Huntsville (Walls) Unit

LETTERS, PHASE 2

December 3, 1878–May 1, 1881

"You may have seen in the papers where I undertook to capture The armor with 50 other convicts."

HARDIN ENTERS HUNTSVILLE PENITENTIARY, WHERE HE SPENDS THE NEXT FEW YEARS TRYING TO OBTAIN HIS RELEASE BY ANY MEANS, LEGAL OR ILLEGAL. HE SEEMS TO TRUST HIS FELLOW INMATES, BUT IT BECOMES EVIDENT TO HIM THAT HE IS BEING TURNED IN AT EVERY OPPORTUNITY. DESPERATE, HE TRIES TO SEND OUT SLIPPED LETTERS, WHICH NO PRISON OFFICIAL WOULD SEE, EXCEPT PERHAPS FOR A TRUSTED PRISON GUARD. HE FINDS OUT, HOWEVER, THAT NO ONE CAN BE TRUSTED. CAUGHT ENGAGING IN CLANDESTINE CORRESPONDENCE, HE IS PUNISHED SEVERELY, HIS WRITING PRIVILEGES TAKEN AWAY COMPLETELY. HE HAS BECOME VERY ILL; HIS OLD WOUNDS ARE STARTING TO HAVE A DAMAGING EFFECT ON HIM. BOUND NOT TO BE BROKEN, HARDIN'S DEEPLY HELD PRIDE IN HIMSELF IS PUT TO THE TEST.

91. J. W. H. to Jane (undated envelope with slipped letter)

FORT WORTH U.S.PO——

———

9
TEX. THREE CENTS

Mr Jno. W. Hardin
Care Huntsville
Warden S.P Tex—

Jane Dearest this is monday night I am well. this is the 23rd & I Send this out By J.C. outlaw my guard He is all right and wil give me any thing you Send me write to me & Direct to Him. J.C. outlaw no one wil See it but Him and if you or ma or Jeff Should ever Send me any thing Be Sure & Send to Him then I will get it all right write to M and tell Him to write to me & Direct to J.C. outlaw no Hardin about it tell Him to Slgm His name Roberson Dearest Just to think of you is a pleasure above all others & you Bet I think of you day & night Separation onley Binds my love to you my dearest So write at once Dearest J.W.H

My loving wife write me How you are Standing the cooll weather and the Jeneral news and when you write to me through outlaw write one at once throug the Superintendants offis and Sign your name (Jane. Hard— Thene I wil Know al is right So ever remember you loving Husband

John W Hardin

Let me Know if you get this (Jane Hardin

---

92. J. W. H. to Jane Hardin

Dec the 3rd 1878 Huntsville Texas
Mrs Jane Hardin

My Dear loving & Devoted wife. this is tuesday night but I take this chance to write to you one who I yet and allways will Love & adore above all others for Dearest I Know that you are True & always have & will Be to me nevertheless we have had great trouble & the Strong

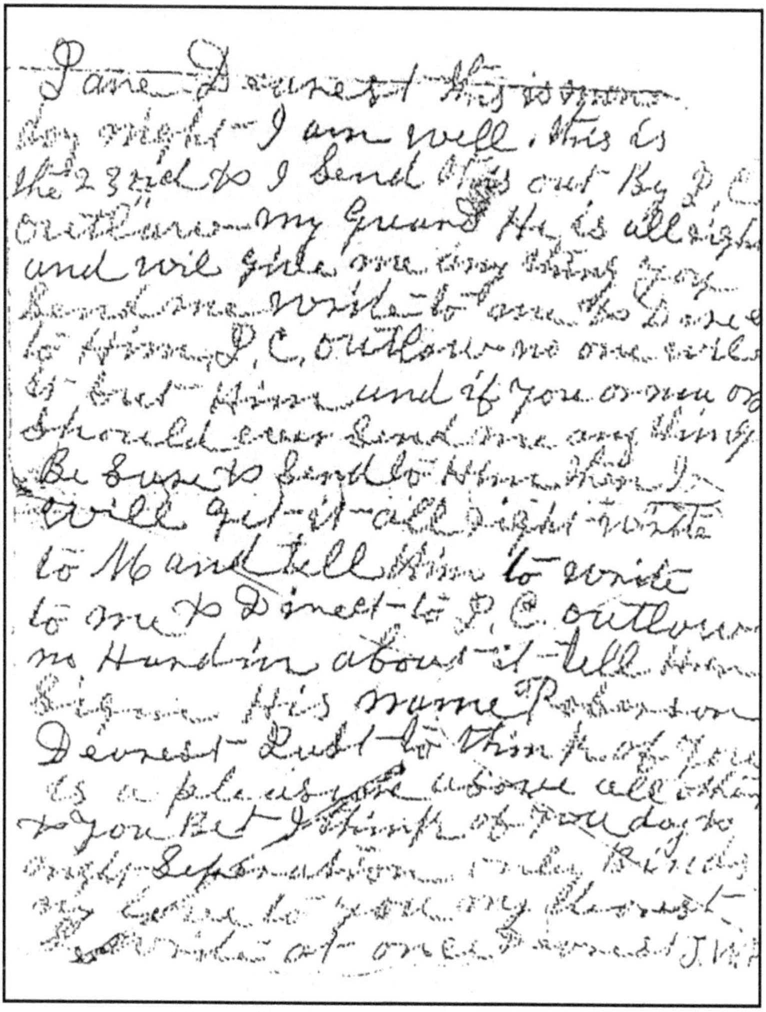
Jane Dearest this is mon-
day night I am well. this is
the 23rd & I send this out By P. C.
Outlaw my guard He is allright
and will give me any thing you
send me write to me & Direct
to Him P. C. Outlaw no one will
get but Him and if you or any of
should ever send me any thing
Be sure to send to Him then I
will get it all right write
to M and tell Him to write
to me & Direct to P. C. Outlaw
no Hardin about it tell Him
sign His name Robinson
Dearest Just to think of you
is a pleasure above all else
to you But I think of you day &
night Seperation only Binds
my love to you my Dearest
write at once Dearest J.W.H

Slipped letter (text appears opposite).

Hand of man Have Seperated us but my Love for the as I Know yors is unchangeable Dearest what I Say I mean & I Know you will believe me, be in cheer. Dont for one instant Despair for my Darling one if Death Dont prevent in less than 2yrs we will be together and I Know we can be as Happy as Days passed and gone by & I Hope even Happier. I Heard through a particular friend of mine that Judge Flemings Said He would Sign my pardon at any time but that at present He did not think it adviseable But that in the course of a little time He would get one & circulate the Same in Comanchie and that I would Be pardoned out without any trouble So Dearest you See it is onley a matter of time you my Dearest Know that patience & percevereance is bitter but loved one you again Know it fruits are Sweet Dearest Dont you ever think I wil fool my Self for I am two old for that and I tell you if I cant get out Legal as I wish you can rest easey I wil be bound to Have my Liberty which Dearest I can get if I must So be cheerful I am as yet Doing well & Have many visitors ladies ever now & then and the guard allways tell me that the Ladies compliment me for my fine apearance &C But all goes I aim to look out for no 1 in the end Dearest you do not Know How anxious I am to Here from you at all times & How I long to receive a Line from my Dearest on earth you bet it in courages me to Live Just to think of you Dearest is a pleasure & a Source of Hapiness to think of you let lone to get a letter So Dearest I Know you will write often and I will write ever chance I have missed two weeks but excuse You Know I wish to write you Dearest you I Know would be surprised but I can Build a wagon all right I received your Kind & affectionate letter Dated nove 28the this letter wil be taken out by a guard it is a sliped letter So dont answer it Direct but you Bet the guard is all right but to let me Know you get it Sign your name (Jan. Hardn)then I will Know you get it Dearest and if you Should Send me my money Send it to J. C. outlaw for me He wil give it to me other wise it wil be Kept in the office but Dearest you need not Send any but use it your Self Kiss all of the children for me Sweet Little Jiney two and ma and all of the family Jane Dearest I do Hope you and my Dear mother Sisters & Brothers wil all live Hapy together dont fret or notice foolishness give my love to one and all & tell aunt nan that I do love her that She is mistaken for She Knows I visited Her when I Had a chance Her advice was allways good So dearest I wil close by saying good by to one & all swet molly & J W papa wil be So glad to get a letter from you So dearest be cheerfull a loving good by my Dear wife

John W Hardin

I wil write ma Soon write to M C for me & tell Him to Come to See me this Sumer if you write a private Letter adress to outlaw (no care about it

if you Should Send me any money Just send it in a letter & Back it to J.C. Outlaw Huntsville Texas J C Outlaw if you Direct a private Letter to me Direct to Jack. C outlaw Huntsville Texas

---

93. J. W. H. to Jane and Elizabeth Hardin (slipped letter)

Dec the 8the 1878 Huntsville Texas Mrs Jane Hardin

(this is a Sliped)

My Dear wife it is with pleasure that I now endeavor to pen you a few Lines this Leaves me well & injoying moderate Health Hoping that this may find you & famly injoying eaqually as good or Better it is true I Have no news that amounts to any thing onley time is rolling on and I Do Hope & pray that the time may come when I Shall be a free man once more for Dear you Know How I appreciate Such a boon as Liberty as to the winter & cold nights I am Standing them the Best I cam But you Know Dearest that there is never a night that passes over my Head But what I think of you my Dearest and wonder if you are well Besides I hope & pray you are and that you Sleep warm But Dear I Know you wish for your Loved one and dearest I do Hope your wishes will be fullfilled in the end Dearest you Know what I think of one who Stands the test and believe that a true & Faithfull friend through trouble & trials as well as prosperity are the nobelest work of god So Dearest remember me for I cannot & never will forget you my Darling & true wife So I Send you all of my love and Hope & pray that we may yet live together So Keep in Hopes never give up as Long as life Last not even for one miute Have more nerve than that or else more faith in me So give my Love to all Kiss all of the Children for me & Dont forget Sweet Little Jiney So adieu from your ever loving Husband John W Hardin

Remember me to all tell aunt nan to write me a long letter So good By all

John W Hardin

Dec the 8th 1878

Dear mother taking this oportunity I write you a few Lines Hoping this may reach you in Due time now after Sending my Love to you all which you Know is more than my pem can tell I do Hope you all are living in peace and Hapiness & that you wil continue to So Live and be Cheerfull ma Dont think for one moment that I am Hopeles for I am not but I am ——— remember me to all Sisters & Brothers tell them that I am never to —ken and that after all Hopes fail for my Liberty You can bet I wil try that noble confidence I Have allways Had in myself you bet I am trying to act my Sport nevertheless it may Seem poor ma you an Jane write me a long Letter But be carefull Just Back it to. J. C. outlaw no Hardin about it J. C. Outlaw Huntsville walker county Texas Be Sure then write one at once a long good one & Direct it to John W Hardin in care of T. J. Goree any thing you may right that you Donot wish to Be Seen Send to J C outlaw all wil Be right I direct this to Mattie Smith for purpose outlaw is my guard and is all right as to favors So love to all write Soon my Dear & Dear Sad Mother J W H

this is the 2nd Letter wrote this way

Jane Dearest be carefull in answering this letter for it is a Slipped one So if you chews write me one But Direct it onley to Jack. C Outlaw Huntsville Texas & to Know one else /But to Let me Know for Certain that you get this one write at once on receipt of it to me & Direct to J W H in care of T.J.

Goree But Sign your name thus (Jame Hardin) then I will Know all is right Adieu John W. Hardin

Dearest M C is at or wil be Soon Cuerro court write to Him at once

94. J. W. H. to Jane Hardin

Dec the 28th 1878 Huntsville Texas Mrs. Jane Hardin

My own Dear & Loving wife Having Just received your Kind and most affectionate Letter Datted Dec the 24th I now by the mercies of the allruling power endeavor to write you in return: allthough my Darling & Sweet & true wife I Have not failed to write you allthough it Seems that you Have failed to receive the Same Dearest you can Bet I never am: to fail to write to you as long as allowed for Dearest you well Know I Love you above all others for my Darling true wife you Have ever Been my Best frind both in Know & in unknow countries and Both in prosperity & in adversities and Dearest I well Know when I am from you allthough you may yet & Have at times past Been thrown in with my enemies & Traitors yet too well do I Know that I allthough absent from the ——— always carry the Key too our Secrets and that no one else but me can ever unlock the Same. and Dearest never think for one minute or even one instance that I Shal or ever wil Doubt you my own true Loving & ever Devoted wife for Dear I assure you that if I Did life would no longer be any inducement for me to Stay in this Deceitfull world But. OH! what a Source of Happiness it is to me to think and Know that I Have a true and Loving wife who Sobs & weeps for me while I undergo punishment for what She well Knows that I did to Save my own life: and one that I well Know even if the whole world is against me & even frown on me with disgrace yet She wil cling the closer and claim me as Her one Dear and Loving Husband. Dearest Sweet Jane OH How Sweet the nam is to me for I know that one of the nobelest & trusst of the fair Sex is of that name and what is Still Sweeter to Know that She is my own true & ever Loving wife & one that will ever wait watch for me to obtain my Liberty as a free man once more no difference How gloomey the prospects my Seem to Be. for my Darling Knows me to well that as long as Life lasts there Hopes. Yes my Darling Sweet Jane you may Hope for I Know you Have grounds to Be Hopefull and Dearest if it was not So I would Be far from telling you my Loving wife So Dearest we I Hope may yet Be the Happiest pair on earth in one anothers embrace of love as once Before So Sweet Jane Be patient Be Cheerfull Dont grieve nor get old or Said But do all in you power to make all arround you comfortable by an Honorable means and I do Hope & pray to god that you & my Dear mother wil Live together Like a devoted child to a devoted mother & a mother to a devoted child is the Heart felt thanks of your own true Husband John W Hardin & all So may you & my Dear Brothers & Sissters ever Be the Same Know no ofence & never give one is to you all my wishes amoung one another. But Be Kind and affectionate to one an other in ever respect. Dearest you Do not Know How Bad I Hated to Here of my Sweet Little Brother Jeff Being Sick But Dearest it is my Hearts wish & faithfull prair that Brother Jeff will Be well Long Before this reaches you for Dearest I wel Know He is a noble Boy Sweet Jane you may Have Seen in the papers where I undertoock to capture the armor with 50 other convicts and that I am now receiving punishment for the Same Dear there was a brake contemplated Here Some time ago and it was Said they onley Liked 2 hours work of Having the armor captured when the alarm was given & given By a convict or convicts and it is thought that in 2 Hours longer the convicts would off all Been released and as the work comenced in my Shop of course they Said Hardin was leader Yes ever thing would Have it Hardin was the one So they put me in a dark cell for 5 days But you Bet the guards & convicts treated me well and I Had all of the candles extra grub tobaco & Beding I needed none of which a man is allow in a dark cell now dear I in person as yet Hant tried to get out yet But you can rest easey if this place must Be Beat no telling what I might do in time to come write to. M. C. & tell Him that I said for Him to come down this Spring that Horses wil Bring a good price Be Sure tell Him to Be Sure & come Love to all Kiss all for me as a new yrs gift your Loving & ever True Husband John W Hardin.

John. W. Hardin.

in writing to Mannin Tell Him that I Say if He wil onley come to See me this Spring that I can get a pardon Shore tell Him I Say to write to me through J. C. outlaw and all wil be right tell Him I Say to Be Sure and come

write to me at once Both ways let me Know if you get th by Signing O-your name J ÷ Hardin

this Letter is ceiled By me in my cell in a new white envellope Let me Know if you get it all right.

Jane Dearest this is a Sliped letter answer at once but Be Sure & Direct to. J. C. outlaw Huntsville walker county Texas whenever you wish to write me a private letter Direct J. C. Outlaw with 2 envellopes one with this address on the outside & the other a Blank envellope with the letter in it to me write to me through outlaw for awhile

---

95. J. W. H. to Jane Hardin

Jan the 9 the 1879 Huntsville Texas Mrs. Jane. Hardin

My. Dear, Loving and Devoted But Troubled wife. it is by the mercies of god alone that I now endeavor to Comunicate to you my Darling and true wife. yes Dearest to me of all on earth, one that I well Know Has ever proven true to me Both in Known and unknown Lands. yes my Dearest Both in prosperity and in adversities. and not that I wish to flatter you in the Least. But in the Latter you my Darling true wife have ever Done your part: as a true friend or as a loving companion and as a True & Devoted wife Should or even would do for Her unfortunate Husband: (Se) in (72)(74) and even in other places & times: not necissarry to mention taking everthing in consideration: But. Oh My Darling true and ever Loving Jane whose name I cherrish Dearer yes Dearer than all names or even Jewels on earth. Simply Because I can Look Back over the past and Say that I found one yes one true true Friend, who Has never told to me a Lye. not even from the Beging of our friendship. and then above all I can Say yes and She is my true and Loving wife. Dearest there is nothing more consoleing to me, and in fact there is nothing els that Does console me onley the thoughts which I Believe and Hope is real, that there is a bright future for us and that we may Live and injoy each others Hapiness as once before. Yet Dearest you well Know we are Sepperated at present by the Strong arm of man in the Shape of Law but Dearest Lovlist Jane & my Devoted wife I Do Hope it can & wil not Be So always Oh Dearest & truest if it were not for faith & Hope what would or even could we do. But Hope that Beautifull Bird How could we live without (Her). Dearest I even at times Go Back to our courtship. I often think of what you told me when I was going on an expedition to the mountains. allthoug we wer then engaged to Be man and wife at Some future day you my Dearest understood my conditions you Knew again what my Journey in the mountains called for I told you then and called you my own Darling Jane that I Did Love you above all others, and that Should I live to come Back from the Mountains. that we then would no longer perlong our engagement. you my Dearest Look me in the face and Said Wes. oh West. is there not danger of you never coming Back alive I Said there is a good chance. and that is the reason I prepose to postpone our engagement you Said that Shall Be no reason. and should you never get Back after telling me this. Life would no longer be any pleasure to me. you Knew my mision to great, or thought too much of me to ask me to postpone. But I then Said to you Dearest my Life is uncertain I am Safe nowhere my Life is uncertain my enemies Seek to take my Life, Daily and nerly Hourley. then I added at present you Know my enemies are Strong. But if I mistake not you Spoke up and Said. yes. but they are cowards and midnight murders: and I Hate them for there Bloody crimes: then I asked you then if you would Be mine untill Death would prove unkind. then you Said Wes your Troubles are Honerable. and (I love you above all others) you have no comparison in my eye. and if you were to Be Killed before I could Claim you as my own by Law. I would allways be the most miserable of my Sex. for West I Know I love you and I believe & Know you love me in return. then I Said Sweet Jane we Shall no Longer Live apart then you Said if our days together Be few or many which I hope they may be many my Heart I wil be Satisfied to Know that you are or was my own Dear Husband then I Said Jane I love you, you Know it. therfore I donot wish to get you into trouble. you Said Wes if you love me dont talk that way for wes all of my Hapiness on this earth depends on being your wife. I fell that I can Share your troubles in everthing without you I am desolate & unhapy. So my Sweet Darling Jane you Know we were man and wife in two days afterwards. your Kindness and your Lovely afections I never Shall forget. and sweet oh Dearest you Know I paid you in return when allowed we promised to Be true to one another Both Before & after marrige Untill Death would prove unkind we fortunateley lived 6 yrs together as Happy as two could Live with the exception of trouble caused by misfortune actions that we Had no controll and dearest of all if I must Say So in that our Troubles Have Been great But Sweet Jane we did Subdue the Best we could and Have Said together god gaveth and He taketh away. So we Said it cant Be Helped. it is So our grief Dearest was Great. But Dearest Jane we tried. we did take all for the Best. and Dearest Sweetest that must Be our motto now no other relief. So we can onley Hope Hope and as Long as Life Last never must we despair. no never no matter our conditions So — Loving wife we Have three Children I am not allowed to Be with them to adv— them they of course at present Like a fathers care. Oh I Do Hope there traing while young will Be Good and that they may Be trained never to to Stoop to any thing ——— Low But to Live Honorable an Honest no diference How poor there circumstances may Be and teach them to never do to there companions or fellow creatures what they would not Be perfectley willing to Have done them Sweet Jane I Know you wil do all you can my mother Sisters & Brothers wil Help you I Know Sweetest on earth and Dearer than my own Life for if it were not for you I now say Life would Be a misery But your Sweet name revives me and dearest if I must Be So weak I am now onley Living for your Sake alone my troubles I am proud to Say would end were it not for one that I Love & adore above all others Her Sweet name Jane and what Holds me up is this

I Know you my Dearest Love in return So good By Sweet Darling wife Jane Write Soon I Send my love to all Keep in good cheer Adieu all your true and Loving John. W. HARDIN
Jane Dearest write me often tell ma Sisters & Brothers to write dont you forget I will write ever chance Let me Know if you ever got my Sachel from ft worth if not write at once to Tom Dewit Ft worth write to my friends & tell them to write me write at once to Barnett Hardin Hill county Texas woodberry. PO. Jane Let me Know How many letter you Have got from me in the Last 6 weeks answer at once a Sweet good By

JWH

---

96. J. W. H. to Jane Hardin

continued part 2 Jan the 10the 1879

My Darling Sweet wife Jane / Huntsville Texas
I thought I would write you a few words more this morning Dearest wil you write me a letter and Let me Know How you are Getting along. and How you are cared for by my relatives and if they are Kind to you or not and if you are Satisfied with your home / oh / I Do Hope and pray that you are well cared for By all of my Dear Sisters Brothers and By my worthy mother for Dearest I Know you to Be worthy of their care and Kindness wich I Know Dearest you Show them in return. tell me what you think of Sister Eliza Sweet Jane Do all you can to make my relatives Love you by Honorable means: for Dearest I Know they cant Help But Love you for my Sake. Sweet oh Dearest Jane Be cheerfull and try and console yourself with Hopes. and think of the Happy hours we Have Seen together when no one Knew who we were But our Selves (Oh) Dearest remember me, and never think that I can or could ever fail to think of you my own Sweet Jane, no mater what may ever be my condition you are the Joy of my Life. my own Sweet wife. and if it were not for you to day: I would think Death a blessing Sent. but Dearest on your acct I consider I Have more to Live for than most any one could imagine. Oh/ Do the Best you can Be Sure & train our children not to Lie not to tell tales out of school besides Teach them to respect you and allso people that are older than themselves. Deares Jane Teach them to Be Jentle and to Be Kind in there man-

ers in ever respect. So Dearest I will close by asking you to forgive my pen as it wont write what I wish also excuse me for exposing our conversation Before going to the mountains I Hope you can come to See me in the course of 5 or 6 months you Know it would Be imposible for me to say How I Long to See your Sweet Smiles. once more give my Love to all. tell Nannie to take good care of Her Little niece M tell J. W. and J. G to Be good Boys obey there mothers be Kind and attentive to there Little Sister & niece Jane M. Dearest the Last Letter I Got from you was dated the 24 of Dec write at once to M. C tell Him I Have writen Him Several Letters & no Ans as yet. So Sweet Jane Do you Know How you Signed your name to the Letter you wrote me on the 24th of Dec if So let me Know But Dearest I Do not Supose any one but me would of ever noticed it except you (Let me Know) Sweet Jane you asked me to write you a long-Letter this is the Best I can do at present for the want of paper But Dearest I Hope paper wil be no object in time to come wil you write me one as Long as you wish, So my own Loving wife I Bid you adieu a loveing adieu for this time By Send ing my Love to all So I remain your own Husband

John W Hardin untill Death

Ma wil you excuse me for writing you So Short a letter if you Knew my excuse you would Say nothing ma wil you Have my Dear wife to write how all is getting along wil you Do the Same ma I well Know you will Do all you can for her & those Sweet children of mine. ma comfort Her and cherrish Her as you would me (She is mine) and I Know She will reward you Some day Dear ma I am in Hopes you get along Like a Devoted mother to a child and a child to a mother Do not think Hard of what I Say. I Say or what I Say is for the Wellfare of all I Do Hope Jeff is well ma you must incourage Him to Stay with you ma write uncle Barnet Hardin a Letter at once write to all of our relatives & See what they can & wil Do for me you can explain all to them Be Sure remember me to all and Kiss Jane & the children for you Son **John. W. HARDIN**

---

97. J. W. H. to Jane Hardin

Dearest I

Jan the 26the 1879 Huntsville Texas Mrs Jane Hardin

My Dear & Loving wife having Recived and read your Letter with pleasure I now through the mercies of God wil endeavor to answer the Same . Which I assure you my Darling Sweet Jane I Do with pleasure and as often as circumstances will permit : Nevertheless in your Last Letter you Spoke as thoug I never wrote or in other words that I Had Forgotton you Well Dearest Do you not think that it would be impossible for me to forget (you) one who you well Know I Love and adore above all others Yet you Seem to think So or Do you not (if you Do Let me Know) you Know what I Have Said as to you you allso Know whether I am a traitor or not and whether or not I Have not allways been true to my vows or word or not

2 Besides you Know what I think of a Traitor or Deceiver I Hope I wil never fall in there Hands But a true true frind there is no value to Be Placed on them But of Late I find them Scarce . But Still I Know of Some I Have as it is: got my roe to weed and you can rest assured it is very grassey But I Do Hope by the mercies of god to Be able to weed the Same. and if I fail it will Be the 1St time. and then I wil Blame nobody But my self time wil tell, Now you asked me Some questions conserning my work Now I ans this way I Have not done a days work in 6 weeks nor Since the Break you Speak So much about . My Health Has not Been good atall Since the 1St of Jan therefore I Have Been Keept in my cell a good matrass plenty of covoring and plenty to eat and Drink and a docter Whenever I wished the Latter only 3 time and am on the mind at present

3 I think I wil Be able to go to work in a few days.. Now as to my trouble Here I Have thus far Bore it the Best I could and Take all for the Best Believing it gods wil or it would not be So and think in the course of time I can Live over it easey.. at Least I Hope so.. Dont Bother about my punishmen for I am doing as well as a man could do under the circumstances the Sup & Lessees Have thus far Been very Kind in extending me favors Now My Dear Jane I Do Hope you wil Say Know more about the Brake or about my punishment for one can Here any thing these Days Hoping you wil now Be Satisisfied with my answer Dearest Do you ever Here from Gonzales Let me Know or from M c or from any of our relatives I Have received 2 Letters from you this mo one Dated the 3 and the other the 14 teenth Dearest I hope you wil cheer up and write me a long Letter (I Know Dearest you wil not for Get to write me) So Dearest I wil close for this time Hoping that this may reach you in due time

and find you in good Health and Good Spirits Let me Know How the Babes are doing Kiss them all for me So give my Love to all So a Loving good By My own Dear Wife Hoping to Here from you Soon I remain your True and Devoted Husband.

John. W. Hardin untill Death

Well. J.W.H & J.G.H. how are you Geting along I Know you are Kind to Little Jane & mind your mothers & Grandma So Be Good Children you wil if you Live Be men Some day and I hope usefull men So good By Dear children Mollie How do you and Budie get along does He Bite yet Kiss ma for Papa Adieu My Children
Let me Know if Sissie Has moved or not John W H How about the Satchell at Ft Worth be Sure and Let me Know Tom Dewit Ft worth So Kiss all of the Family for me Adieu my Dearest Jane JW. Hardin

---

98. J. W. H. to Jane Hardin

Feb the 9 the 1879 Huntsville, Texas

Direct to Mrs Jane Hardin
Bennit Station Redriver county Texas Huntsville, Texas
Mrs Jane Hardin
My Dear & Loving Wife it is with pleasure that I now endeavor to write you. I received aletter from you Last Sunday one from Ma also which I answered fourthwith. I received one to Day from M. Clements of SanSaba He Sends His Love to you and Family allso to Ma & Family He Says that He Has beat all of his casses in Gonzales and one in dewit the rest Now He Says amounts to nothing. and He allso Says that he is getting Now So He can attend to Something else besides court. but Says up to the present He Has Been Quite Busy He Say that He will not forget you and my Sweet Little Babes He allso Said that He would Be at austin to attend Court on the 3rd of this mo in the county court. and would probabley Be there for a week or Longer. He allso Said that He Bonded William Phillips out at austin in Jan and that Bil had Gone Home. Bill & M Last Winter directley after you Left austin Got in to a Difficulty with Some of the citty authorites So M Got out at once Bill Had to Lie in Jail untill M got Back from court in Dewit He Says His case amounts to nothing

at austin Bill wrote me 2 Letters while in austin Jail He Says His case wil not amount to much I would of writen Long ago But I thought you had enough to think of at the present and Have Been waiting for further Devellopements. Jane Dear I expect to Surprise you a little your Sister Mattie Has Married on Oliver Odum. So Chew on that for awhile. Jane write at once to William Phillips. of Gonzales. tell Him that I wrote 3 Letters to Him while He was in Jail at austin tell Him to Be Sure & write me at once and to Give me all of the (News, tell Him my chances are onley of a Sunday to write But wil write him the 1st Chance Jane Dearest M told me to Cheer up that he Did not think my time would Be Long He allso Said He Hoped I would from this on obey all comands from the officers in comand Jane Dearest I Donot think they wil ever have Grounds to complain of again as my motto is from this on to Strictley obey all orders and to (Do right Let who wil Do rong) the Sup Says He wil Give me a fair Trial which if He does I Hope He never wil regret Jane Dearest my Health is Still improving, and at present Doing as well as circumstances wil admit, Dearest remember me to all of the Family and Kiss those Sweet Babes of ours for me So I wil close for this time By Sending my Love to all Hoping to Here from you Soon and often I remain your Husband John W HArdin untill Death
Direct to Mrs. Jane Hardin Bennit Station (PO) redriver county Texas

---

99. J. W. H. to Jane Hardin

Feb the 23rd 1879 Mrs Jane Hardin Huntsville Texas
My Dear Darling and True wife it is with pleasure that I now endeavor to write you thoug I Have no nuse to write only I received your Letter to day and was glad to Hear all was well you cannot imagine How proud I am to get a letter from you my own Darling Jane besides to Know that all thoug a convict yet I Have a True and Loving wife the Best property on earth oh Dearest Donot think of my troubles for I consider them nothing Besides yours oh that I could onley Bear yours with mine and that you Had nothing to Bother you But Dearest truest Be only Have patience and remember you true Loving Husband can do nothing But wish you good Luck and Happy days at present But Dearest I Know time wil chang everthing it Seems to me that my Love for you increases and I know

yours to me must for Such is the result of true Love No other on earth could take your place with me Dearest Dont think I am flatering you for you Know it So (oh) My Darling Sweet Jane treat Ma as a mother my Brothers and Sisters as you would your own they will and Do love you they are our Best friend Do not Suffer your Self to get angry with them onley Teach your Self to love them as I now you Do Teach the children the Same Grand ma H is there Best friend Sweet oh Dearest Jane I Dreampt the other night of coming in the House wher you and Sweet Little 2 Amigos I though She was (Sucking you) I thought I Huged and Kissed you So Happy was I in my Dream to Be with you I thought you Said Jiney is Jealous She Looked Mad at me as though She thought I was an intruder But when you told Her I was Her pa I though She Huged and Kissed me and called me papa oh How often I think of you my Dearest Sweetest & truest Jane you cannot imagine rememember I think of you Hourley though it is a pleasure to think of you my Swet wife Yet Sadness is mingled with it only to think I cannot Be with you. Jane Dearest we are both young and I think and Hope we may pass our Latter days together in perfect Hapiness then we can talk over our Hard Ship & trials of Life Swet Jane remember me often to our Sweet Little Babes which I Know you Do. Jane my Sweet wife I cannot find words to express my Love only think of time past and you wil Know) J.W.H

Do not grumble at this letter for it is Done in a Hurry by candellight and wil not go throug the office Be carefull of my guard He told me He Had writen to you Be carefull in writing to Him Be Sure and give Him no clue He Seems all right But is He is a question you Be Sure and tell Him you think I can get out Legally & that is the only way you wish me as you Know I can in a Short time till Him you would of sent me sone things But you Did not wish to incourage me in

Tell Ma I would of and intended writing Her But No Room at presen

Write me a letter My Sweet ma

Sister Mat excuse I wil write you when I get somemore Paper But Deliver this Let me Know if you receive this By Signng Your name Thus —Jane Hardin— a mark Before and behnd

Ma Kis all for me excuse in Hast a cop is coming now So god Bless you all **John W Hardn**

100. J. W. H. to Jane Hardin

Excuse this Badly writen and composed let Dear
March the 2nd 1879 Ad Mrs Jane Hardin, Huntsville Texas
My Dear and Loveing wife it is with pleasure that I now endeavor to write you on this Small piece of paper Dearest this Leaves me well at present my Health Having improved no Little I am Doing as well as a man could Do under the circumstances Dearest I Hope your health is good and our Little Childrens allso Jane Dearest I do Hope you wil try and make your Self contented for the present and teach our children to both Love and fear god and to be honest an honerable in all there Dealings never Doing any thing to any one but what they would Like to Be done them (the golden rule) teach them) Jane I am So Glad you are getting along So well nothing afords me more pleasure than to Know my loved ones are doing well write to MC for me

Tell him to write me you can tell him my chances to write therfore I cannot Both for the want of paper and time write to those I would like to write to. Jane I heard from Gonzales again all are well Bill Phillips Says he wil come to See me this Sumer or fall Jane tell ma to write to uncle Barnett for me tell her to tell uncle to write me at once (Be Sure) allso tell ma or you write to Jim Anderson and tell him to write me that I wil answer allso to uncle Ellack Dixson I would like to Know his opinion about rota Jane Dearest Give my love to Sister Mat & Brother Bright and the Little Smith Jane write me as often as you can tell Jeff I hope He wil Have good Luck farming this yr I Send my Love to all and ask you to Kiss the Little Children once more for me having no nuse nor time I wil Bring my Short and uninteresting letter to a close tell ma I never got tired of her letter read it over 3 or 4 times So Dearest adieu you Loving Husband

John W Hardn

---

101. Matie Odom to Jane Hardin

March the 16 1879

Deare Sistr I take my pen IN haND to write you A few line this leve all well aDans hope that when this come to hanD Ite finsD youe the same Jane I have No nuse to write JAne iam mareD i mareD on the

last Day uf December i mareD mr olver oDom We ar living at fank ASher plase tims is so harD here that we canat harDly mak a liveig k frank is goen odom th both sanD teh lover to n you JAne kiss the chilDren for me tetl moly that S She muse forgot
--nt matie fo i wooD give teh inythiNg to se you all Jane unk ben ses i that you out to writ to him pa ses that he is going to senD you & me mony when he sel his cat—e

Jane i waNt you to writ sos suNe as you got this So iwill cloese for this time

kinD Sistr untill Detih
Matie ODom
Dereck you leter to yorkton

---

102. J. W. H. to Mattie Smith and husband, and Jane Hardin

March the 16 teenth - 1879 Huntsville Texas

Mrs Mattie Smith & Husband
Dear Brother and Sister
it is with pleasure that I now endeavor to write you a few lines this Leaves me well and in as Good Spirits as a man could Be under the circumstances though I have No nuse of importance to comunicate to you I here you are going west I hope you may Make a good move and that you May Be Blessed with prosperity if I new where you expected to Locate probably I could Describe the country But at present I supose that makes No difference But I may if it is god will fall in your Section time to come So when you get Settled write me a long letter that I may Know your wherebouts I would of written you long ago But Doubtless you are aware of my chances to write I am only allowed to write once a month with Material furnished but to day I am imposing on the (Sup) and I must Say wil Be the Last time and unless I am fortunate enough to Get material wil only write one letter a month I suppose you can imagine who that wil Be too having Nothing at this time to interest you I wil Bring my Short and Poorly composed Letter to a close Hoping you wil write me a letter at once as a line from you Both wil Be thankfully received Give my Love to all of ma's Family and remember me Kindley to all that may

inquire after me So I wil close for this time By Sending Love to the Little Smith So I remain you. Broth with respect

John W Hardin

Mrs Jane. Hardin
My Dear Wife Having received No letter from you in Some 3 week I thoug I would Drop you a few lines in this one this Leaves me well and in as good Spirits as circumstances wil admit Not receiving any Letters for Some time from your Section of course makes me anxious to here from your Section Dearest as my time is up for writing I wil have to post pone hoping this may find you all well an in good circumstances So I send my Love to all Kis the children Adieu my Darling wife **John W Hardin**

Diret to Mr Bright Smith Bennit Station Redriver County Texas

Major Send this if you please and I hope I can return the favor at Some future time if it Should ever Be in my power yours with respect **John W Hardin**

---

103. Mollie and M. Clements to Jane Hardin

March 23rd. 18.79 Sansaba Co. Texas Richland. PO
ps tell all to write. to us tell Wes to Hold up his head. think he will come out all Right M.
Mrs Jane Hardin) Dear Cousin I seat my Self this lonsom sabath eavening. to write to you to let you know that I havent forgotten you, nor dont want you to think I have. I often think of you in my lonsom hours. Manen got a letter from Wes dated March, the.. 11th. and was glad to hear from him he spoke of getting letters from you often, and I know it is a pleasure to him to hear from you and the Children, as eny of the connection Manen Writes to him often, and Writes for both of us and all ways puts in words for the children. to cousin john.. tha often seaks of you and.. children and Cousin john.. jane it is very dry here thare is scarcly Water for Stock, and hardly enugh for people. I dont think thare will be eny thing raised in farming this year, in this part of the Country. we havent had rain enugh in 3 monthes as ——— ——— eny Season in the ground. Spring has opend — but not mutch. grass is putting up sme. times is very

hard in this Country but I believe its So every where.. or at least every Where I hear from.. jane I hope you are doing well and Satestfied. try and content yourself and dont study and greave so mutch look for the future and pray for things to change, and I do hope and pray thay may I hope john will not have to stay thare long, it is the genearl opinion that he wont have to stay verry long Try and bare your troubles as easy as you can and I think all will come right yet. I want you to write to me as soon as you get this write me a long letter and tell your Ma to write. We are allways glad to hear from eny of the Connection. We havent heard from the boys in a long time We — heard from Joe & gip last thay were well at that time

March 23ird 1879. Mrs Jane Hardin.

Deer Cousin

as Mollie has Writen you all the news I Will not Comment. Well Jane I Recd 2 letters from Wes: the Last mail Jane you must not think hard not writing oftener But i thought Would Wait to Receive a lettr from Wes the Last letter was March the 19th 1879— he wrote like he was better Composed then eny othr letter he wrote, give my love to Aunt Elizabith & all the Children tell Jeff i admire his staying at home With his ma tell him to Look at Wesses fate for exanple and you must not — take Every thing as Easy as posible. Eny thing in the World i can doe for you i would Redy doe it i have to be in austin in or on the 20th of next month will Write you from their soe write soon Kiss the children for me

i remmain your cousin until Death **M Clements**

We got a letter from james Denson last mail thay were all well at time Mary jane. has another boy. manen Kimbro came up in the winter and stayed a while with us he said your pas folks Were all well then. We heard While manen was up here that matt Was married but I dont no how true it is heard that she married Olever odam if She has Married Olever she has got a very good man and I hope her all the good luck that may befall her Well Jane I have wrote about all the news and Will Close as Manen will finish it for me this Leavs all Well Write soon I Remmain your Cousin untill Death

Mary A Clements, To Jane, Hardin

P.s. Jane sallie & ——— sayes tell Cousin Jane & the children Houdy for them good By Write Soon as you get this we are all at home to night good By

— By Her cousin M.C

---

104. J. W. H. to Jane Hardin

J. W. Hardin
Apr 13/79

Apr the 13 teenth 1878
Huntsville Texas

Mrs Jane Hardin
My Dear and Loving wife I received yous of the 4the inst which Brought me the News of your arrival at austin I assure you it was thankfuly received for I was more than anxious to here from you. Besides to Know that you and the children Had arrived Safe at austin there is nothing more incouraging to me than to here of you and the children Doing well Dearest you Said you would Be there untill the 20ith. then you Said you would Go to San saba I hope you wil injoy your Self while there Knowing that you wil find Friends there that wil Look after your interest Dearest I received a letter from ma Staiting how well you all had gonton along But how much She Lamented at your Departure But She Hoped it would all be for the Best She Said that She Loved you and the children Dearley and Believed She was Loved in return By you Jane Dearest you Spoke of onley going South to obtain what Belongs to you I Know you Need it much But my advice is to Do as I have told you Before in (person) if you wish any advice concerning the Same I refer you to M Clement as he Know the circumstances But Dearest I Leave the Subject with you as I have No time to Spare Concrning it. Dearest I wrote you on the 1st in care of D. Corwin I hope you got it Give my respects to Joe A. also to others that you may Desire hoping to here from you Soon I wil Bring my letter to a clos By telling you that my Health is good as comon and am Doing as well as a man can under the circumstances Hoping to here from you Soon I wil Bring my Short Letter to a Clos By telling you to Kiss the children once more for me So I remain yours Most affectionateley John. W. Hardin your Husband till Death
(PS) Dearest you can tell M C that I wrote to him Last Sunday Jane as to him you Know him therfore there is no use to Speak you Said you would come to See me this Sumer you Know how proud I would Be to See you and the Dear Little Babes But Dearest Let Manin Be the Judge allthough it may Be Hard But Dont fret nor grieve But Look to the Bright future which I hope yet awaits us give

my respects to capt Hendricks allso tell M C to See Joe Steward or get Mr Hendricks to See Him conserning my writing at austin Be Sure allso tell Him to write me His intention concerning it Give my Love to Mollie and the children allso to M Hoping to Here from you Soon I remain your Husband John W Hardin
Tell Joe Anglemieer to write me and Send Some reading mater a Sweet adieu my Loving wife

JWH

you can tell M Bill Tempelton is here and Says The Sutton party no good/But can git a man in But not out tell Him/ ed Steadman who come Here for Braiking John Ringo and Sco cooley out of the Lampases Jail is Dead died of Sickness on the 11th

---

105. J. W. H. to Jane Hardin

Apr the 2Oith —79 Huntsville Texas Mrs Jane Hardin
My Dear and loving wife. Having received your of the 14 teenth inst with pleaseure and contents Noticed. I now endeavor to answer the Same Hoping you wil receive the Same in Due time This Leaves me in Tolerable Health and am Doing as wel as my circumstances wil admit Jane Dearest I Have no nuse to Day to comunicate you of any interest. Jane my Dear Keep in cheer and Drive Dul care away by Looking to the Bright future which I Hope yet awaits us. remember me to my inquiring friends Give my Love to Mannon tell him to write when He has time allso to Mollie & the Children When you See them No nuse from Ma Since I wrote you Hoping that you may meet friends and that you Wil Be Satisfied for the present I wil Bring my Short Letter to a close By asking you to Kiss the Children once more for me and that Little Jinnie may be well by this time Hoping to here from you Soon I remain you Loving Husband as ever affectionately adieu **John W Hardin**
(P.S) Write me when you wil leave Austin Tell Mannin to try & come to See me this Sumer or faul he might come as a guard with prisners from his county which would Save expenses. So a lovin adieu my Loving wife **John W HArdin**

---

106. Elizabeth Hardin to Mrs. Jinnie Hardin

Fannin Co. Apr 27th. 1879 Mrs Jinnie Hardin) Austin, Texas) My dear daughter and sweet little Children I am here at Mr. Cobbs eight miles North of Bonham all well we have been here a week it was Severl days before I could Send to the office. I received a letter from Johnnie and one from you I have answerd his. Jane after you left Bennett we lost the black horse we got from Mr. Sinclare Jeff Spent a week in hunting him though could not find him. we left there on the tenth. the first night we camped about twelve miles from home there we lose our two year old yearling and Bright a cow we Supposed they had gone back. So Jeff went back to look for then spent three days returned with out then did not hear any thing of them. last thursday started back home to take another Search for them Bright and all are waiting his return. I am afraid we will loose them. Jane another of Doctor Moody's pacients died Since you left. Mrs Moss. Gray her first husband took his little girl from Moss. the Robberson's was very much opposed to him having her. Jane I want to see you so much it appears So long Since I parted from you. when I returned home I missed you So much and we ware so lonesome I could See so many plaything of the childrens and their little Stick horses ware all over the yord a many a tear I Shed about you and the children we received a Telagram from Johnnie the morning after you left wishing you to go on with us. I wrote him a letter and received an answer from him before I left. Jane answer this letter the very next minute after reading it. direct to Bonham I think we will be here long enough to hear from you. and tell me what you are going to do. Jane I am deeply interested in your well fare O how I do want to See my Sweet little children. Sweet Mollie Gran ma misses you So much you must have your Ma to teach you and Johnnie how to write So you can write to gran Mama Jane Kiss all the children for me dont let Johnnie and little M. forget me let me know when you herd from Johnnie last Sissie inquired a grea deal about you. she Sends you and the children her love. Nannie Says tell Sister Jane to write to her and She will tell her evrything. Jane Mama wishes you all the happiness a Mother could. it has not been long Since I Saw you though it appears like a year has passed write me a long letter good bye my Sweet daghter and little Mollie Johnnie and Sweet little M.

Your Mama
Elizabeth Hardin

---

107. J. W. H. to Jane Hardin

May the 4 the, 79 Huntsville Texas Mrs Jane Hardin
My Dearley and Beloved wife
having received yours of Last month, which was more than a thankful visitor in ever respect Dearest I am Glad to Know you Still Find Friends and that your health is good ailso the childrens I received a letter from ma today all well they are at M cobs in Fanin and wil Be there Some time write to her at once She Says She wants to See you and the children So much (oh) She Speaks So High of you all She Said She had received one letter from you Since She Left She is more than anxious to here from you Jane Dearest Do all you can to make all around you
2
you happy by Honerable means Be Sure and Keep the children under good moral instruction Tell molly to write me a letter as I have written her Several or notes Kiss Little maney and Sweet Little Sallie For me tell them cousin John thinks of them often Tell Little Sallie that She can have Mollie H for a play mate but tell Little Manin that the rassul Betwen him and J W dont go as he failed to come up to contract But take Good care of him for Some Special accasion which may yet come as to little Jane I Know Mollie C wil not forget her Jane Dearest I am Glad to Know you have a mind of your own and can use Good Judgment on Special occasion you Have mad a good Selection for a Home I Know that you wil Be well cared for in ever respect Besides I am glad to Se you independant of you Know who yet I wil Leave this Subject with you and my Dearest wil indorse any thing you may do in refference thereunto the Best and truest advise
3nd
that you can find is Manin C and I think you can Gain Some of your property throug him in Gonzales But take his advice in ever respect for I Know he wil Be a Father to you as well as a cousin I am dearest doing Splendid at present and See no reason why I shal Not continue to Do well for this place and I Know if our lives is onley Spaired

that a bright Future yet awaits us So cheer up Be patient Dont fret at what cant Be helpt But train your Self to Be contented for the present and Look to the Bright future which I hope yet awaits you and yours Jane Dearest and Truest I Know your disposition is to make Friends which I Know you cultivate By your Mild and pleasant maners So dearest I wil close for this

4th

Time By Sending Love to all Kiss the Children once more for me and remember me to all inquireing Friends tell M C I have writen him in this and wil Send in this one Hoping it wil Suit him But that I wil try and write Him Soon again

Houston powel is Here He Sends His regard to you an Family allso to M C & Family So adieu for this time My Darling and affectionate wife I remain your loving Husband till time Last

affectionateley yous **John W HArdin**

Major Goree please Send Both if not please return. I am yours obedient prisner J W Hardin with

---

108. J. W. H. to M. Clements and Jane Hardin

May the 11the 1879 Texas State Prison Mr M Clements

Dear cousin Having received yours which informed me of your arrival at your Ranch with My Beloved ones and finding your family injoying good Health I assure you it was thankfully received and read By me in each & ever particular. Mannin I have No nuse of interest to communicate you at present onley this Leaves me well and in Hopes of Better Days When you go to austin See Lieu J B Armstrong & Capt Lee Hall Tell them with proper management the Scrap Taylor case can be worked up to a certainty you can imagine How I am informed the party Says that if allowed He wil Show up allso you See there will Be no use of making a State evidence of those who are Bound to hang this winter Manin I advise you to Be very pruden in all Such maters But the matter is Just as I have told you all Stood in and it is so. rangers an any (Now Be Prudent) even in your Small maters Such as the Agrivated assault with intent— at austin allways consider motives. Know you are right then go ahead. Hoping you May Be Sucessfull throug Life and that we may yet meet on this earth and Shake Hand over our troubles with out reference to malice or otherwise I Send my Love to you and Family and ask you to give me the Jeneral News of west and South Texas remember me Kindley to all inquiring Friends most especialy (in a Hurry) to those who desire it So Adieu for this time my Faithfull cousin **John W Hardin**

May the 11th 79

My Darling and Dearly Beloved wife this leaves me in fine Spirits and Health and am glad to Know you arrived Safe at M C ranche I Do Hope that you will Be contented and not Despair in the Least for I Believe truth and Justice wil yet prevail Dear Be carefull with our Little Children Kiss them Kindly in rememberance of there Father write to me as often as can tell Mollie to write Give me all of the news in your next So adieu my Loving wife I remain your Loving Husband untill Death John W. Hardin

Manin Besure and write m at Austin received one issue of the austin Statesman

---

109. Mattie Odom and Oliver Odom to Jane Hardin

May The, 13: 1879 Gonzlas Co texas Mrs Jane Harden

Dear sister I receaved your Kind letter A few days Ago and was glad to hear from you and the Children and you was all well the folks is all well here frank is living with me now She says you must rite to her and nettie is bording with us going to school.

Packey was here to day She wantted to know where pone Freman is she has written seaverl letters and has never receiveed any answer well Jane I cant think of any thing else to rite tell J W Harden that I would like to see him William and nancy is talking of going up there before long to spend the summer and you can come back with them I would give any thing to see you and the Children so I will Close you must excuse my short letter I will try and do better next time Kiss the children for me

from your effectionate sister good by **Mattie Odom**

May the 13 1879 Gonzlias Co texas Mrs Jane Harden

Dear sister I will rite you A few lines and send it withe mats as we havent but one invelope and it is all the same any how Jane I havent any. news to rite tell mannon that they have got Marcus tyler in Jail and they say he will never get out I heard they had seavon bills Agin

him for Cow stealing and one for the Brasell murder I heard well I cant think of any thing else to rite so I will close for this time they all Join me in much love to you and the children
rite soon good by **Oliver Odom**

---

110. J. W. H. to Jane Hardin

May the 25th 79 Texas State Prison

Direct to Mrs Jane Hardin Richland Springs San Saba county texas in care of M Clements Mrs Jane Hardin

My Dear Loveing and affectionate Wife it is with pleaseure that I now endeavor to write you thoug I have no nuse to communicate you of importance onley this Leaves me injoying good health and Spirits as a man can have to Be in my unfortunate condition which I know you wil Be glad to hear of. Dearest I have not heard from you now in 2 weeks But at prest I Know you Mail Matters is very inconvenient Therefore My Darling wife I will be Glad to receive a line from you when it Does come Dearest Be patient Do not Grieve or take trouble to heart but Look to the Bright future which I hope yet awaits you and yours. be carefull with our Sweet Little childrem teach them to Both fear and worship God, and remember that it has been Said the Darkest hours are Jus before day So my Loving wife make all the friends you can by honerabel means be kind to all of your associate and do Not be to hastey in giving or taking offence Give my Love to Moley and the children Kiss Sallie & manie for cousin John Ma Says She is So anxious to See or heare from you She Says it Seems So long Since She Saw you and the Sweet Little children She is on the move and dont know when She wil Stop or where She expected to Be in or near fort worth this week Give my best wishes to all inquiring friends Kiss our Dear and Sweet Little children for me once more my my loving wife X. Donot Grieve over Dreams for you Know I would not Nor never have done what you Dereampt So a loving Adieu for this time my true and loving wife

John W. HArdin

Manin Dear cousin I hope you can by this fall come to See me I Know you wil take the Bes care of my Little family imagineable So Be prudent in all things is the advice of you unfortunate cousin give my regards to all inqiring friends this is done in a hurry excuse till next time So adieu your cousin John W HArDin

111. J. W. H. to Jane Hardin

June the 1st 1879 Texas State Prison Mrs. Jane Hardin
My Dear and Loving wife. I received yours and Mollies Letter Last Sunday Evening after I had writen you they were welcomed by me with Know comparison for you cannot imagine how anxious I am to receive a line from any of My friends or relatives and most especially from you my Darling and Beloved wife Thoug to day I have no nuse to write only this leaves me well and in as good Spirits as one could expect and am Still Living in hopes of injoying free air with my beloved ones and ask that you wil not Give over to trouble in the Least But Just take all for the Best for there is nothing So Bad But could Be worse for Dearest I do Believe that: at least I do hope God wil Spair our lives that we may injoy Life and Liberty to gather as once before and I do hope the time wil not Be Long Be careful with our Sweet Little children Kiss them for me once more my Darling and true wife Kiss manne and Sallie for cousin John. tell molley that I will write her Soon and to take good care of Little Jane I have not heard from maning Since he went to austin But hope to Soon and wish him all the Sucess a man can which I believe he wil have Jane Dearest write me me a long letter tell me all about the Lower country (&c) tell Manny to write as soon as he gets home I wil close By Sending my Love to all of the family hoping to here from you soon. I remaim your Devoted husband Adieu a sweet adieu my loving wife **John W Hardin.**
Please Direct to Mrs Jane Hardin in care of M Clements. Richland Springs PO Sansaba county Texas

---

112. Mattie Odom to Jane Hardin

yorktown June the 15 1879

My Dear sister
I receiveed your kind letter A few days ago and was glad to here from you all and you was all well we are all well here Jane you said you rote to me while you was at Austin and have never receiveed any answer aswered it as soon as I got it and directed it to richland springs I did not get it in time to send it to Austin so dear sister you must not think that I have forgotten you for I had rather see you than

any body but it does look like the rest has forgotten you all tut uncle Ben and aunt Margret they have written to you and have never receiveed any answer uncle Ben said he was willing to do any thing for you he could Jane I heard from cousin Caroline and Mary Camal they wantted to know where you was and said for you to rite when you stopped well Jane I beleive I have written ever thing that will interest you tell M C and Mollie they must write to me and Oliver so I will close Oliver Joins me in much love to you and the children from your true sister

Mattie Odom

---

113. S. J. Clements to Jane Hardin

June the 19th, 1879 Junction city Kimble Co Tex
Mrs Jane Hardin

Dear Cousin I this morning Seat my self to answer your most welcome letter it found us all well hope when this comes to hand it will find you all enjoying same blessing was glad to hear from you all Jane I would be so glad to see you and your children I seen sweet little Mollies picture when I was at your Aunt Margets this spring I want to see Mollie and her children I reckon the Children have growed so I would hardly know them Jane my children are both going to school they both grow fast well I have no news to write only the Indains were in week before last and I reckon you hav heard of that before now they Killed a woman and two children about ninty miles west of here Jane ma has gone home Jims and Gips familys were well when I heard from them last Gip has two children girl and a boy his boy is a smart little fellow he will talk to any body you could not scare him to Save your life talks as plain as my boy now we are needing rain here very bad well Jane you must write as soon as you get this tell Mole & Manen to write Joe is over on devils River look for him back tomorrow if he was here he would write but as the mail goes out today I thought I would write now I hope to heare from you soon my love to all Your cousin asever **S J Clements**
3—1
Jane tell me when you heard from Wes and if he is well I never hear any thing away here

---

114. M. J. Cobb to Jane Hardin

Gonzals. Co. Texas Julie 2 the 1879 Mrs. J. Harding

Dear neis I rescev you welkcom letare and I was glad to her from you wonce more I began to think that you had for me times is dul her money is scearsc I nevar hav scne as dul a time in my life our crop is veary sory we havent had but too rains since last febuary Stock scufeard for gass and waytor Ben is trying to sell out he is the worst dissatsfid purson that you evar hav seene he wants to get away as soon as he can The childran is going to chool Mollie has got the ——— and all the present at school the childran cant say that they love daisy eny betar than they did litt Mollie daisy is veary mucl like litt Mollie in her ways Jane I cnt tell whye you culd think that I was mad at you you nevar give me enney case and I am not a unresenbu purson I hav mor simptis for you and you seet littel childran than evar undar the scicumstants jane you know that I nevar varing. nor weare too facis undar wone crown I am as true and as scentsear as evar Jane you must exscuse musteakes and bad writing for I am all most dsstracted with the toothake you pa has sold his plasce for 1.2 hundared dolers you uncel joshua is gone to florida he writs that crops ar good out there Edward and Beney is with ows yet they ar ging to school I must cloce for Ben is wating for letur as he is going to the post offest this leavs all well I truley hope thees few lines you all injoying the. same good blessing giv my love to Mollie and the seet littel childran, and giv my love to Bet frieman tell her that her peopal is all well min they has gote a fine girle it is for weeks old yestarday tell litte Sallie that mollie says that she regret not giving her somthing that was th ——— as she preschates the dole that she give to her for it was a sorry present write soon and ofting I remain you aunt as evar

M.J. Cobb jane kiss the childran for me

---

115. J. W. H. to Jane Hardin

J W Hardin 7/6/79

July the 6 the 1879 Texas State Prison Mrs Jane HArdin

My Dear & Loving Wife Haveing received yours of the 1St inst I now endeavor to answer Which wil inform you my Dear that my Health is good at present Besides I am Doing as well as any one could expect my work is in the Shade and for the Last 2 month very Light I received a letter from B H Jones of Polk Co he wishes to Know where you & the children are you and M write him a Letter Jane Dearest Do the Best you can and Take Good care of our Sweet Little Children Teach them to mind you But I think Jentler means is the Best to train children under But teach them Right from rong Give my Love to Mollie & the Children tell Mollie I answered her letter and if I Dont here from her again Soon I wil write again Kiss all of the Children for me tell Mollie to Be Good to Little Jiney aliso tell J W to not Bite his Sister M So Adieu for this time my loving wife Hoping to here from you soon I am your Husband

Affectionately John W Hardin

Dearest Do not get uneasey about not getting letters from me for I hardly ever fail to write you once a week oh Dearest may we yet Be to gether as in time Past a Sweet adieu my Loving wife John W Hardin remember me when this you See oh the past wil it never come again I am yours

JWH

---

116. J. W. H. to M. Clements

M tell me how John ringo got Killed Be Sure you Said he was Killed in Kansas

July the 6th, 79 Texas State Prison Mr M Clements

Dear Cousin This Leaves me in good Health &C I have Got no news to write only it has Been very Dry Here for Some time but on the 4th we had a little Shower and it has Been Showery ever Sence Manin cant you write me Something that wil make me feel Good or Bad one and what my chances are for ever Being aloud my Liberty. you Live in adjoining (Bad english all goes) Comanchie & Brown Co you could acertain very easy as to my chances if I could See you I could post you who wil help me in Comanchie allthoug they Have Been in time past my Deadly enemies Write to mart Flemings Comanchie Texas he come to See me while I was there uncle Bob & Aaron Staid at his House during my trial tell him I refered you to him as he ask me to Be Sure and write me a long Letter ad Libitum

John Ringo
—Courtesy Arizona Historical Society / Tucson.

and if you cannot come down this fall or think it to Soon to try a petition Let me Know as I am easey Satisfied Do the Best you can with my Beloved ones remembering me to all inquireing friends So I wil close By telling you this is my Last Paper & envelope But Hope to get Some one of these days I am as ever and allwys wilbe your cousin till Death

John W Hardin

---

117. Mattie Odom to Jane Hardin

gonzales Co texas July the. 22. 1879
Mrs Jane Hadren

Dear sisster

I receiveed your kind and welcome letter A few days A go and was glad to here from you and the children and you was all well I beleave all of the folks is well here except lizzie she has got A big girl I have never bin to see her yet but I am going as soon as I get time Jane I told pa what you told me to tell him about the money for your shoes he Says he sent you five dollars before you went up to mannons but you know how he is Jane you said it had rained up there this is the dryest Country here you ever saw ever body wants to move we had to move on the account of water we are living at Mat Vancleaves I dont know what the people will do here for they have failed with there crops every body is talking about moving there stock some where to water and grass Oliver says he is going to stay and skin what is left he says he is going to move this fall and if he does he says he will come up that way and look at that Country wel Jane I beleave I have written all I can think of write soon dirct your letters to —o Rancho Oliver Joins me in love to you all from your true sister

Mattie Odom

---

118. J. W. H. to Jane Hardin and M. Clements

July the 27th 1879 Texas. State. Prison Mrs Jane Hardin

Please Direct to Mrs. Jane Hardin /in care of M Clements Richland Springs PO Sansaba County Texas

My Dear and Loving
wife it has Been Some time Since I Received a Line from you my Dear and Loving one But Nevertheless I wil Drop you a few Lines which wil inform you that I am well and Doing as well as circumstances wil admit my work is not very Hard at Present Nor has not Been for Some time But the heat is terrible for it is very warm and Dry in this Country and has Been for Some time But Dearest I hope to Be able to Sumer it through and trust that my health wil not fail for when a person Looses his health he Looses all Dearest and truest I hope you are Doing well and the children also Dearest Be carefull with our Sweet Little children for the way a twig is Bent the way it wil Grow I hope you are making friends and I do wish you to Be Satisfied an await future Developements Sureley I wil not Be here allway or 25 yrs for a crime they Know I Did to Save my own Life you can write to mart Flemings at comanchie it wil Do no harm men that were once my enemies promised to have my time reduced to 5 yrs when I was at comanchie he was one remember me kindly to all inquiring friends Give my Love to Mollie and the Children and Kiss our Sweet Little children once more for your Loving husband So a Sweet a dieu my Loving wife

your husband **John. Wesley. Hardin**

July the 27th. 1879

Mr. M. Clements
Dear cousin No nuse at present cant you write Send or Bring me Some words of incouragement I Know you wil take good care of my Dear Little Family without asking and you could Do nothing Better at present to Please me Manin I am Doing the Best I can I Do hope on that I wil yet See the day when I am free from these or any other Bond whatever M Do all you can in reference thereunto all the Comanchie people wants is to Be insured that I wil not renew the old Grudge then they wil pardon me they Know I am not Guilty of the crime I am convicted of now maning you Know how to work and I hope you wil See to this mater and Keep a close Look out for the future for from Small acorns Large trees Grow and Little Streans Large rivers flows so give my Love to all you think Deserves the Same Your own cousin till Death **John W Hardin**

---

119. Elizabeth Hardin to Jane Hardin

Ennis Ellis Co. July 30th, 1879

Mrs Jane Hardin) Richland Springs Sansaba. Co.)
My very dear deaughter.
It has been a long time Since I wrte you I recived your kind letter which you wrote me while at Auston I answered it while I was at Lizzie's and my apoligie for not writing before now is that we ware moving So long and unsetled. you must not think hard of Mama, you know how I neglect poor Bell it is not because I do not love you. O how I do want to See you and the Sweet little children tell them gran Ma loves them you must not let them forget me. well Jane we have had a long and wearysome move, we traviled through ten or eleven counties went away out to Graham Citty young Co. the country did not Suit us no good water no grass evry thing parched up from drought. we all Started for Palopinto we did not like there the country So dry poor crops So Bright Said he would go to Bosque Jeff and my Self not willing to go there. Jeff Said he would go to Hill Co. and we had to part with poor Bright and Matt. we could Scarsley Stand it we parted in tears Sadness and grief. though with the kindest of feelings no falling out by the way. we Started for Hill. parting with Matt at Palopinto the town, it took us one week to reach Barnetts Hardin's they ware all So glad to See us and Said we did Just right in not going to Basque I rested a few days then I left our wagons at Barnett's I visited my relatives at Hill bourough all So glad to See me Spent two weeks there. Squir Tarver. Johns Cousin by marage wrote Johnnie a long letter Sent him a fine chance of writing material. I returned to Barnetts rested a few days Jeff took us to Ennis on a visit it being only forty miles from Barnetts Jeff returned to Hill. I am looking for him to come after us now. though I may be here a week or two longer I have been here four weeks I have enjoyed my Self So much here considering my great troubles. my Sweet babie Sister is So kind to me and the children She is Such a noble Sister I received a letter from John last week. I wrote to him this eaving. I got a letter from Matt Since I been here they are in Denton County She Said they liked there very well I expect we will Settle in Hill Co. our kin are all very anxious. I think I will visit Bell Soon. as She lives but thirty five miles of Barnett's Har Jane write me a long letter direct to. Oceolia Hill Co. Jane write to Johnie often

his kin all talks So hopeful of him I think his Cousin Barnett and Jeff will go to See him this fall now my dear child do not dispair try and bear your troubles, ask God to help you. may the good Lord bless you and my dear little children

adieu dear children **your Ma E. Hardin**

P.S give my love and kind wishes to my big Nephew Mannon and my kind Niece Mollie and their Children tell them to write to their troubled aunt I thank Mannon a thousand times for all his kindness to Johnnie I hope he will be rewarded on earth and in heaven amen E.H

little Gip talks about Sister Jane So much and little Jinnie Mollie and Johnie I feel So Sorry for him Nannie Says tell Sister Jane to write She wants to See you So much Write to me Sweet Jane E. H.

Kiss the children for **gran Ma**

---

120. J. W. H. to Jane Hardin

Aug the 10the 1879. Texas State Pris' Mrs Jane HArdin

My Dear and Loving wife it is with pleasure that I now endiavor to write you my Darling and beloved one which wil inform you that I am as yet Still No with the Living. by the mercies of the all-ruleing Power. My Health at present is good with the exception of frequent pains from internal injuries which you my Dearest one are well aware but as yet are not of a Serious nature. it has been very warm and Dry here this Sume but at present it is raining and pleasant enoug as far as the weather is concerned we had a Good rain yesterDay with prospect for more rain Dearest I Got your Letter which Stated that Maning & Mollie were going to austin this Mo I was more than Glad to here from you my Darling and True wife. I hope you wil be carefull with our Sweet Little children while they are young as Dearest I fear they wil never Know the care of a father yet Dearest I Live in hopes that I may be able to finish there Lessons taught to them while young I Believe If my friends and relatives wil go to work that they could get me out Sooner than Most any one expects I have now Been here Nearly one year and I hope they wil Do Something for me before a nother yr rolls around I Know I have the facts and the Judge himself told me that he would assist me nothing can be done without making a begining and I would Just

Like to Know what the govner would do with the papers Such as I Know can be got up in my Behalf But pardon me and it only wants attention as to any other cases they Need not Stand Back on them for I know Just what they are and have No fears whatever. tell Maning to write me a letter in reference. if I have to Stay my time out I would Like to Know it and Stop the expense of writing &C and would feel Better Satisfied than to Be Living on probably Blasted hopes Dearest and truest give my respects to all inquiring friends my love to all of the connection and Kiss our Little children once more for me. So I wil close for this time and Live in hopes of Better day I remain your afectionate husband till Death

John. W. HArdin

Well Mannin Dear cousin it has Been Some time Since you wrote me I hope you wil take time and write me a Letter M I am Doing as well as I can under my circumstances and I Do hope and pray that the day wil come when we can Shake hands as free men Give my love to all you wish and take good care of my Dear Little family Hoping to here from you Soon I remain your Cousin untill Death

John W HArdin

I wrote to the Gonzales imquir after he had writen to me for a Statement and received 3 copies of which I Send you
one afectionately yours

J W H

M I wil Do the Best I can and try to gain all the friends I can by my my conduct and I hope all wil be done that can be done for me Surely truth and Justice wil prevail

JW

---

121. J. W. H. to Jane Hardin

Aug the 17teenth 1879 Texas State Prison Mrs Jane Hardin
My Dear and Loving Wife having received your Kind and welcome Letter Dated Aug the 12the I Now endeavor to answer though I have no nuse at present onley this wil inform you that I am Still No with the Living and am doing as well as my circumstances wil permit and am Stil in hopes of Seeing Better days it is very Hard to think and Know I have to Stay here for a crime I Did to Save my own Life But I do Believe and hope truth and Justice wil yet Prevail and it Does

Seem to me that if my Friends and relatives would onley try that my time would Be Shortened but if they never make a trial Nothing of course wil ever be done But I wil try and Be contented and wil allways Know that I am fortunate to Be allowed my Life for the opposition that has Been against me has Been wonderfull on the extreams But Dearest I hope there wil yet be a change in my favor as great as ever was against me but time wil onley tell and I wil try and Do the Best I can hoping that we wil yet Be together as once Before. remember me often to our Sweet Little children Kiss them for me once more and try and Bear your troubles the Best you can there may yet Be a Brighter day for you give my Love to all of the connection tell mollie I wil write her Next Sunday if it is gods wil Hoping this wil find you in Good health and Spirits as it thus Leaves me I am your Affectionate Husband till Death John. W. HArdin Wel Joe a few words I was glad to here from you and Know that you had not forgoton me Joe Dear cousin remember me Kindly to all inquiring friends Give my Love to Sallie & the children I am Doing the Best I can and as well as could Be expected of a man in my unfortunate condition I hope my relatives wil Not forget me and I assure you that your letter was a welcone mesanger. When I Knew Dell Doublin he was a Square man and if you can assist him Legally and not interfere with your private Busness do So give him my resp So I send Love to all adieue for this time your cousin till Death

John W Hardin

---

122. J. W. H. to Jane Hardin

Sep the 21st 1879 Texas State Prison Mrs Jane HArdin Dear wife it is with pleaseure that I now indeavor to write you thoug I Have no nuse to write onley this Leaves me in good Health and Spirits considering every thing that Surrounds me wel I hope Dearest you and the children are well and doing well Besides I do Hope that the day may or wil yet come when we can be together as once before allthough at present the dark cloud hangs over us Still, but I hope we may not hope in vain. tell maning that I received his postal card to day and wil excuse this time But that I would Like to get a long letter from him as I wil Look for one tell him I want to

Know how and the Jeneral News tell me how Capt Hays is Doing any thing wil be interesting to me be sure and write MC So Dearest Give my Regards to all inquiring Friends and my Love to all of the connection and Kiss our Sweet Little children once more for me and tell them they Both look Like me So adieu my Loving wife for this time Your Husband afectionately untill Death **John W Hardin**

Mollie C Dear cousin a few words I wrote you two weeks ago and wil write you Soon again my Health at present is as good or better than it has been Since I first became a prisner and I hope wil continue give my Love to Manen & Sallie tell them cousin John say for them not to forget him Hoping to here from you soon I remain your cousin till Death

John W Hardin

tell Mane I wil write him Next Sunday if nothing Hapens and Hope he wil write Soon and oftener than he has been **JWH**

---

123. N. D. H. to Jane Hardin

Sept 21 / 1879 Sister Jane

Dear Sister Jane

I write you a few lines in Ma's letter We are here at Mat's arrived here last Tuesday Sister Jane I intended write you all about our western trip, but I would keep neglecting it untill now and now I have forgot it. Sis Jane how cone Bright and us to part he wanted to go to Bosque Co and Ma did not want to g there and So there we parted but we Soon got back to one other So when we left them they turned around and went to Denton when we got to Cosin Barnett & they were So glad to See us in about 2 weeks Jeff took us to See Aunt Nan's She was So glad to See us Stayed a month I will Send you a peice of cloth like the Suit She gave me She gave us So many nice presents Jeff left us there and as he went back he went by and Saw Sister Bell Stayed a week & went and Spent the week at Hill Borrug the week before we left Tell Moll that I an going to write to her next tine I have not wrten half enough Good By Sis Jane

N D. H.

---

124. From Elizabeth Hardin to Jane Hardin

Denton Co. Sept 21th, 1879 Sansabia Co Tex
Mrs Jinnie Hardin

My very Daughter
It has been a Long time Since I received a line from you. I undersood you wrote me a letter to Bonhan Sissie wrote me and forgot to Send your letter to me. I wrote to her to send it yet. for I would be glad to get it a year from now. Jane Hill did not suit us in the leas I would rather Live in Red River Co then there no crops there Scarsley. the people are living a centuary behind the times. Jane I visited my relatives in Hill Bourough I enjoyed my self So much Jeff took Nannie Gippe and my self to Ennis. I remained with Sister Nannie a month She was So glad to have me with her Jeff went back to Barnett's he visited Bell while I was at Ennis. Bell was So glad to See Jeff. She did not know what to do. She made Jeff a presant of Jodie's Saddle Besides other nice preasants and mad Jeff promise to go and bring me amediatly to See her. though he did not take me. Jane the day before we ware to Leave Hill. my Dear Brother Elec and Sister Mollie came over from Navaro Co. to See me O! I was So glad to See them. it did my very Soul good to be with them. So we remained together for Severl days. So we Started for Denton County We reached Brights and Matt in one weeks travil found them well. We have rented a farm very good land a neat fraim house a kitchen box house I think this is a good country Bent and Sissie are going to move out here Soon. Lizzie has a little girl about three months old She come very near dyeing, poor child. Jane I Supose you have herd that it is published in the papers that Johnnie had acknolledged killing Holdeman, and the Editor of the Gonzales Inquirer asked John for a Statement John wrote him a true Statement giving it the falsehood. the Ed published it and Sent John a coppie and he sent it to me. and I had the Hills bourough Prarie Bee to coppie it perhapse you have Seen it. Jane I want to See you So much little Mollie Johnnie Jinnie So bad. I cant tell you half I want. I wrote to you while I was at Ennis and I cant get a line from you tell Mollie She must learn to write So She can write to Gran Ma Kiss all the Children for me, write and let me know how you are doing. good bye Sweet Children **E. Hardin** Your Mama
Jane direct your letters to Pilolet Point Denton Co. give my Love to

my big Nephe and my Niece and their Children tell them to write to me be Shure **E. H.**

---

125. J. W. H. to Mrs. Jane Hardin

Nov The 2nd 1879 Texas State Prison Mrs Jane HArdin

68 1496
2 11 1496
136 2992

Dear wife

HAving received your Kind and welcome letter a few days ago I Now by the mercies of god endeavor to ans the same which wil inform you that I am Still No with the Liveing, and must Say doing as well as my unfortunate Condition wil permit. hoping to Be able to out Live my present Situation and that I may even yet Be able to injoy the Happiness which liberty yet ows me Knowing as I do that I am Suffering for an act I Did to Save my Life Though I hope to be able to bear it Like a man. And if it is gods wil for me to put in the Ballance of my day in Bondag. I hope to Be able to Be contented with my Lot.. but it has Been Said the longest Lanes have a turning and the darkest hour Just before Day. So I may in case of future events be restored to those I Dearley Love. and whose burdon I would readily Bear were it in my power and which troubles me more than my own troubles Yet Deares Jane I hope in a few yrs that I wil Be restored to those I Dearley Love Hoping Dearest your ever efforts through Life wil be cround with Sucess and that you may be able to train our Sweet Little children up in the right way impressing the golden rule on each of ther minds Hoping you wil injoy your Stay in Gonzales I wil now close By asking you to Kiss our Sweet Little Babes once more for me Hoping to here from you often I wil Close by Saying adieu my Sweet Jane Your Afectionate Husband

John W HARDIN -

Dearest I hope you wil have a nice time in Gonzales But Let By gones alone is the advice of your Husband as to the Charge I am perfectly Satisfied Hoping you wil be Write me a long letter when you can Affectionately **J W H to Jane H**

---

126. Nannie Hardin to Mollie

Forget Me not Forget Me never Till younder 5
Shall Set Forever Your faithful friend

Nannie D. Hardin April 27 1880

Dearest Mollie It looks like I cant never get to send off this letter no one has ever been to The Office to get Johnnie's letter since I wrote this. Bright has gone to get our mail to day I recon we will hear from Johnnie. If he tell where you are living I will Send this off as soon as anyone goes to the office again I am so anxious for Bright to come back I know there is a letter from Some one. Mabe I will get to Send this off Some time this week. Now Mollie I want you and your Mamma write me aslong letter I would rather hear from you all than any one. Jeff went to the Oil Springs a few days ago, He also went after his horse and got him. I recon Ma wrote to your mama that we had lost him in Red River Co. Mollie Mattie Parks is married to John Towns and Miss Pink Norris to Dr Clark Mollie I have forgotter how old you was Febuary was you 6 or 7 I was 14 in March well I will put up this letter again Good By Sweet child

Nannie D Hardin 6

well Mollie this is morning Bright got back last night. got a letter from Mr Goree but not from Johnnie So I am disapointed again I going to Send this letter off am if it is a mont from now Matt came over here yestarday evening to get me to go home with her and Stay all night So I went and a bout the time we got to bed Bright came.. Lillie is Sick Little Gippie has gone over to See Sister he went by hin Self Ma has just went over to Matts to See Lillie So I an by my Self Oh] Mollie if you was heare with me I would not get lonesome Sis Jane. dont you think you can come I do want to see you So bad I have So many things to you and Something alful funny but I cant put it in a letter.

Nannie D Hardin

April 29th 1880

Mollie I went over night before last to see Sister and Stayed all night and day. We had quite a Storm last night never was in Such a Storm in all my live it came very near blowing down our house Sister and Matts also it blew down our fence and every body els fences well I

will quit for this time And Seal this letter up. Dont mind your Mama will get mad at me for writing to you So much and not writing to her Good By Darling honey
Direct Your Letters to Valley View
Cook Co Texas
Your Aunt Nannie Hardin

---

127. Elizabeth Hardin to Jane Hardin

n Co. May 27th, 1880

din

My very dear daughter ——— whareabouts untill ——— I received three ——— —nie. he tole me whare ——— morning I hasten to write you a few lines.Bright is Just Starting to Town and I have but a few moments to write and So you must excuse brevity. I could write all day and then cold not tell you all I want to Say. O you can not immagine how much I want to See you and my Sweet little babes Kiss them all for me tell them Gran Ma loves them So dearly. poor Johnnie writes very Sad O how my heart aches. he Says ——— herd but three times ——— this year he Said ——— like to hear from ——— felt like writing, ——— mater write ——— the particulars. John has been debared of writing for Some time on account of being caught in clandestine corispondance with Mannon C. in order to get his liberty from that place by force he aught to quit that way of doing Jane, write and tell me what is done with Mannon. We have a good prospect of fine crops both corn and Cotton we had our wheat cut this week. Jeff wants to See you So much he Says he is going to See you Gipie, also Jane write to all of us and tell us all the news Since you last wrote my Sweet precious child I often dream of being w-— you ——— and ——— us ———
Adieu love to all

---

128. Joshua Bowen to Edward B. Bowen

Whiting Ala July, 15th 1880 Edward. B. Bowen

my Dear Boy I take the pleasure to answer yours of June 28th which

I Just recieved yesterday and was glad to hear from you and to hear that you was well and going to school for I think that is as good a thing as you Can do well I have know news of any importance plenty of work going on here but it is hard to save any money Out here I thought I would of Been out there be four this but I never got Exactly ready and I recon I will stay and Timber untill next Fall and try and be able to fix up the place.

I was at a big Barbacue at Pollard last week they had some good speaking there will be a Picnic to morrow at Hollys Ferry I Expect that I will go to it tell Uncl Ben Passmor that I have not forgoten him and send my best respects to him and famly give my best respects to Jane and the Children and would be the gladest in the world to see them.

I am glad to that there is good Crops made Out there hi— —ear — I wish you would fine out what the Taxes is on my land I want to know so I can settle it up it is tow much to loose and we hav done tow much work on it Engage me One Hundred Bu of Corn and have it Kept in reserve for me untill I Come.

I want to see you and Beney vary bad I imagin that Ben has groad afoot cinc I left there this leavs my self well at present and hope in fined you all well give my respects to all while I remain your Father

Joshua Bowen

Mr E. B. Bowen gonzales County Texas

Bowen is the best this is the Key that lock Mis. T—na these too hearts Mr EB Bowen

th— to ——— Bowen

Mr JR

heart of the of all my ——— Shure it is ——— Gingo

---

129. Elizabeth Hardin to Jane Hardin

Denton Co. Aug 30th (1880) Mrs Jane Hardin Rancho Tex.

Jane be Shure to Send Johnnies letter back. please

My very dear child I received your kind letter Some time ago. have been waiting for you to answer Nannie's letter I do not think you are going to So I will try my pen again you can not immagine how glad I was to hear from you and to learn you ware keeping house, that your people ware all kind to you I wish you all the happiness this life can afford. my Sweet child I know your troubles are great and you are quite young but dont dispair. look for a moment at my troubles, what I have bourn and what I have to bear yet Sometimes the Storm is So heavy that the wheels of life are all most ready to Stand Still a few more beating winds and Storms and my troubles will be over. then I hope to go whare Storms and trouble never comes. I received a letter from Johnnie the other day he said he was doing the very best he can he sayed he believed he would get along better there then he ever has. he Sayed he took the Testament in his cell last Sunday has read the Chapters of the Acts and Romans both through he says now he likes to read the testament. he wrote me a letter Some time a go he said I could Send it to you if I wished. So I enclose it to you. Jane please Send it back to me. you know I allways want evry letter he writes me. I am going to visit him this fall. Jane, Bell is married She and her husband and little Jodie has been to See us her husband name is Pierce he is a fine looking man a man of considerable property little Jodie is the very image of his Pa he reminded me So much of my own Sweet Jodie when he was a little boy. Bell looked better then I ever Saw her She inquired a great deal about you and tole me to tell you to write to her. direct to her at Mt Calm Limestone Co. O I never tole you how I liked her husband I think a great of him he did not appear like a Stranger and Bell was Sweet and amiable as ever. now Jane if you want to hear from me you must you must answer my letters promptly. Jane whare is Dr Bockeas Bell inquired about him. write me a long letter kiss all the children for me tell them that Kiss is from Grand ma tell them I love them press them closely to your breast for me. God bless you and them forever O how I do want to see you. if I could See you we would talk old times and things over Mollie Grand Ma Sends you the blossoms I pressed for you in Red River that grew in my yard.

E.H.

Jane write Soon I am so anxious to hear from you goodbye my Sweet daughter and little ones remember your troubled Mother adieu to all

E. Hardin

130. Mattie Odom to Jane Hardin

March. th. 5. 1881 Mrs. Jane. Harden

Dear sister
I seat my self to rite you A few lines to let you know that weare all well at present and hopeing these few lines will find find you all the same Oliver has got back from cort his triel was put off by the state I was at A mask ball on the 26 of feb and had A nice time tell Mollie that frankey can crall and is as bad as ever Jane have you ever heard from Elizzie where she is and what they are doing and pa and the children I heard they was gone but I dident here where they was gone well I will close for this time till frank to rite
give my love to all good by

Mattie Odom

---

131. Mattie Odom to Jane Hardin

April the.26. 1881 Mrs Jane Harden

Dear sister I seat my self to rite you A few lines to let you know we are all well at preasent hope ing these few lines will find you all the same I have no news of interest to rite only frankey has got two teeth at last I have bin quilting for A weak I have got out two and have got two more yet to cuilt and I have got more little chickens than any body and ducks Oliver has had his pictures taken he says you can have one if you want it tell nancy to rite if she is there tell frank to rite too tell Mollie frankey says She must rite to him give my love to aunt Margret well I will close excuse my short letter I will try and rite more next time rite soon Oliver and frankey sends there love to you all from your true sister good by

Mattie Odom

---

132. P. A. Bowen to Mrs. Jane Hardin

Santa Rosa Co May <u>the</u> 1 1881 Mrs. Jane. hardin

Dear daughter
I Seat my Self to answer your kind leter which came to hand the other day I was glad to hear from you and to hear you was well this

leavs us all well except me and edna we have the third day chills yet Jane there is a grate dele of Sicness it is mosly cold old uncle willis Jones is dead lizzie Jones is dead Steave Jones got kild by lomax Jernagan they went to polard and go to drinking and felout and lomax kild Steave with a liderd not they arrested him and caired him to milton but he is out on bon

Jane I have bin over to see cosin mary mc millain She Said you had never wrote to her they all in quired about you we have got a plase abot a half a mile from mary Cobb She is a good nighbor Jane I wish you was here with me to day me and dode and beasly is here by our selves netty and ed is gon to Suday School your pa is gone on the river with your uncle Josh tell frank the children Said they wished She was here to go with them after may hause and Sweet gum Jane tell lizzie to write to me for I have not forgoten her give my love to all inquireing friends and Shere a portion for your Self write Soon and writee all of the newes **P.A Bowen**

John Wesley Hardin, surface embellishment with pen & ink.

—Courtesy Robin Campbell

LETTERS, PHASE 3

June 3, 1881–May 29, 1893

"As for death I did not fear it"

SLOWLY JOHN HAS STARTED TO REGAIN HIS HEALTH. WITH HIS IMPROVED HEALTH COMES A NEW GOAL, STRONGER THEN BEFORE—AN INTEREST IN THE LAW. NOW HE SETS OUT TO STUDY EVEN HARDER AND WITH GREATER DETERMINATION. JOHN TRIES TO IMPROVE THE QUALITY OF HIS LIFE AND PERHAPS SHORTEN HIS TERM IN PRISON.

133. J. W. H. to Jane Hardin

June the 3rd 1881 Huntsville. Texas Mrs Jane Hardin under the circumstances which have Seperated us: while I am confined to a felon cell you are alowed your Liberty: but I cannot Say freedom for I am wel aware that you nor no one else can feel that Freedom which inspires the Human Heart Nor are you able to apreciat its Liberties with out Being able to Be and injoy the company of one that you Love above all others. This my Loving one is doubtless far below the factes in our case thoug I Deem it unnecissary to call you any pet Names for Doubtless you Know my Heart to well to Speak, Though I wil take this opurtunity to Say that our union was Not for any other purpose than for Domestick Hapiness and it was accompanied with Domestic Love & purity which onley rests in the Bossome of the Faithful. Dear I once thought I never would write to you Simply because I rather wanted you to try and forget me for your own welfare as my chances at that time Seemed very Doubtfull of me ever being allowed my Liberty, thus for the Love I had for you & my children I thought it advisable to Stop corresponding with you that you might be at Liberty to act in any maner you felt Disposed Nor Do I by this imposition claim any rights what ever more than you may be willing to grant as I hope you wil Ans this or till it was Not on account of any unfaithfulness but Simple from motives purely Derived at by my Situation: for at that time my Heart was filled with Such Desperate Ideas that I knew not what moment my end would be in this world by Some rash act of mine and how it ever turned out as it Has I cannot account only by gods mercies for as for Death I did not fear it Nor did I have any Dread for the grave but Some How another I have escaped I hope for Some worthey purpose (and I hope that I may Never Die a foll) I was well aware that I was giving you much trouble by Not writing you but Jane you Know when I cannot

J W Hardin

7/3 Speak plainly to you that then & then only Do I fail to Speak you ought to Know me well in that respect then if I Should have writen to you I would have had to have wrote you a lie Which would onley Been ading Fuell to the Burning Flames to have Spoken the truth would have been Disgracfull in ever respect. But Being concious of all though Despirate. I realy refused to write to any one for a long time allthough I received Numerous Letters from friends relatives and even you/ the onley woman that I have ever Loved with faithfulness though I failed to write you in my Degraded Stat but it was Not for the want of faithfullness or Love but from Secretives motives purley for your good thoug a many a tear I have Shed in your Behalf and for our childrens Sake Yet I can only think with what courage we have loved but Dear Hope can Love wher courage Dirpairs. but it was only by the persuasion of my Respective and worthey superintendant that I again Began to write when my mother Had writen time and again. to Know what was the mater with me why I Did not write &C that I finalaly gave my consent to write but I asure you that I never wrote to any one else Not even to mc Since you Left His House. / Jane there Has been a great many Life and Long time men pardoned out Here of Lat, who have Been here from 5 to 20 yrs Simple on accout of meritorus conduct and I asure you it has been a Great Stroke to incourage all to Lead a Life of Humbliness. as for my part I have Long ago gave up any Disposition on my part to get out of Here by any other means than by Leagal process of Law as I believe I would be better off to Say nothing of those I Love Dearer than life if I was Dead than again to Become an outlaw for if I was an out Law I would Be true to its principles thus I Never again wish to Be But would rather Spend the Ballance of my Life in a Dungeon than be the outlaw I might Be wer I to gain my Liberty by any other means than by Law I believe By gods mercies I can out Live my present trouble My Friends & relatives think So I am young to Speak and I hope as Lively as ever courage I hope Not wanting patience Surely wil deliver me (as for hope I have) Dear I an getting along Spendid and of late have no trouble and believe that the Keepers of this place are above treating a man confined to there care with any thing else than with Humanity & Kindness as to my treatment when severe I alone was to Blame but when I have conducted my Self in a meritorious way they Have ever Been ready to assist me an even when I did not thus I Look upon these officals as being my Friends an who would Frain from Doing any one intrusted to ther care an injustice my work is the Shad and am admited By all acquainted with the Shoe & Boot Busines as being a Splendid Fitter that is doin all the Stiching on Boots Shoes gators &C fixing them ready for the Last Jane I realy admire the work I am following in refference Now my Dearest Kiss the children for me talk to them for me if you Have or Have Not concluded to discard me it maters Not it is with you if you can be benefited by Doing So Do it but I know your Love your Faithfullness when I ask you to write wil persuade you to write So answer me at once for I am more than anxious to here from you Space Does not permit me to write more

affetionately J W Hardin

Look over all mstakes for this is Done in a moment warning Not by any means a well composed Letter full of error but wil inforn you of my sentinents

---

134. J. W. H. to Jane Hardin

Hensley Gold	2	The prison Debating Club
Henney Chas	2.	was called to order by the
Hasse Jus -		president July the 3rd
Hadley Hilliard	6.	minutes of the proceeding
Hepp Wm	8.	minutes of the preceding meeting

Read & adopted Debate being in order the presiden anounced that the Judges were ready to hear argument three Judges were answered

July the 3rd 1881— Texas State Prison

Dear Jane it is Now about 8 o clock Pm I am Locked up in my cell for the Night and by Spescial permition from my Keeper I now write you I wil first Say that I have Spent this day in allmost perfect Hapiness as I Jeneraly Spend the Sabath here something that I once could not injoy Simple Because I Did not Know its causes Nor results. therfore I had no Idea of its Benefits to man in my condition. thus we though prisners Sureley are on the Road to prgress. J.S. Spoke of our Societies in His litter to His aunt of which we are both members and even Looked upon as the Leaders by our associate of which we have a goodly Number thong Neither of us are president of Said Societies yet John is Secretary of the Moral & Christian Society as I am allso Sec of our Debating club of which we Both attend with prompness J.S. Spoke of our Debating this evening the Subject of womans rights eaqual with man John held that woman Should be alowed equal rights with man I held that She Should not we Had a lively time John made the closing Speach on womans rights but I followed him winding up the Debate for to day John is the champion for womans right but he failed to convince the Judges after they Had Listened to my Argument thus I Scored another victorey over John this evening

wel Dear Jane if you wil allow me the privolage of calling you Such for your name alone is Dear to me, though I feel from the maner in which I have treated you that I have Lost all claims upon you as Dear or Love and Finaly my wife. Something that I wil Not insist upon for in treating you as I have I Sureley forfeited all my right to your Love in reference and Dear it wil Be with you to Say & determine whether we Shal Again renew our once faithfulness Thougt I have Never Doubted your faithfulness to me for I never have had the Least cause I an wel acquainted with the History of woman from the Beging to the presant day Not that I wish to flater you But I have never Seen in History Nor in any print wher woman has held to her Lover or her Husband with that Benevolence & faithfullness that you Have held toward the Notorious John Wesley Hardin (all) is Familliar with me) I say for the truth you Have ever mantained my cause both in time of prosperity & adversities against Brother & against father to say Nothing of Scandalous reports of that day but I hope they wil be forgoton and Looked upon as decades of the past. Suerely allthoug you have remained quietely in your Sphere yet if the truth in reference was mad known you would undoubtedly cary off all the honors in reference in pride in virtue in Love & Finaly in Faithfullness and Should I ever write the History of my Life in full which I have gave Some thoughts I wil with truth make you the Heroine of your sex (for I know you are) in Deterring as I leave it with you intirely Look at your own & your childrens intrust and not mine for you Know I am a convict you suerely are aware of my condition and to conclude that we wil be as we once was wil take more courage more hope than I ever have Seen in Humanity to Say Nothing of the Female Yet I wil say though I do not wish to affect you in the Least that (I) though Silent Have Never faltered Nor wavered in my Love to you and my Dear Darling Babes and to Night I would Frely & willingley give up my Life for your Suport Let your circumstances in Life be as they may Just remember that it is something incomprehensible for me to not Love you as warmly as ever you sureley Know how true my Love Has Been for my Friends to say Nothing of my Love to you Look over old Letters call the past to the present when you and I have reaped imortal fruits of Joy in blissful Solitude do not my Dear hesitate to make your Descision if you Se your condition can be improved what I have Said is nothing to Be compared to your good or the childrens welfare it is only relicks of the past but Let your Descision be what it may my Love thoug I may fail to express it for maners sake yet I Know I cannot Nor wil not ever try to not Love you for my Love for you canot Die though I am prepared to Stand the worst Now Jane it is all with you Just as Soon as you can write me a Letter Let it Be Long or Short I of course prefer a Long one but tell me plainley what I can depend upon Just come out plain and Say I forgive or Not write at once Do not fail you only said you wanted to here fron me Now come out plain you hav Had 4 yrs test of this Life you know what it is Jane Should I ever write you again which is Now with you to Decide I will give you all the news in reference to our Families and I sincrley Hope and Believe I am sure to write you again if spared by god (I know you to well) So I wil close by sayin my love for you canot die I dont Like cold letters but afectionatley I am and wil ever be your Lover if Nothing else though you know I am called by some Stuborn Love to my children Kiss my children and think of me for one moment give my Love to Mrs Anglin & her Husband an my best wishes to all you See fit a kind and an affectionate adieu my Loving one Yours with respect

J W Hardin

Mrs Anglin please deliver at once and if She Desires to write please mail ——— letter is a request to J—

---

135. J. W. H. to Jane Hardin

Aug the 14 teenth 1881 Mrs Jane Hardin
Texas State Prison

Dear Jane.

I received a letter to day with your Name attached to the Same. but can onley say that I was Glad to Hear from you. and my Loved ones I mean My children. whom: you Say I had deserted. God forbid that I ever Shal Desert Loved ones as those you Speak off. circumstances may Seperate me from Loved ones. Position: to Say Nothing of pollicy: may Keep me from writing to those I love Dearer than Life. which Has been the case. Thoug Seperated Divided & Surrounded by almost insurmountable difficulties. yet I Say for a truth I never have forsaken you for on moment in my Heart Nor my children but god Knows that a many a tear I have Shead for you & my children Silently in my cell to Say Nothing of those in publick as I am Now an god Knows were it possible my Blood would pour from my veins as free as ever my tears have droped for you my Loving one. Jane I say it was not on the acct of any unfaithfullness on my part that I Stoped writing to you but policy in Several respects one was to give you a chance to find a nother Lover one was to Keep you out of a disgracefull correspondence Something I cannot mention Now. an other was to Keep Certain parties whom I Knew would be glad to Hear of my misfortune from Knowing too much & Several other of as much importance I hope it Needs No more explanation But Dear you Say you have not nor never will Love any one But me: thoug circumstances have Somewhat changed. I hear your Pa is in Florida &C Well Jane if you love me to be plain write to me in that maner you know that I wil Be Sure to reciprocate I attach no blame whatever to you & to Say I Love you Dearer than all others would only Be a truth my children Next a truth. Now Dear if you expect to ever Love me as in the past and cherrish my interest as yours of old I would be glad to hear from you in your own hand writing when sick I can excuse you for Borrowing a Scribe & wil Look over this time but if you want to Renew and Live in hopes of future injoyment as of days of old Just use your own Hand when you write to me if I Look upon you atall I wil Look upon you as I use to Look and when you write reckolect that it is No bodies Bussiness what you Say to me for I am yours and you Have a right to Say what you please But Say it with your own penn & Hand. Jane dont doubt my Fidelity in Deserting you at the time. Now as to renewing my comunication it is all righ I consider I have a right to write you and I assure you I had rather here from you than all others put to gether So write me at once I mean at once dont put off But at once & if I get it by Sunday week I wil ans it at once Jane Dearest in my next I wil tell you a heap. Kiss my children tell Mollie papa is well tell J W H to Be a good Boy & tell Sweet Little Jane to Not cry papa is well tell sister mat I indeed Sympathize with Her tell Her to write me at once tell Her I love Her as well as I ever did may She yet Be Blessed with fortune Now Jane I hope you wil on receipt of this write me a long Letter and I wil Say I never wil under No circumstances Fail unles

Reasonable fail to write you Jane my Dear Loving & true wife write me at once Kiss my Loving children & Sister Mat & give my Love to all you wish be Sure & write at once to me an give me all the News I am getting along Better than I ever have Since a prisner and am not Jealous of any ones privilages May god Bless you & my children & ever prepare means for your Suport is the prairs & wish of your own Loving Husb

John. W. HArdin

Direct this to Mrs. Jane HArdin Sedlers Mills Gonzales, County Texas

Now Jane if you forgive me Say Say So. I Know you Love me and you Know the Same of me as to you ever flinching from your Duty towards me I have never Doubted but read the Last Letter. Now write me a letter from your Heart I will Ans y— Sweet Adieu

J.W. H.

---

136. J. W. H. to Jane Hardin

JW Hardin — **Sep the 25th 1881**

9/25 — **Huntsville Texas**

Mrs Jane Hardin

I wrote you Some 5 weeks But Have received No answer. it may Be that you Never Received the letter.. I explained to you in my First Letter all that I though Necessary to explain in refference to me Neglecting to write you. I wil Say to you this much I wish to Know if you Still Hold me as when I Last Saw you as to falts I am croweded with them and have my own ways I hope Not coppied from any one you Said you Had almost Despaired of ever geting a letter from me. Jane you Know me to well and you ought to Know when any one does the Square thing By me, that I have Never failed to do the same by them Now I wrote to you Because I Loved you as warm as ever my children allso I though that you wished to here from me for I Know you once Loved me Dearley. You Know no one can influence me in refference to You & my children and there Has Been a time when you could not Be influenced against J.W.H But if that time has Past Do me the favor if you please to inform me of the Same. I donot wish to Be a Burdon upon you in Your unhapy condition I wish you to Live Hapily and I hope Honorable and raise our children as they Should Be if you wish any advice in refference to the Children & your Self from me State the circumstances &c to me I want my children educated and I Know How it Should be Done under the circumstances. but wil Not give my Advice or aid untill I Know How you Stand in refference to me I have Been in Prison a little over 4yrs I Do mot Know whether you have lived true to me or not. if you have I Donot thinK or Have I any reason to Believe otherwise but Know you to Be above Suspison, Now I think in 4yrs more by the Help of god I wil Be a free man for if Justice dont Strike me probably Humanity will I feel this morning like I might Live 100yrs — 50 by gods aid or wil. Now Hope may Have ruined a many a man as Love I Know Has pulied down thousans of women (but Solitary made a cincinatus Ripening the Hero & the Patriot. It gave De Staell. Self Knowledge it gave impirial Charles Religion for ambition That which Scipio Praised that which Alfred practised which fed the mind of Milton that whic fired Demonsthenese to Eloqunce by all thing Just & wise How truely Solitude thou art the fostering nurse of greatness) Now Jane I am not pleased in the main which I write you But if you wil write me a letter as I think you Should you wil relieve me much Let it Be plain. I fear to Speak to you in any other manner than I have as you Had allmost Desparid But then circumstances changes operations Now write at once and let me Know if you wish to Be a regular coresponder of mine But you can rest assured My Dear that I wil allways Love you and as for my children I pray that they may Be Blessed with prosperity & that they may yet have the advantage of a fathers counsell Kiss Mollie My Little Texas girl Kiss JWH. & Little Jane tell my Boy gofer to Be a good Boy and mind ma tell Sister Mat to write me a Letter Kiss Her allso You Loving Husband until (Now ans at once in Pain)

J. W Hardin

Adieu

Please Direct to Mrs Jon Hardin Sedlers Mills Gonzales Texas

Please Send this off

---

137. Mattie Odom to Jane Hardin

Janary 18 1882 goliad Mrs Jane ha—

Dear Sister —

I senD you kinD letere afue dase ag i was glaD to haer from you all We ar all wel at presen hoping thes fu line wil finD you thes same ——— move to mi ove luane evilan anD Mat live with me iso much beter SaDfde to miself i comeing up thare befre long long after frank or Moley to Sty with m- tel frank to writ to me ——— wrot to here aD Saley but never got any anser iwoD b So glad to See you all give mi love to Mrs Wright famley tell deler to come Done give love to mrs. angle famley teel here to writ to me Wal i wil clse for thas time Writ as Son you get this your kinD Sister

Mrs Mate E ODom

---

138. J. W. H. to Mrs. Jane Hardin

Feb the 26th 1882 Huntsville Texas Mrs Jane Hardin
My Dear wife it is with pleaseure that I Now write you. But wil first acknowledge the receipt of you Kind & welcome letter which came to hand Some Days ago. and be assured Dearest that there is None that I had rather receive a line from than you My Dear and Loving one. Besides when I read and See that you have hopes even yet of seeing me a free man. with the Hope of inJoying life together. I am bound to Admit that I am incouraged to no Little extemt.

2nd

it in Spires me with a hope of fuuture Happiness for I wil allways consider the Happiest Days of my Life was Spent in your presence where you gave me Love for love No Distrust No: not even a Shadow Oh this Life Seems a hard one But fate Has Decreed it and may we Both have patience & courage to bear our part of it as for my part I am Satisfied) or at least the past is Secure,) may the future yet produce Some thing that wil eleviate these Bonds Jane Dearest I must admit that I think of you Dream of you

3rd

and infact you are on my mind more than all other objects My wish is that you may enJoy yourself that you may Live Happy raise your children up Honorably and that you may Never want for a friend. Some may call it the weakest act of my Life in as we all have week places in secur ing you as a pardner for Life But I wil allways think it and Look upon it as the crowning contract of my Life one which I Shal Never regret but Look to as an emblem of wisdom in choice

there is many a false face and Smile. but I Know there is one that wil & has always proven true to me one in whom I
4th
have Never placed any Doubts though I may at times treated Her unkind I Know She Has forgiven me and even feel unworthy of her Love but I Know She Loves me Still. may god Bless You always is my prair my Dearest truest and Loving one. Dearest you Spoke of Josh writing me I was in hopes of receiving a letter from him before Now But none as yet I Suppose he Has forgotom it You allso Said that uncle Ben was So Kind tell him that I am under many obligations to him for his Kindness and Hope to Be able to retaiate if ever permited to again apear in
5
Society by Showing him that I was worthey of it and Did appreciate it by conducting my Self in a maner worthey of my calling to Say Nothing of any thing else I Do not Se why any of your people Should have ought against me Never in my Life Have I Done ome of them an inJustice But you Know that I have ever clung to them when Surrounded in Difficulties even against my Relatives I hope that if any of them has Beeen talked to by Designings
6 th
parties in reference to me that that wil Look at in a wiser Sense Ben use to Be my Best friend and was when we last parted and as to his famly you Know I Loved them Dearlly Aunt Margret for instance and all of the Children and they all Seemed to me to retaliate I would think it very unkind to Be a friend to a mans face an an enemy to his Back I dont Believe that Ben cob & Family has ever Been any thing else to me than a friend I am truely glad to Know that he wil help
7th
for I had heard to the contrary Give him and family my love and as to Mr Wright I am glad to heare of him and to Know that he is my friend allso tell him Dearest Jane that I would be pleased to write him but would have to defer writing to you for one month if I was to but that if he should write me a line that I would try to Ans it and allso appreciate it But Dearest I treated you cruel once I cant do it again though I was the chief Suffer in reference to writing tell uncle Josh that a line from him or unc Ben wil be received with pleasure at any time
8 th

I received a letter from ma She Spoke of her & Bright & Mat receiving letters from you She Spoke So Kind of you and the children So glad to hear from you and Said She had Ans them or would Jane you Say for me to try to get along with the officers that my friends wil at a proper time do all they can for me I hope So I have Been getting along Splendid here for Some time and it has Now Been Some time Since I even Have Had a cross word Spoken to me by any oficer for we have a good many my Health is good to Speak and the Boys all Say I look younger than I did when I came

9th

Now Dearest I believe I would come Nearer of Doing what you wish me to do than any one else and if you wish me to do any thing with a Hope of future Happines please Say So as for my Self I have Had enough of adventures and Never wil I again Become a fugitive from Justice unless circumstances demands it When I take a glimpse at the past and See how I Became an outlaw See How me & mine were driven from our homes

10th

our property Destroyed our relatives lives taken &C and See How often my life as it were hung upon a thread. and See to day that I am Still Spared makes me hope for Some worthy purpose. I hope to that one wil yet Be to comfort & love you and yet to provide means for the Suport of you and my loved children Jane Dearest why Dont Frank the Little raskel write me She use to Love me But now She Dont write or even Send a kiss tell her to write

11th

Now about the Boots J W wants tell him he has plenty of cheek But to Send his measure I wil try and Send as Soon as convenient after the receipt of measure But he cant cut My Little Sweet mollie out you Bet & little Jane Sweet Little Babe, Has got to have a pair of Buttons, to, So Send me all three of there measures Let them Stand up on a piece of paper mark all around the foot then take a tape line and measure the in Step to Heel. around the hollow of the foot & in Step, also the ancle & Calf, for Boots or Butons I believe I Know your measure.

12th

I Dont promise to Send at once but first chance Jane Dearest remember me to all of your Friends & relatives Kiss the Children for me and tell John W. that he must Be good to his little Sister and to

Mollie to I Know molli is good to Both of them She is my Little Texas girl Jane Dearest write me as often as you can I can write you on the 4th Sunday in every month So adieu my Loving & true wif A Sweet Adieu for this time Afectionateley

J W Hardin

I send you Nans Husband's card it came in my Christnas Box on a cake Ma Says you Know him write to Nan often as you can I think She is a Noble sister Jane write me al long Letter JWH

---

139. J. W. H. to Jane Hardin

J.W.Hardin
4,2,82

Apr the 2nd 1882
Huntsville Texas Mrs Jane HArdin,
Rancho Gonzales, Co, Tex

Dear Jane it is with pleasure that I now write = Though Having Nothing to communicate to you that will interest you except my Health & C But wil 1St acknowledge the receipt of you Last Letter which I received with pleasure and was highly appreciated by me . in which you Said you would rather See me than any one on earth but when you Saw me you wanted me to be a free man. Now this need no reply But Be assured that I had rather See you than all others But Not with these Bonds, But would rather See any one or all others than you Here though my Desire is great. in fact, the Neare my friendship and Love exist towards one the Less I care to See them with these Stripes. though I am Degraded in the eyes of the world yet in my Heart I know that I am thus Degraded for an act I Did to Save my own Life. I would Do it again I regret nothing on my own acct. though my relatives has Been made to Sufer in the extreems for an act done by me to Save Life. Besides Had Not my Brother My Father Have passed to the unknow world I Never would have Been here to Say Nothing of other Friends & relatives who fell in the Hands of a cowardley mob and were executed by Judg Lynch My Habit of thinking Has Somewhat Changed in regards to many things But in the main they are the Same and think that an Honest man is the Noblest Work of God. (But He Seldom Has a Job) I am proud to See you So hopefull I hope you Hope Not in vain. . my Desire is to Live for you and those Loved children of ours & my

(mother) if it were not for you all Be assured I never would ask for Mercie of man thoug I failed to Get Justice
Be assured Dearest that I wil Do the Best I can and for your Sake I would Do allmost anything to Say Nothing of my children Jane Dearest I am getting along Better than ever before here. Have Not had a cross word Spoken to me about my work nor anything else this yr I hope it wil continue Dearest my paper is runing Short this time So I wil have to close I am injoying good Health to Speak I wrote you to Send Shoe measures I have not Heard from them yet it was writen Just a week before your Last Tell me Dearest where Nancy is if advisable I mean your sister Remember me to those you Desire and give my Love to my Children (with a Kiss) I am as ever yours Afectionately

John. W. Hardin till Death

(I am in Hopes your eyes are well before this time Besides I Send you much Love and hope that though years may pass and forest Decay that our Love wil ever be fresh and ripe & Never Die

JWH

Write when you can
and as often as you please

---

140. M. A. Smith to unknown

Dodd City Tex **May 1st 1882**

Dear Daughter
I am thinking long of the time between letters Why dont you write to me I want to hear from you so bad I started to s— once last Summer to see you got to Brights took Sick and could not come so far by My self My health is about as usual some times up some times down I am still living at Loides I want you to write to me and if some of you can come out I will go back with you if I am well enough I have not heard from Jasper's mother for a long time Loides folks and Dicks folks are all well now be Sure to write Soon for I want to hear so bad Tex is married and doing well and Dick Smiths Mary is Married to Will Grear Tish is not Married I have heard that Bright house and all he had was burnt up I will close hopeing to hear from you soon I remain
your Mother

M A Smith

---

141. Elizabeth Hardin to Jane Hardin

Gainesville Cook Co May 25 1882
Mrs. Jane Hardin Rancho Gonzales

My very dear daughter I wrote you Some time ago have been waiting with patiance to hear from you and dear children. I am living here in Gainesville doing the best I can have many warm friends when I wrote you last I tole you Nannie had left her husband. he was any thing but a kind husband to her he let his tongue runn for three months Stayed right in Sight of us all the time. we all could See him evry day. Nannie did not Speak to him during the three months he and Jeff got along fine untill Nannie left him then Jeff would not have any thing to do with him he Still let his tongue runn. finely Jeff asked him about Some of his gab they had quite a Combat. So after all the dificuly and troubl She is living with him. Jeff has not been home Since, he does not know they are living togather. I do hope he will be at home soon, Jeff was doing well. was So kind to me and was proud of Nannie he would have been a true brother to her was very kind to little Gippie I have a good garden have my own milk and butter, Cobb lives joining lote to us. did I tell you Bright got his house burned and evry thing last January it was thought it caught from the Stove pipe it was insured they get the policy they left for Fannin Co. last tuesday on a visit to his Mas then they are going to Waco he will Sell Scroubs of Mclellan Co you need not be Surprised if they visit you his Summer. O! how I do mis Matt I can Scarsley live from her the little children think So much of Gran Ma. Jane tell me if you have made any effort for John's relief if we are going to do anything for him now is the time. it has been three weeks Since I herd from him. Nannie had to tell him all the particulars about her Sepperation I did not want her to. for I would not, and when I wrote to him last I tole him they ware living togather I know he is mad and no wonder, my pride is taken down considerable John tole her not to compromise on any terms for She would lower herself —y notions ware the Same. I have not changed as yet. Jane I do wish I could See you O I have So much to tell you I cant write it if I was able I would visit you this Summer tell Sweet little Mollie and Johnie

and little Jinnie not to forget me that Gran Ma loves then dearly. Bells Dora wrote her aunt Lizzie a letter not long Since. Jane what has become of Dr. Brockies tell me evry thing you can think of Jane John has become a Bible reder I believe he has had a change of heart. Jane do teach your children the precepts of the Bible may the good Lord bless you and them for ever and Save you all high up in heaven is the Prair of your troubled Mother
good bye Sweet loved ones

Your Mother E. Hardin

direct your letters to. Gainesville Cook Co, Tex.

---

142. Mattie Odom to Jane Hardin

May 28th / 1882 Weesatche P Goliad Co Texas

Mrs Jane Harden
My Deare Sister I will right you a few line to let you know how I am geting along Molie Keeps Well and seems verry anxious to get home and go to school. Jane you Will have to come down and get her for it is imposible for me to leave home now you and sally must Come down about the midle of June for there Will be a picnic and you can have a nice time be Shure and bring Sallie ever body is Well down here and Crops is fine I am going to Singing School every Saterday and Sunday and learning to Sing verry fast Frank is leaning to Talk most any thing he Wants to Mollie is going to Sunday School every Sunday We have had plenty of rain and evry thing look nice Well I Will Close for this time give my love to Frank and the Children bring little Wesie down With you
right Soon and often to your sister

Matie E Odom

---

143. Elizabeth Hardin to Jane Hardin

Gippie Sends a kiss to all Mollie write me a letter G.H

Gainesville Cook, Co. Aug 13th, 1882
Mrs. Jinnie Hardin Rancho Gonzales, Tex

My Dear Daughter
I recived you letter Some time ago So very glad to hear from you.

Jane I have not heard from Johnnie for three weeks he was not very well the last account Sissie Nannie and my Self Sent him a box of nick nacks, week before last, Sent it by express. I will tell you we Sent him light bread, Crackers, butter, pound Cake, Jellies apples and peaches, all weighing twenty forur pounds. I have not herd from him Since. he wrote me he Sent little Johnnie a fine pair of boots he Says he does not know whether he got them or not he requested me to write to you and know if he got them. Jane if I can raise the money I will go to See him this fall and take Gippie with me. O: how I do want to See him he Says his long confinement is begining to tell his weight being only one hundred and forty lbs poor boy I would take his place if I could, Jane did you know Bright and Matt are at Lampasses Springs. Jane I have not Seen Jeff Since I rote you last. I am nearly dead to See him. Ed. Nannie and myself are living togather. I am not as well Satisfied as when Jeff and myself ware keeping house togather allthough we are doing very well and I do Just as I please I Support myself I have plenty milk and butter milking my own Cows. I have had a splendid garden Some yet Squashes ce— and water mellons yet. Jane I do want to See you So much I could tell you So much is your children going to School, Jane I recivied a letter from Bell not long Since one from little Dora. little Joda wrote a letter to his uncle John for me to Send to him I sent it. I have recived an answer to it I will mail it for him this eav Jane write me all the news you can and tell me Just how you are getting along I do wish I ware able to help you and your dear little children if I had money I would visit you and remain a month or two. my dear child you cant immagine how dear you are to me. I am nearly dead to See Sweet little Mollie Johnnie and Jinnie kiss them for me tell them Grand Ma loves them dearly. Jane teach your little children to pray Jane my dear child do you pray if you do not, begin right now to pray for your Self and little children and dear husband. Jane I believe John's heart is allready changed Jane our heavenly father is the one to tak our troubles to he has Said ask and yea Shall recive nock and it Shall be opend.Bells husband has professed religion and Joined the Methodist Church Bell also you do like wise. may the good Lord bless you and your dear little children forever kiss all the children for me tell little Jinnie to kiss you for Grand Ma,adieu my dear child

Your Ma. E. Hardin

144. J. W. H. to Jane Hardin

Sep the 3rd 1882 Huntsville Texas

Mrs Jane HArdin Zedlers Mills Gonzales Co Tex

Dear Jane I received your Letter a few days ago and be assured it was received & read with pleaseure I must congratulate you in regards to ——— and hope that its association may make your unfortumate Life a better & Hapier one, I am Tolerably well Doing as well as can under the circumstances & present Situation Jane tell Mollie yes when I can I wil Send her Some thing I am Sorry I am not able at present tell Little Jane I wil not forget her But Jane Dearest Send them to School as much as you can & when Not at School have them to Study their books at home Say 2 or three hr a Day tell them I am proud to receive the mesage of a Kiss as well as from you Remember me to them often wil Close by Sending My Love to them my Love to you My respects to all you Desire to have them tell Little Sallie Cobb that I wil be proud to get a line from her Kiss your Name Sake for me & Be Sure and have Buck to write on his arrival or Shortley afterwards Hoping trusting that Shall we Never meet on this earth that we may meet in heaven where neither moth Nor dust Does corrupt Nor thieves Break through and Steal Jane it is hard to Be Seperated from one's that we Love But there is a final Seperation of the mind and Body may we be prepared for that Seperation is my wish your Afectionately as ever Kiss the Children for me..

J. W. HArdin

Direct to Sedlers Mills. Mrs Jane. Hardin Gonzales, Co Tex

---

145. J. W. H. to Jane Hardin

Oct the 1St. 1882 Huntsville Texas

Mrs Jane Hardin Zedlers Mills Gonzales County Tex.

Dear Jane it is with pleasure that I Now write you. but will First Acknowledge the receipt of yours received a few days ago. and be a sured that there is nothing that goes further to Aleviate my Sorrows than to receive a line from you one that I esteem above all others. it found me in moderate health to Speak. and Leaves me in better and as good Spirits as circumstances wil permit. am getting along Splendid. Have Not Been punished this yr, 9mo hast past this yr.

though I am not Braggin for Bragg Jeneraly meets with misfortune Before he reaches the woods. Well I am Doing Just as well as circumstances wil admit.. Jane Dearest I was glad to Know that J. W was able to Help you Some I am in Hopes He wile be able after while to Help you more & more I am in Hopes that he wil ever Be a Dutifull Son. incourage Him in what is right. and Teach him to reject what is rong. wherever it may Show itself Teach Him to Say (No) when it is rong or right for Him to Say (No) Tell Him that No one whom So ver he may be wil ever give Him advice with out a motive either good or Bad and to (allways) consider there Motives Well Before acepting or rejecting Jane Dearest I am glad to Know that mollie & Little Jane Keeps well I Know they are Lovely Besides I am glad to Know that you have Thus far been able to find Friends that have administered partley to your wants in your unfortunate condition. Jane Dearest it may be that I may Never See you or be with you again thoug I am Hope full There is one thing certain that you wil ever have my esteem and Best wishes Some th— that No other has or will ever have in comparison with you. Now over five yrs has past Since we were together a round our fireside your memory your name is as Bright to me as it was the Last time we parted you have ever Been faith full and done what but few of your Sex would do. and none but the purest. may you ever be Blessed with prosperity and may we yet Se each other yet on this Shore. if not may we meet each othe on the Bright terrestrial Shore yes may we meet each other there Jane Dearest Kiss the children for me I Send all of my Love to you & the Children Best wishes to all you Desire to have them Hoping to Here from you Soon I am as ever yours Afectionately **J W HArdin**

PS) I am proud to Say up to date you have been the Most faithfull in writing though ma has been very faithfull JWH

Jane in your Next if posible and convienient give me Some Florida News as well as Mountain News Adieu Dearest **JWH**

---

146. Mattie Odom to Jane Hardin

Oct 4th 1882 Weesatch Po Goliad Co Mrs Jane Harden

Dear sister I reckon you think I am along time ansering your letter but I havent had no news to rite havent got much now I Was somened out to pleasent yesterday if I dont go out there I will be up there in november if I can get off mr. White is talking about moving out West I dont no Whether he Will go or not mat has got back from uvalde he got back last Week Jane rite and tell me Where Lizzys Children is and how tha are geting along I havent heard from them for a long time you must come down and see my fine dress I have Just finshed it Well I Will Close for this time give my love to Frank and the children I remain as ever your kind and loving sister

Mattie E Odom

Miss Mollie Harden my Dear little niece I will rite you a few lines and see if you can read them I Will bring your trunk I promised you When I come up mat sais you must not forget to come down the last of november for he Will have a big Cake laid up for you you must learn to rite and anser my letters if you Was down here now you could go to School we have got a good school now Mat sais he Will send you another dress whin go up there well good by be a good girl and maby your ma will let you Come home with me from your loving aunt

Mattie. E. Odom

---

147. Neill to Wad

Pollard Ala nov the 26 1882

Friend Wad

it is with the greatest of Pleasure for me To write you A few Lines it seames Like I am A Talking To you Pursonly & I am Also A shamd for not writing To Sooner I was not at Home when your Letter arrived & Some neglect But excuse me this Time & I will do Better you Said Something About me A mooving Back To Texas old fellow I would of Bin Back their now if I could of raised the means my famly was Sick So Long that I got thrue what I had they aint A damn thing A doing hear nor nerry dollar in the Country I rode three weeks To Seel Two good mairs & finly Sold one for Sevety five dolars they is no money hear Been has Bin gon About A month out in Jackson Couty I dont no how he is A doing horses has Bin dull Sale hear every thing is high hear yet corn at Miligan mill worth $1.40 cents pur Bushel meat 20 cent A pond they has Bin A good eal of Sickness hear this fall Nety has Bin Sick About three weekes they is no nues hear that would interest you Lis has Bin mighty Bad off But She is Better Balance of your conniction is well arkey & Bud is A geting A Long fine Bud Told me To give you his regards marry thadies Swaped Horses with Wade & got the Black mair that he got from Pierce She pitched hur off the other day & Broke one of arms & Sprand the other So She has concluded that She cant make A Buckcaro She is Two old give all of my old Friends my Best respects also give your Famly my Best respects & except A portion your Self while I remain yours as ever Wad excuse this Short Letter write oftun for it is A greate satisfaction To me **Neill Bowen**

Pute & the Childrn Sends their Best respect To you & Famly give my Love To Jane & Frank & Beens Famly

Neill

---

148. Mattie Odom to Jane Hardin

fewuary 16th 1883 Middle Town Goliad County Texas

Mrs. Jane. Harden

Dear Sister I Write you a few lines I Would have Writen Sooner but havent had time I Was at a Singing the other Night had a nice time Frankie is Well and the Worst boy you ever Saw Mat is living With me We have got the prettiest garden You ever Saw ever thing is up and growing nice Ma Was out to See us to day her family is all Well Milam and Mat is going down about Victoria to Marrow after a horse that Was stolded from them I heard from Jim and Mollie a few days ago tha are all Well Mat Sais tell Mollie She must come down and stay With us a while this Summer and eat Wattermellon We are all fixing to go down to Goliad to a big Circus on the 22ed and a big Makurade ball on the 24th if nothing happens tell Frank I will Write her a letter next time Well I Will close for this time give my love to all and a portoin for your Self. Write Soon to your loving Sister good by

Mattie. E. Odom

---

149. J. W. H. to Jane Hardin

Louis

Adieu my Dearest JWHArdin

Mrs Jane HArdin Rancho Gonzales County

Riddleville Texas

Caffall Tom Has been here

Huntsville, Texas, Jan the 6 1884. J W Hardin

Mrs Jane HArdin

Dear Jane I received your Letter Last Sunday and was glad to hear from you you Speak of not receiveing any Letters from me in Some time Deaest it has been Some time Since I wrote you or any one else and to day I write you with much pain I am Sick Down in the bed with my wounds have had them Lanced 3 times and expect wil have to be Lanced again it has been over two months Since I have worked any been down in the Bed all the time part of the time not able to get up when down (I am now improving (aperiantly) I hope I wil Soon be up. though I cant tell how Soon as I have allready had Several relapses I can only Do the Best I can ——— wil try to indure all Cheerfull evin Death it Self which must come Soon or Later Jane Dearest Do the Best you can for your Self and the children what ever you think best will please me remember me to then often (with a kiss) Ma Sent me a box of eatables for Christmas I am treated well Mrs Goree and Mrs McCuloch Sister came to See me a Christmas day with a Christmas diner god Bless you is my prayer

---

150. J. W. H. to Jane Hardin

Just received a letter
from Ma nan up & ma
better John, W, HArdin

Mrs Jane. HArdin
Zedlers Mills
Gonzales county Texas

Huntsville, Texas, Dec the 7th 1884

Dear Jane it is with pleaseure that I now write you. I received your Kind and welcome letter a few days ago. Which gave me great Satisfaction as all of your Letters do. and must Say it is a pleaeure for me to heare from you I an Glad you are all doing well as you are. there Surely is no one that wishes you and yours more happiness tham myself Jane Dearest I felt better Soon after reading your letter I hope I am improving I cant Say for certain Some times I feel better I believe I am. Some Stronger but my Sufferings are constant and intense at times I hope I may get well cant tell by the help of god I shal try. I am not Yet in a State of Despondency but very bad health. tell mollie being Sleepy is no or at Least a poor excuse for not writing me. tell Molly that I have a nice gold ring I shal try to Send her by her next birth day Dearest Nannie was very Sick the Last account I had Ma was better I wrote you about Mannin being here I hope you got it. I am glad you wrot to Barnett concerning me Jane Dearest I hope to hear from you Soon Again and I hope I Shal have improved much by the next time I write you give Mollie John W & Little Jane a Fathers Love yourself a Devoted wife's portion. I hope I Shal hear from you Soon I am Affectionately Yours.

John, W, HArdin

(I Send my Love to all you wish to have it)

JWH

---

151. J. W. H. to Captain McCulloch

8/26/85

Capt McCulloch (Sup)

I Do once more earnestley Appeal to you for (medical Aid) this Disease or Maledy or whatever you may call it unfits me for Any use it Seems to me that my Life is threatend every moment and that the final Assalt is Likely to be made at any time I have for two years patintly bore all and hope to be able to bear the rest with christian fortitude. I do not Know whether I have cancer of the Stomachi Bright's Disease Heart disease or what else fit whatever it is it give me much pain both mental and physicaly

2nd

beyond Description at this present time. I Do respectfully request that you See Dr. Bush and Accertain the facts in my case a thourough examination migh uncover the Disease (I have no Disposition to complain unecessaryly) . I may be beyond the Point where a cure is possible : but I hope not. I Do believe with common Sense treatment my condition would be greatly improved . that I have an internal Disorder no one can deny. and that my Heart Longue's Liver & Kidneys are affected I have Little Doubt Please See Major Goree and tell Him that I say I have become incapacitaled and Ask for human treatment or at Least a place where I can bear my pain & Sufering unmolested I have been trying to

3nd

work I can do but very Little I Donot wish to be worked to Death.nor punished to Death for my inability to Do the required Amount of work. the court passed Sentence on me for 25 yrs in the penn, and unless you See that I am treated in a diferent maner I fear I Shal not be Able to Serve the 25 yrs.to make a long Story Short I am Sick I am Suffering Death as it were by Degrees and ask you to take cognisance of the fact I make this plain unvarnished Statement to you hoping you wil be favorable Disposed. I am very respectfully

John W HArdin 8/26/85

---

152. J. W. H. to Jane Hardin

John Wesley HArDin — Mrs Jane. HArdin
Sedan Gonzales County Texas

(Tell JWH I would Like to hear from him)

Huntsville, Texas, Sep the 27th 1885

Mrs Jane Hardin Dear Jane it is with pleaseure that I now write you. I have no other Appology to offer to you for not writing than my inability through sickness. to day is the 1st letter that I have attempted to write in the regular writing room in over two yrs. and we are positively forbiden to write in any other place: therefore I have writen few letters in the Last two: yrs because I was not able to go to writing room. I received a letter from you & Molly in July and answered at once. have not heard from you Since Hope you and our Dear little ones are well I send Molly ten Stampt Envellopes to write me once a month and if She is not willing to write give them to JWH & if he is not use them yourself or (burn up I have been very Sick Since I wrote you nearly all of Jully all of Aug & a good portion of Sep confined to a cell 21 days. 7 days in the Hospital but have been at work 7 and in Justice to my Self. I feel better than in two yrs can get about better and have hopes of getting intirely well or at least a great deal better though I am thiner than I ever was a least Since I reached 2lyrs from 1651bs I have fallen to 1351bs but hope to gain the most of it back by Spring. Jane Dearest Keep up a courageous Industry and dont give up life yet. We may yet be blessed with fortune but keep a carefull guard over : or continual watch over our children. I hope they Shall never deviate from the paths of rectitude So inculcate in them: imbue in them right principles teach them to Say no. as well as yes. hoping to hear from you at once

I am Affectionately yours
John W. HArdin /
Kiss all th Children
For me /

H B C.
Mr J. E. Cam—
Dear Cousin

en en
Frankie
Bowen

Frankie
Bowen
Frankie
- - MB
Jane Jane

---

153. J. W. H. to Jane Hardin

[UNDATED]

John. W. HArdin
I think my health is still
Improving (at Least I hop So)

Mrs. Jane. HArdin
Sedan, gonzales County
Texas

Huntsville, Texas, Nov the 22nd 188

Dear Jane it is with pleasure I now write you and will first acknowledge the receipt of your's Molly's & J.W.H.'s of Oct the 15th to be Sure I was very glad to hear from you all and to Learn you were all doing well and enjoying good health Jane Dearest I shall offer an Appology to you to day for I have very little to write of or about. But Shall endeavor to Answer: at least Some of your questions Mats' PO is Gatesville Coryell co Tex Elizabeth's is Gansvill cook co Tex Nan & Gip's are at .Enis Elis co Tex Jeff the Last I heard from him was in the former and had married to whom I do not Know Now I very Seldom here from any of them. Nan is the only one who has wrote me Since Ma's death I hope they are all well and Doing well I am very proud to have Molly & JWH to write me and hope it will not be long before my Little Sweet Baby Jinney will be able to write me tell them I love them dearly and wish them to write me often that I read their Letters with great pleasure tell them they do well for new beginers tell them I hope they wil learn all they cam that is that they will improve ever moment they cam while at School be obedient to the Teacher's will get good Lessons and try to excel in every. thing they under take Never Say cant (but)(I will Try) I am allso glad to hear that are not Afraid to work and praise them for there industry and ask of them that they obey there Ma in every thing hoping they will make good and usefull citizens I send my Love to each of them and tell M I have not forgotten the ring and wil Send it Soon Kiss each for me and as for yourself you have my intre Affection as you have ever had I am very affectonable yors **John W HArdin**

---

154. J. W. H. to Jane Hardin

John W. HArdin It has been over a month Since I received a leter from you all I Shall by the mercies of god try to write a Specia and Seperate letter to my children Soon my Love to you all my intire affectons to you Dearest JWH

Mrs Jane. HArdin Sedan Gonzales, county Texas

Huntsville, Texas, Jan the 3rd 1886

Dear Jane. It is with pleaseure that I inform you of my existence: though deprived of the greatest Blessings preserved and reserved to mankind. perfect health and untrameled Liberty: without which Life is hardly worth Living Yet Dearest I feel constrained to offer my humble prayer and thanks to that omnipotent, all wise god one who holds the Scales in which the Destinies of Nations as well as man are weighed for my, being, even in this condition and ask his bountifull protection in the future. Jane Dearest I have received two Letters from Nan one from Aunt Nan one from Mat Since the 20 of last month Gip is with his Aunt Nan. Nan at gatesville Jeff allso. the Latters wife Died Last Sep Nan and Mat Spoke very Affectionately of you and the children. aliso told me of Bright receiving a letter from J.W.H.Jun. Mat aliso Said that She had become more attached to you than ever while She Staid in gonzales She commended highly the way you tried to teach your children the true course. (way) Jane Dearest you cannot be to carefull or too earnest in that one but all importun duty I can hardly expect that there education will be as libral as wide. as children povided with means and an abundant opportunities, but dearest I do expect that their elementary training Shall be of the very best Truth honor Virtue &d charity Sentiments the cherrishing of which will make them Ladies and a Jentleman there is great Need of impressing these Sentiments these principles upon them at present So long as a lady keeps her honor though She be poor She wil comand the respect of all honest people and the admiration of the world teach my boy th-- to Suceed in any Business he must be (honest) tell him honor &d ability can Allways find imployment. tell Molly & JWH that their Letter give me much pleaesure and comfort in this: my present but I hope not my final abode Kiss Little Jane the other two allso you Still have my intire affections I hope I Shall Soon be able to write them a Seperate letter yours **JWHArdin**

---

155. J. W. H. to Jane Hardin

John. W. Hardin　　　　　　　　　　Mr John. W. Hardin. Jun.
Sedan. gonzales County　Texas

tell your Ma that I heard from her through a preacher who was at her hous Mrs Mcculloch Delivering th message

Huntsville Texas, March the 7 1886

Dear Son.

It become my duty and I assure you it is a pleasant one to write you in answer to Several letters received from you my Son. Let me assure you that your letters as well as your Sisters are highly appreciated and accepted as well as eagerly read by me. I am in hopes your baby Sister will Soon be able to write me a letter: you write and compose well for a boy of your age: but there is great room for improovement there fore Let me Suggest that when you go to write a letter think over carefully what you wish to write: that is what has happened or transpired that would be worthy to Speak of if you was brought face to face with the person address Since the last time you Saw him or address him untill my Death Sign your Name (John W Hardin)(Jun.(younger) I have made these Suggestions to improve your maner of writing hopeing you wil profit by the advice. as I have Said before you do well but I wish to See you do better: large

Streams from little creeks flow: Tall trees from Small Accorns grow: then great men from little boys you Know. Son let me advise you in your Studies in School make Arithmetic gramer Spelling reading and writing a Speciality especially the 1St and Spelling. be indoustrious have honor then you wil have intelligence and with this trio you wil be able to Succeed: teach your Self to think for yourself in all things: and when any one gives you advice: allways even if it is your best friend consider his or her motive: do not doubt there is allways a motive it may be a good one or a bad one then you wil be able to decide the proper course I Send my love to your ma go an Kiss your ma for me and your sisters

allso tell Mollie She will here from me Soon

---

156. J. W. H. to Jane Hardin

John W Hardin — Miss Jane M. Hardin
Sedan. Gonzales. County Texas

I send you and your Brother amemen to Each JWH

Huntsville, Texas, May the 2nd 1886

My Dear Little Daughter I thought I would Surprise you in the way of a letter. Which wil convey to you a Fathers Love. you have promised to write me at Some future time I hope this will Stimulate you and incourage you in your Studies and that you will Soon be able to write Pa a nice little letter commenceing Thus Dear Papa) (and ending Thus your Daughter Jane M. Hardin) I wrote your Sister a letter Some time ago I recived a letter from her Last night but if She got it She failed to mention it in her welcome (Epistle) She allso told me of the where abouts of your Ma your Brother your Self: but again failed to disclose her own position. Daughter by the next time I write you or your Mother I Shal try to Send you all Something as a token of regard in the way of reading matter which I hope will be read by you all. as it will be for you all. Now Little Jane be Kind to your playmates never offend them by any word or action Love your Brother and Sister as yourself Love respect and obey your mama in all things: and in rememberance of your unfortunate but Devoted Father go embrace you Sister your Brother and Last but not Least your Mother and tell them Pa Still Lives, and Sends Love to each of you. May peac hapiness and prosperity be you heritag on this Earth and eternal Day be your crown in the Future but unknowm Yes tell your Aunt Frank that I appreciate her Kindly wish and that chicken is my Favorite Dish but must Decline the relished Dish

Very Afectionately Your Father John W Hardin

---

157. Mattie Smith to Jane Hardin

Gatesville aug 3rd 1886 Mrs Jennie Hardin

Dear Sister

I Know you will be Surprised at me for not writing Sooner I have no excuse only negligence. Well Jane it has been So long since I wrote you. I hardly Know where to commence Mr Smith raised a very good crop last year and has been in the machine business ever Since as he can make more at that than farming or at the carpenters trade We are getting along very well Mr Smith has bought us a nice home here in gatesville an acre lot With two front rooms a hall with an ell back of it with a little galery and a portico in front

2

I like here very much the people are very Sociable I often think of you and those Sweet little children and wish to be with you. nannie has been with us all winter and spring is at Ennis now will be home in a few weeks has ben gone a week. Gip has been to See us left for Ennis yesterday he is improving So fast is going to School all the time they have a fine School at Ennis a real College. he will Stay ther til his education is complete. he loves aunt nan and uncle Dr So much. Jeff is in kansas with cattle his wife died 6 months after they were married. I Suppose you have heard of my other girl She is a month over

3

a year old can walk She has been in bad health ever Since christmas I fear we will not raise her. tel Frank to write me a funny letter. Kiss all the children for aunt Mat. Mr Smith Says of all the boys he has Seen Johnnie is the boss with him. Will often talks of you all and frank acting the negro. ther is a fine college here Jane. Willie & Lillie Will Start in September how I wish you was living close So you could send them cant you consent to let Mollie come and go to school I would take all paines in my power to make a lady of her and it would not be long before She could make you

4
and her a respectful living We will be glad if you will consider this. & let her come, for an education is to be valued above gold. Mr Smith Says he would be So glad to See Johnnie have an education & will give it to him if you will allow it. then by that time Jinnie will be the right age to come. Jane I suppose nan will Jump the broom Stick before long her fellow lives here but is in Arkansas now. he is a real nice young man has a great many friends Jane I fear I have the consumption. I have hardly been able to be up in a month have a dreadful cough. give my love to inquiring friends. Mr Smith is not at home he Says he will write has not written to his ma in a year I have not writen to sissie in a year and a half
Write Soon and I will answer immediately tell all the news
your Sister **Mat Smith**

---

158. J. W. H. to Jane Hardin

John W. Hardin — Mrs. Jane. Hardin
Sedan. Gonzales county Texas

Huntsville, Texas, Sep the 5th 1886

Dear Jane. It is with a desire on my part to inform you of my, being, that I penn you these lines hoping you will be able to find Some comfort in the word 'being, though that being. be far away from you yet he is pleased to assure you that you are ever near him in head and heart. Dearest do not ever think that I can forget thee: no not untill the leaves forget to fall in autum. the brooks Sease to flow down Stream. no not untill the marinier forgets the Star that guides him no not untill love goes out upon the alter of my heart, and memory empties its urn into the gulf of forgetfullness. Dearest tell Jane that I am highly pleased with her photograph and that the cords of merit were immense tell Mollie & John. W. H. that I will be pleased to hear from them at any time and from this on will try to answer their letters with promptitude not before exhibited remember me Kindly to all inquiring friends give my love to the children Kiss each one for me and retain a reasonable portion for your Self. I hope you have been blessed with rain I ailso hope you will be able to Send the children to School Soon teach them that honor integrity and virtue are necessary qualifications of true man hood an womanhood teach them to Know right from. rong and then to have the courage to uphold right if for no other reason because it is right. and then teach them to reject rong no mater from what Source it may come if for no other reason than because it is rong eternaly rong. in other words teach them to Shun hate vice and to Seek and love virtue. I heard from gip the other day he is at Enis Hou is their on a visit. acept the love of your unfortunate but fortunate JWH

---

159. J. W. H. to Mollie E. Hardin

John W Hardin

Miss Mollie. E. Hardin
Sedan Gonzales county Texas

Huntsville, Texas, Oct the 3nd 1886

Mollie. Dear. Daughter. Enclosed you will please find a gold ring 18 carrat fine. with the enitials of Donor and donee: and the Date it became yours. The Souvenir my dear child appropriately represents the love of your Father: as the ring is round therefore it has no end: So my love to you in it. I Send a love that can never bend. I donot Send it to you for its intrinsic value though it is worth five dollars: but permit me to Say again as a memento of your Fathers affections. his love for his Daughter M. E. Hardin. He desire you to weare it at all times as it is pure and from a pure heart. and Should you ever be tempted by an evil Spirit that a glance at the ring. will be Sufficient to drive, off. Away, that Spirit that would tempt, would delude you from the paths of rectitude and virtue this ring is 18 carrat pure gold therefore one eightteenth of it is alloy, or Some base metal: but my dear Daughter I would have you know that there is no alloy in your Fathers heart. a love appropriately compared to the form of the ring which has no end not the quality of the gold: for in all gold rings there is alloy. there is none in the love I Send you this love is from the heart of a devoted Father: whose heart is effervescent with love for his own true virtuous Daughter. I cannot close this without requesting you to Attend church Sunday School Prayer meeting Singing School every day School. That is let every day be a day of School to you, but my Daughter give your Sould to god. nothing would be more pleasing to me than to Know that you were leading a christian life. I would not have you enter upon a life of Austerity and Solitude. I would not abridge your happiness. I would not check the outgoings of your young and buoyant heart but dear daughter please permit me to point your joys your Desires your affections to the only object worthy of your Soulds esteem. Space forbids me from further exhortations. therefore I will leave for the present. the rest for your Mother your Teachers a- yourself. Tell Little Sweet Jane that her Letter was So nice in form. So Sweet in words So consoling to her Father. therefore I send ———.John. W.H to you and your Ma ——— Ad— tell your Ma I ——— the ———

---

160. Mollie G. Anglin to Jane Hardin

[UNDATED]

Mrs J Hardin

Dear friend little Jennie is not here is gone up to Mr Papmor's. I will bring or send her in the morning.. I want you, if you can, to go with me down to John Anglins tomorrow if you can get a horse. meet me at Mr Winslets in the morning.. if you cant go I guess I shall have to go alone.. go if you can.

Rect Mollie G. Anglin

you might have come up here and stayed to night I think

---

161. J. W. H. to Jane Hardin

John. W. Hardin — Mrs. Jane. Hardin
Sedan Gonzales County Texas

Jane encourage the children to write and have them all write any time that is each a Separate letter

Huntsville, Texas, Nov the 7th 1886

Dear Jane it is with pleaseure that I to day renew the affections, the Love that has So long existed between yourself and the Writer. Though years have passed Since we gazed in each others eyes. Since our hearts beat responsive to the real Love of two beings. yet to day it becomes me to assure you that the Laps of yrs has not in the Least Disturbed my love for you. My chief desire is that you and our children may prosper I am duely grieved to Know that I am totally forbiden to contribute to your wants. to those to whoom I owe So much. but dearest Such is the case while I cannot do any thing within my self for the welfare of you and our children. let me assure you that concious of the rectitude of my course the justice of my cause. I can appeal to him that doeth all things well: for the peace prospeiity and happiness of those who are at the mercies of cruel world. Jane Dear as there is more Sunshine than cloudy weather So there is more pleasure than Sorrow then let us Strive to obtain as much of the fomer as possible observing our duty to ourselves and those around us. but trusting in him that doeth all things well. for the ballance Jane Dearest I am highly pleased with the promptitude of the correspondence between myself and children I derive more relief from their letters. tell J.W.H. I hope he can Spell (Sow) by this time, and tell him that he must learn now how to receive a repremand; though it was not intended except to instruct. I hope to hear from him Soon, tell little jane that I could trace a Similitude between her hand writing and Mollies. I think however that Molley wrote the Letter if I am mistaken I will Stand corected Let me Know. I am truly Sorry that you have no Schooll Dearest have the children repeat or recite lessons to you as often as circumstances will permit. hopeing you will write Soon and often Send you and the children the Love of one who is unfortunate. —ccept my Love and affections as ever Yours **J W Hrdin**

---

162. Nannie to unknown

[UNDATED]

5 oclock. Thursday.
Have done pretty well to day. The Germans Cam at nearly every place. The Me- Shi— ——— I expect I could do fine at Fredrics burg but dont Know that I shall go there, as it is off the K.R.
Bye. by. **sister Nannie.**

---

163. J. W. H. to Jane Hardin

John. W. Hardin

Mrs Jane. Hardin Sedan Gonzales county. Texas

Now my Dearest ones I take pleaseure in acknowledging your Soothing letters: but to you children I desire you to be more pains taking en large upon your letters See which one of you can write the prettiest letter tell the most in the Shortest Space give my love to Wes Mcgee love to you all

Huntsville, Texas, March the 27th 1887

Mrs Jane Hardin. Missis Molly Jane and John W Hardin. My dearly beloved wife, and affectionate children, it is with love for you, and it is allso with an eagor Solicitude for your present as well as your future happiness peace and prosperity that I write to you to day, and my dearly beloved I take pleasure in assuring you that I do So with a heart effervescing, yes. (ebullient) with love for those whoose names appear at the head of this epistle. words may describe but they cannot define the love that goes out from the heart of a true husband to a true wife and (vice versa) nor the love the Solicitude a true a courageous father has for his children. Love I Say my dearest ones is an emotional quality and you cannot define an emotional atribute but it is more and when Suported by patience by hope makes life cheerfull beautifull happy in expectancy and brings joy now, it aradiates the future it allso makes trials temptations troubles pain Sorrow all radient with the beauty of victory of Sucess of comfort. Yes all that is dark or dreary vanishes like the morning dew before the effulgence the luster of love of patience and hope. I Say my dearest ones go where you will look into whatever house hold you may and if you find not these (pandemonium) reigns Supreme, all is rong there is no Symetry in any thing. but I Say my dearest ones light that cavern up with the torch of love of hope of patience, then view the change, yes my dearest ones where all was dark without form: you behold its beautiful ligh, and the Symetry is perfect. then may the god of mercy give you love hope and patience in all things. I Say to you my loving ones carry these with you to School that your lessons may be easy, and in your labor forget not these for your arduous work will be made light. and when you go in company lay not these aside for they will make you cheerfull, they will enable you to entertain all in whoose company you may per chance to fall in a royal hospitable maner. you not only have my word that these will chang darkness into light hatred to love. but, christ tells you to, "Remember without ceasing your labor of love your patience of hope in the lord Jesus christ in Sight of god our father". Then again "May the god of hope fill you with joy with peace in believing and may you abound in hope. in the power of the holy ghost, then

my loveing ones live a life of love of hope of patience and may god give you courag to walk according to the light these may cast upon your pathway in this life and may they Shed there effulgence more and more as the years go by and may each of you live a life of love not for fears Sake but for loves Sake and may you find at last the joy and peace that dispeleth the puns of the dying that removes the fears of the grave that drives of away your doubts in the eternal joy beyond the grave peace be with you and ever abide is my prayer
2nd
without this their education well be worthless. but jane I have ever reason to believe that you are now have been and will continue to teach our dear children Truth honor virtue religion and the Bible: for these are a few the important principles that underlie all true manhood or womanhood ah Jane if you can but fix impress upon their minds the value of truth of honor of virtue of religion: of courage to observe these. you will have Succeeded in crowning them with a coronets of far more value than gold their fortune in my estimation will be Secured. Jane Dearest I Speak from experience that Honor truth virtue courag and religon makes the man or woman who dares to point the finger of Scorn to a virtuous girl though She be poor. who has the temerity to asperse the name of a truthfull honest up right Boy: who has the courage I say to Scorn honor and virtue Truth religion not the wise the rich or the good: but as the miners of India of South m America Seek to find the brilliant diamonds of the field So do the wise the rich the honest the good Seek to pluck the virtuous for their own use and like the miner who cast aside the inferior diamond So do they cast aside the untruthfull the dishonest however Shapely they may apear. Jane Teach these children to take christ for their example I point him to you as the only object worthy of their Soulds love. teach them to love one another to love you to obey you. not through fear, but throuyh love teach them to love their teacher to obey him for love Sake. Their is no fear in love:
but love casteth out fear, because fear hath a torment: he that feareth is not mad perfect in love is John 4:18. Then again come unto me all ye that labor and are heavy laden, and I will give you rest: Take my yok upon you and learn of me: for I am meek and lowly in heart and ye Shall find rest unto your Soulds: For my yok is easey and my burden is light Math 11:28. Jane then let us today thank god for his loving mercies bestowed upon us in the past: Let

us ask him to cleans us from mistakes to cleans us from Superstition cleans us from ignorance: To give us believing hearts trusting hearts not for fears Sake but for love's Sake: and may the Ladder which Jacob saw with his head upon the Stone be given allso to those who have been tought to lie upon the ground with nothing but a Stone for a pillow. may the angels of heaven be Seen ascending and decending, and though the bottom of the lader rest upon the ground. the top reaches into heaven. Now this is my peroration. I to day beseech the oh god for thou dost love us: to teach us to love the: and to live a life of love. for christs Sake. hoping to hear from you Soon I will close by asking you to Kiss our loved ones for me with a deep Solicitude for your. your childrens welfare I am affectionately your **John W Hardin**

---

164. J. W. H. to John Hardin Jr.

John. W. Hardin To Mr John. W. Hardin. (Jr)
/Sedan Gonzales County Texas.
"and god Shall wipe away all tears from their eyes. and their Shall be no more death. neither Sorrow. nor crying. neither Shall their be any more pain: for the former things are passed away."

Huntsville, Texas, Apr the 3rd 1887

Miss Molley. Miss Jane and Mr John. W. Hardin. My affectonate my beloved children. through the bountiful mercies extended to me by the allwise by the allseeing all powerfull the ever present god, the lord Jesus christ. our Savior, our Redeener, your earthly father is again permited, to day, to offer you his greetings, and he takes pleasure in assuring you that this Salutation this address is actuated by love the love a true a devoted father has for his offspring or descendants. yes my admrable Daughters & Son this love is distinguished from all other forms of love one that cannot be defined by words but can be partly described by actions and words, and is promoted with a desire to make glad the hearts of those whoose names head this epistle. to Kindle the fire of hope of patience of love that is inclosed in your dear mothers heart, to regale to cheer to ameliorate one who is now and has been for years Suffering with a bleeding a broken heart. Truely the Heart disease is a dangerous one in any form, Stop it, is to Stop life, therefore we Should at the first approach of threatened danger to So vital a function as the heart, proceed without delay to move the cause of the maledy and Stop its progress. oh my dear children their is Such a heart disease that craves gold that pines and dies for fame which is common enough in these days but which is detestable in the Sight of god and intelligent mankind. your mother's is an intirely different form from this and is known only by those who have been cruelly Seperated from their husband by the Strong arm of the law by the perversion of the law. by the mock trial of an incompitent bias court, who but a few years before had counseled the taking of his Brother and four own cousins, and who had express on more than one occasion his hatred for the one he at last Sits and judges. My children I wish you to Know that I was tried and convicted by my eternal enemies who were at that time the court. Oh my children I pray god to comfort to cheer to console your ameable mother untill he can in his own way entirely cure her by yielding to the desire of her true Sincere heart. Now my Sweet children your father desires that each of you go in your own gentle affectionate way or maner and throw your arms around your mothers neck Kiss her and tell her that I live. and that I hope. tell her that I can See a gleam of light in the distant future that aradiates my Sould that fills me with hope and joy in believing that it is gods will that I Shall be returned restored to those whoom I So dearly love and who mourn my fate my abscence as only a devoted wife and loving children can tell her to raise up that drooping head to wipe away those tears. and when She thinks of me to hop and trust. not in man but god.

Adieu

J W Hardin

---

165. J. W. H. to Miss Jane Hardin

John. W. Hardin Miss. Jinnie. M. Hardin

Sedan Gonzales county Texas

Huntsville, Texas, May the 1St 1887

my beautiful my intelligent my Sweet and my brave children. your father desires to give you instructive lesson to day. and in So doing he will use the most Simple words at his command --ress himself to you. he will Speak to you in the languag of children. but he wishes you to know ---these words are your fathers words. your fathers advice to his three lovely children. I do not wish ——— make you feel Sad. or depressed. or to check the pleasures you now or may hope to enjoy. but I wish to point out the way for you to secure pleasures far more than you have now and which will increase as you grow older. I desire to add Strength to the virtuous energies that move. that inspire your young buoyant but brave hearts. listen to your Father untill he tells you how to live. believe the bible because it is gods book, and in it he tells mankind how to act towards each other. love god because he is your creator, and he is love, the first thing — wish you to do is to learn by heart the ten commandments. then obey them. the next to learn by heart the lords prayer ——— repeat it over to your mother when She has time to hear it. repeat it to your Self every night before you go to Sleep.——— ashamed to ask your mother for any thing you need. then be brave and ask god to guide to protect -------- -----ou in the paths of virtue. he is a merciful god he will answer your prayers. when each of you ——— commandments and the lords prayer let me Know. Now my dear children I wish ——— and———

---

166. J. W. H. to Miss Jane Hardin

John. W. Hardin — Miss. Jane. M. Hardin.
Sedan Gonzales county Texas

Huntsville, Texas, Aug the 28 the 1887

My dear child. my affecttionate my beautiful daughter. your father is not only actuated urged to write to you because it is his duty. but because it is his inclination . therefore he is prompted by his deep Solicitude for your welfare and his paternal love for his amiable daughter forces him envites me to day to Send to you and through you to your dear ma your Sweet Sister your noble brother there my greetings of love. he hopes he believes that this missive will be a welcome mesanger. that it will cause your young your pure your buoyant heart to leap with joy, and that it will light up the house hold of which you are a member with hope and that all will be glee around the family altar for a brief period: at least until the contents of this letter is made Known may the god of hope of love of patience

Suport Sustain you all is my Sincere wish. your father was highly pleased to receive a Sweet letter from his baby and to learn that She was going to School. to learn your School mam's name to learn that you loved her and that She was Kind and loved all of her Schollars, and your avowal or declairation to learn all you can exhibits a Spirit of a dutiful child and particularly attracted my attention, and for this good resolution I bestow upon you a fathers praise. Now from what you Say I think Miss Molley Shroder a lady of high attainments perfectly capable of teaching the young mind how to think how to (Shoot) love my dear child is a quality a virtue which is indispensible in the School room where Success is attained. Knowledge to Know and wisdom to impart to direct to guide are allso essential requirements which I allso hope I believe your teacher possess in an eminent degree. Now Jinny Some little girls and boys grumble and complain because they cannot Stand head in their class because their teacher dont love them because they cannot excell in everthing. now papa will tell you how to Stand head how to gain the esteem the love of your teacher the love and respect of your Schoolmates the admiration of all who Know you. if you love your teacher then obey her dont grumble or complain about any thing. but Study your lesson untill you can recite it. by heart. So that when your class is called you can recite a perfect lesson then you will Stand head in your class. yes and head in the estimation of your teacher. during School hours Study your lesson dont play or talk but when recess or play time comes lay down your books be mirthful be gay and take just as much interst in your Sport as you do in your books. be Kind to your Schoolmates and never Say or do any thing to depress them

2nd

or hurt their feelings, do not quarrel with any little girl. Sweet little girls never quarrel. remember without ceasing that their is a charm that attracts every one and that charm is love and (urbanity) (or good manners) Now a little girl that will allways Say, please Sir and please mam. yes. Sir and no Sir.. yes mam and no mam. thank you Sir and thank you mam. that has a kind encouraging word for those who are Smaller in Stature or size and weaker in mind. that never makes fun of a person because he is old or blind cripled or deformed, nor never makes fun of a person because their Skin is darker than her own is a little heroine and will make a lady worthy to be a queen. because a child has had Superior advantages has them now and Surpass you in learning in dress dont complain but be content with what you have and Show by your industry by your love for the truth for virtue that you two are worthy of what you possess the love the esteem of all who Know you. the greatest wealth a little girl can own. Trials misfortune poverty is the indelible ink which god Stamps upon his children the image the likeness of his own dear Self his (Superscription). ah my Sweet child look at the Spider he will work him Self to death before he will live without a web. The ant will build its nest or house just as often as the weary foot Spoils or crushes it. The tiny the industrious the indefatigable bee toils labors none the less because the fields the forest are (Parsimonious) or Scarce of flowers, but he extends lengthens his curcuit and penetrates goes to far off Swamps or fields or gardens and valleys to obtain his nectar and their Sucks from the nectary the flower the delicious juce and carries it home and Stores it away for the winter. So you See that the busy bee by his industry his thrift by his frugality Suplies the want the Scarcity of flowers in the nearer meadows or fields. Then my intelligent daughter are you to be rebuked in vain by the Spider the ant and the be. now my dear child Show by your pluck by your love for truth for your ma your Sister your brother your teacher your little companions and by your industrious habits by your general (decorum) or maners. that you will Substitute these for your (deformties) as rather your humble condition. and you will be the pride of your brother your Sister the joy of your father and mother beloved by your teacher admired and respected by all and the prettiest little girl in all the land in which you reside or live just what your pa would have you be. papa cannot answer each one of his childrens letters Seperately. but he assures you that it gives him much comfort to receive a line from either of them. he desires that each of them write him a letter once a month. all can use the Same envelope for the present. I cannot forego or out off expressing my Satisfaction or rather my gratification of two letters now received each from your brother and Sister in which their filial duty and respect. mark. exhibit their commenable appreciation of my advice their promptitude as well as yours in learning by heart or memorizing the lords prayer and the ten commandments are deserving of my hightest commendation praise and gratitude. be asured Sweet daughter that it will be my object in the future as it has been in the past to lead you all in the paths of rectitude and virtue. now your fathers valediction or fare well words are to go embrace your lovely mother imprint a Kiss on her dear cheeks and Kiss your brother and Sister and tell them to live and hope and in hoping be Steadfast accept a fathers love adieu

John W Hard

---

167. J. W. H. to Jane Hardin

John. W. Hardin — Mrs. Jane. Hardin.
Sedan Gonzales County Texas

Huntsville, Texas, Sep the 4the 1887

Dear Jane, Well do I Know that love is an eliment that exist in ever person some in a higher Some in a lower degree. jus as courage exist. that it is a quality that is admirable Wherever and Whenever exhibited even in animals fouls or human beings. See the dog the Hog the cow or any of animal defending their young with all their might even with their life See the barn yard hen fly up in the air to preserve her little chicks from the assaults of the hawk. ah yes see the quail hide at her command the little partrigies While She herself dances around before her Supposed enemy to lead that enemy from her beloved brood. ah She would make you believe that She is crazy and attract your attention to herself in order to divert your attention from the little birds. Some Say She is crazy. they are rong. it is her mode of warefare and is to be admired though deception is her object and aim yet it is prompted by love and often generally protects the little foul. Now my admirable wife as I have Shown you that love exist in this lower form and how it operates that it is willing to bleed to Suffer and to die for the object of its love is it not admirable worthy of commendation even in this form if So how much more commendable is it in the higher intelligent the human form where it is Supported by (patience by hope) it is of all qualities the most commendable I tell you that all difficulties that all Sorrow vanish before its glitering beaming appeasing enfluence. Trials troubles disappear as by magic wherever it abides and the present that was Sad the future which was dark dreary gloomy is changed in a joyful gleeful present a bright a beautiful and a hopeful future takes the place of the one just mentioned. Oh, yes everything is lighted up with hope with patience and with love and there is nothing Sad or dark. but all is exultant arradient with the beauty of love "Fear is a torment. but love casteth out fear". but where love abides fear cannot remain. probably you wish to Know what I mean. of all things I desire is for you to cultivate a Spirit of love in your family. rule them with love with reason. teach them if they love you they will obey you teach them to love this great State of Texas this union of States teach them that the hightest ambition of a Texian Texan is to render humble Submission to its laws. to cling to truth to honor to virtue with an unyielding tenacity. the more So because of my humble condition. the gap betwen poverty and wealth is wide and has ever been but the bridge that Spans this Chasm and has ever Spaned it is is truth is honor industry virtue and upon these the poor girl the poor the orpant boy the widow can walk to wealth to glory in Safety accept my cordial greetings Kiss my children and tell them if they love me to cling to virtue Adieu

---

168. J. W. H. to Jane Hardin

John. W. Hardin Mrs Jane. Hardin
Sedan,Gonzales,county Texas

(I will with pleasure give your Kindest regards to Duffy at my earliest opportunity.) "Where a mans treasur is there well be allso his heart"

Huntsville, Texas, Nov the 6the 1887

Dear Jane. My Sence of duty my irrepressible love for you and our dear children coexistent with my deep Solicitude for your present your future welfare peace prosperity and happiness, impells commands me to write to you to day, my admirable one, and through you my adorable one, I desire to light up the hearts of our, dear, precious, children with hope. a hope that dispells fear, that banishes Sorrow, and obliterates pain. that makes all labor light beautiful. that removes all obsticles in the way of progress. one that cheers the heart of the poor the needy the afflicted. that makes happiness possible in every case. that leads to victory those who dare to follow the bright and the beautiful Star whoose glittering Sheen adorns the head and, embelishes the heart of those who look into the future in a hopeful maner.

Tell them when they think of me to hope "for god will provide. Then dearest one bravest one truest one. the most lovely of the lovable whoom I adore please accept these greetings of love as a Slight token of my plighted faith made years ago, and which I now renew and which no time can alter no distance change no trouble or misfortune Sever. These are but a few links of love in the long the Strong chain of love which has bound my heart to yours. which binds it now, inseperable, and which no human vicissitudes can alter and, I assure you that my heart beats hopefully fervently for you for I firmly believe that the love I have for you is the love you have for me. god bless you is my prayer, and may you and yours be objects of his loving kindness. I take pleasure in acknowledging your Kind cordial welcome and highly entertaining letter of the 1St. ult. and I allso take pleasure in informing you that your letters have a desirable effect upon my head and heart, and act upon my nerves as an Anodyne or as your presence your Sweet Smiles use to do when unalloyed loved reigned in our hearts, as it reigns now. My Beautiful daughters letter was received with parental pride and favor. John Wesley's and Sweet little Janes love was quite a balm Little JW Mc Gees message respectfully acknowledged and will recieve my attention in due time. the disposal of the picks quite Satisfactory to myself Tommy. T Being a Son of one of the bravest and truest of men that ever lived or died. more over my Friend. Jane dearest I have nothing but good will for the people of that country, and believe the feeling I have for them is the feeling they have for me. as love begets love. So dos hatred beget hate. or the (devil) I hope you will impress upon your children at all proper times the great necessity of leading honest truthful upright lives. Educate their hands eyes feet and hearts as well as their heads. teach them to labor and that it is honerable to labor. teach them to be temperate in all things to Shun bad company. teach them to love their books and theirwork. teach them that happiness pleasure is the object oflife. and that any pleasure gotton by Stealth by violatingthe moral laws or organic law is Short lived and fletting will Sop the foundation of the most beautiful womanhood and the most noble manhood and will final bring to the gutter to prison to the galows the boy the girl the woman or the man that perchases pleasure happines by wilfully violating the (ethical) or moral or organic or religious (code) or laws teach them to get all the pleasure they can under the laws. teach them to have no Sympathy with crime or any one who wilful-

ly violates the laws. teach them to discern between the true and the false. tech them to be aware of that friendship which would devour them under the pretense of love. woolves offer their protection to lambs to Simple cover them and devour them. teach them to form no friendship with any one whoom they cannot cast from them as Serpent Should they prepose to them any thing contrary to law and order teach them to consider the motives of every one who may advise them. teach them to rely upon themselves their God teach them to love one another to Suffer for one another and if need be, to die for one another teach them that truth honor industry virtue religion are essential to true manhood or womanhood children pride in the achievements of their progenitors. therefore teach them that no people ever lived who were braver truer or more noble than their ancestors that their fathers father and grandfather with his brothers came to this country in the thirties or about 1832 from Tennesee and helped to fight the battle which mad the State of Texas possible. the men wer ever noted on the field for their valor. no less in council for their wisdom. the women for their beauty their virtue. which only eaqualed the Hardin their patriotism and their love for truth justice and (religion) (I mean the religion of jesus christ as revealed in the bible) teach them that to do a mean a low a cowardly act belongs not to a Hardin. and finally teach them Such principles as which will intensify their love for their country for their fellow man that will elevate them enable them and make them peerless citizens as the Hardins was of yore / Kiss each of our Dear children for M (Adieu)
JWH

---

169. Mattie Odom to Jane Hardin

[UNDATED]

Decnbr 14 Mrs Jane Harden

mi Dear sister itak my pen in hanD to writ you afeu lines to let you kow that me anD the baby is wel hoping thes fue lines wil fi— you thees same your leter --me to hanD afue dase goe ——— ithought you ——— to ans it but irecig it takn you along time to mak it out Jane you neve tole me nattn abot lizza little children iwat youe to writ to me about frank anD the children ——— an gong to huse keping Befare long iam comeig after litle Moley to Stay with me thay

going to ——— the mi hous I close to alf talk ithink iwil be SoglaD to get to hose keping one more tim giv mi love to Mrs angle tel here to writ to me Mrs Wright at ——— to me ——— thare to spen chris— wih you & all wil iwl close for time writ soon So god by
Matie ODome
——— frank iwil writ you afue line on Jane leter than mi time iwil writ to you ——— frank is as Swet as ever he can whisl as larg -if he waes gron he ses ——— ses he is comig to you anD the chilre kis all of than forme

---

170. J. W. H. to Jane Hardin

John. W.. Hardin. Mrs Jane. Hardin
Sedan Gonzales County Texas
Huntsville, Texas, Jan the 22 1888

Dear Jane I desire to Salute you this cold Sombre wintry morning and I cannot at this present time think of words more appropriate more beautiful or more exquisite for this purpose than those contained in the plain Simple and familiar and yet Sweet phrase. how do you do my dear, and how are our dear children. Now dearest I desire to greet each of our precious (gems) and respectfully request that you act as my proxy in this delightful Service by embracing each one by the other. by imprinting a Kiss on their crimson dimpled cheeks or upon their ruby lips. do this in your own gentle Sweet impressive way but in my behalf. tell them that this is no Kiss from a Judas who betrayed (christ) or an Arnold who tried attempted to betray american Liberty, but from their loving banished god fearing and god loving trusting manacled, yet Still achieving and still hopful father whose ambition is as hig as heaven. Who has dared to walk according to the light which Shown upon his way. and who Still dares to think to act and to preform his duty as he discerns. regardless of man or its consequences, but allways remembering that he has a Spirit within and that their is a god over head before whoom he must Stand or fall (forever) according to deeds done. Tell them to be gentle honest truthful obedient children Kind hearted and true. these are the characteristic of the Hardins of old. Tell them as they Know the ten commandments to observe and Keep them. plant impress upon their minds and heart the great principles of (virtue) of honor of Chastity and of probity. these are the great and fundimental principles that underlie all manhood or womanhood inculcate Stamp these upon their minds and hearts with the indelible mint of a mothers love, So that no worldly influence or demoniacal power can drag down trample under feet or Seduce, teach them that it is honest and right manly and lady like to do honest labor for honest fair wages. teach them to be patriotic law abiding god loving and god fearing children. teach them to be temperate in their habits and to controll their passions their desires and their appetites. this last is necessary and escential to a happy prosperous life. I know their tempers are high but teach them that their happiness in this life will greatly depend upon how they control their passions desires &C George Washington had a high temper but his Strength his excilence was the more conspicuous because he controlled it. These my dear Jane are Some of the Principles. I would have you teach our children if you wish them to grow up and be honest upright useful citizens. Now Sweet Jane it becomes at last my duty to Speak plainly to you, my Knowledge of wayward froward men and women is that they lead wicked miserable lives and die reched deaths, the gambler dies a blackleg the prostitute dies a whoar the thief fills a thiefs grave the rober the robers grave and the Sepulcher of the murder is the assassins Sepulchre. This is the general rule. oh their ways are hard their days are Sombrous and Sad. their nights Starless and Sleepless. their draught is as bitter as gall. their hope for time and eternity has faded away and they await their terrible doom with trembling. and fear because their end is dreadful and certain and terrific. yes each of his or her Kind beget children who make men and women of corresponding habits of vice and crime: oh dearest one you have a great work before you. a heavy task but you are brave you are true you have fought many battles and won many laurels. but this is the grandest battle that you ever fought you must win and if you do you will not only crown yourself with imperishable honors, but you will give to the world the light of your example which will inspire hope in many a broken hearted bereaved mother. then nerve yourself for this contest by the help of god you can accomplish this arduous task. then dearest meet it bravely ask god to help you and you may reverse this law god grant that you may. ask gods divine assistance to help you Steer your children in the paths of virtue and rectitude and righteousness. and by your love your courage patience and by your persevering industry and your wisdom you may and can reverse this general rule and Snach our loved ones from those who have broken many mothers hearts by leading their daughters and Sons astray and who gladly look forward to the day when they can lead your children into the paths of obliquity: oh my dearest if you can accomplish this it will fill my heart with Joy. and be communsurate with my hightest expectations, and Should I ever be So fortunate as to doff these tags of degredation and Sever these Shackels of peony. and don those regal vestments of liberty. What ever Suffering I may have borne or anguish and pain I may have to bear will be Soothed washed away by your persevering indefatigable love by the Knowledge that I have a wife and children who are pure and chase this will be glory enough for me. to compensate for all I hope and I hope that god will fill you with hope. Now that the conclusion may be in harmony with the prelude, I bid you a sweet good by. (PS Jane a virtuous Brave Woman has friends every where only last week capt MCcullock the assist Sup my chief boss paid you a high complemnt and filled my heart with joy and Sorrow also he Said you must be a noble excellent woman

---

171. J. W. H. to Jane Hardin

John. W. HArdin — Mrs. Jane. Hardin
Sedan. Gonzales County Texas

Jane if this will be any incouragement to you and I believe it will Capt McCulloch told me the other, day that less than Six years more would let me out. there being a law that Shortens the Sentence of a man for meritorious conduct. Now I hope that it will be much less than that but let us with patience wait hope and labor. (Adieu)

Huntsville, Texas, Feb the 5th 1888

Dear Jane a fortnight ago to day I payed my homage of respects to you and I also remited my love to you and our beloved children in a letter the preface of which I deem excellently appropriate for this occasion: if you will modify the remark in refference to the wintry weather. Since that time we have had rain and Snow and a few bright beautiful days. This reminded me of the fact that in this life Some people have a great deal more Sorrow than Joy. it looks as

An old oak tree.
—Photo by Roy and Jo Ann Stamps

thoug their hearts Suc in Sadness even as a Sponge sucks water. but ah Jane this is all wrong for natures god teaches us to be blithe hopeful and brave. then let us be true to our god to our Selves and to mankind by looking into the future in a hopeful maner. experience teaches us that So the earth will with its broad mantle of vernal green charitable cover all Signs of the ravages of a pluvial

Sombrous wintry Season: and the frond Scent period will Soon be here when the trees in the orchard in the forest will deck themselves in robes of vernal green: and Soon the fructescent. period wil be here when the orchards wil hang with lucious fruit. then nature wil have put on her richest garment and She will be adorned in the vernal foliage which nature provides. Let us hope: it may be that these days: are the wintry Stormy days of our life. who knows but what there is a Spring for us in the future that the frondescent period the fructescent period may come. god only knows". let us hope who knows I Say my dearest: but what victory may yet pearch upon our baner and that our Sorrows trials and resignations will be covered up with Songs of joy of triumph even as natures god covers and hides all Sigm of Snow and Storm. Then let us hope that there is brighter better and glorious prospects ahead Jane I am continually preparing for that day when we Shall meet again and by the help of god I hope to be able by that time to have purged myself of all my wicked intemperate ways in order that I may be able to contribute to you and loved ones Jane dearest you have asked me time and agan about my Brothers & Sisters Nanny and gip are at ennis and they write me often. aunt Nan also. and Send me nicknac. in Nans last letter She Spoke So kindly of you She Said She dreampt that She Saw you and that you was as pretty and lovely as ever. I acknowledg your an Molley letters with my thanks. (Love to you and a kiss to the children) I Send, adieu **John W Hardin**

---

172 J. W. H. to Jane Hardin

John. W. HArdin

Mrs. Jane. Hardin.
Sedan. Gonzales County, Texas
Huntsville, Texas, March the 25th 1888

Dear Jane
I received your Kind welcome and cheering letter. which together with the Sweet epistle from my beautiful intelligent and charming and devoted daughter filled my Sould with hope and thrilled my heart with Joy It would be useless for me to day, this god blessed day to undertake to describe or define the mellifuous love that Sweetly Serenely yet Surely flows from me to you, and when I Say this love is Sincere unfeigned. I feel I Know that I but express the real

Sentiments and give Shape in words to the true inspirations of a reciprocal being, who has the memory of my name indelible enshrined in the parlor of her heart. Then dearest truest bravest let me this estival Sultry morning Salute greet you and our lovely children: afar off: not with the whimsical Kiss alone but with the love of an uxorious husband and devoted father: oh what rejoyping tidings those two antiphon's brought me. and to learm that our little boy and two little girls were going to School and that their Teacher was an old acquaintance of mine. and that my noble boy was deporting himself with Such decorum as to gain the esteem the commendations of his Teacher my old friend and I hope his classmates and companions also. Jane please allow me to Speak to the children. Jus a few words:and: I am done: 'Molley John and Jane' you can each of you, gain the lasting esteem the confidence and good will not only of your Teacher your Schoolmates: but every one with whoom you come in contact and communion by being mild and kind. cheerful and forgiving earnest and industrious in your bearing. obedience to your ma your Teachere is included. be truthfull be honest be brave be courteous and you will gain the unfading admiration of all: You will please God fill your mothers & fathers heart with joy and win everlasting plumes honors for yourseves, but never gain the friendship the favors of any one at the cost of truth of honor of chastity look with contempt treat with Scorn Such patronage. remeber that wolves offer their protection to lambs only to cover them and devour them / Dearest far away from you ostracised from loved ones. this being So for more than a decade: hid away in this dungeon of obscurity and poverty and degradation: having borne this for ten years with the contumely of my enemies misguided men and the calumny of defeat and imprisonment attached therunto. Yet this humiliation has not unmaned me thoug time and again it has Stagored me and allinost Straned me: but thank god there has been a resilience: and thank god that the recoil is upward outward and onward: deplumed as I am: yet I have a duty to preform and by the help of god I am going forward to accomplish that that work. what I desire most of all Liberty not except that our dear children receive a thorough moral and religious education. Let truth honor chastity be the base. any education that is not based upon these in this age of progress and improvement is deceptive is a false delusion. Then I Say in the name of their earthly welfare and their eternal happiness

Hardin's mantle of vernal green.
—Photo by Roy and Jo Ann Stamps

let these and common honesty be the fundamental principles of their education but Stamp these So deep in their hearts that no earthly demoniacal can Shake or Strand. Then if education is intended for the edification of mankind: in order that they may Know how to enjoy life to regulate by just laws their actions towards each other Surely the potency and power of those are visible to the naked eye in order to make honest truthful upright worthy citizens out off Sentient mortal creatures. an educated Scoundrel is worse than unsphistiticated rascal. Yes they are educated frauds if they are anything. and all brave honest truthful enlightened men and women Know this. and they have nothing but contempt and pitty for that class of man kind to See a a man or woman who has a flippant tongue ready willing and able to converse in French in German in Spanish in english or with fluency able to converse intelligently upon the customs the tastes the fashions the politics and the religion of foreign countrys. Who wields a trenchant pen with pollish and power and whoose proficiency and general attainments as peculiarly fit them to draw the highest Salery in the counting room on the forum or at the mechanics bench. These are beautiful worthy attainments yet I will add to them the accuteness of Herod the Strength of Sampson the bravery of david the Grace of a chesterfield and I wil

addorne them with locks of hair that would put to Shame those beautiful tresses and curls that hung down upon Absalums Shoulders but unless truth honor chastity and the religion of our blessed Savior underlie these they are naught a failure, Jane dearest I am now Just now becoming interested in this all absorbing importun Subject: but propriety Says I must desist but the Rev Dewit Talmage has Said that years ago that he longed to Speak to the world through the Secular press. his Sermons at that time only having the narrow circulation of the religious papers. but to day he realizes that his Sermons have a wider a more extended circulation than his most Sanguine expectations through the big daylies and weeklies. all he says in answer to prayer. I believe in the efficacy of prayer. How may I not pray with hope to have my facilities enlarged for the comnunication with you and loved ones: oh Sweet Jane I See a new heaven and a new earth and the former thing have passed away then Standing upon the historic past, I welcome the bright hopeful & glorious future Adieu **JWH**
with all its beauties/

---

173. J. W. H. to Jane Hardin

John. W. Hardin Mrs Jane. HArdin. Gonzales County Texas.
Huntsville, Texas, June the 24the 1888 Sedan.
Dear Jane I greet you my beloved, with a Soft Sweet good morning my dear. and through you I desire to Salute and embrace each of our dear precious children. Jane there is an old proverb which Says "let every tub Stand upon its own bottom" in this Short but beautiful Sentence is compress profound Knowledge, and it Seems to me that it contains the very appex of truth of Justice and its wisdom cannot be questioned for it measures to every one Justice according to truth. Solomon has Said "the fear of the lord is the beginning of wisdom" The Statutes of the lord are right. It is not my purpose to pose before you to day in an austentatious maner as a hero or a philosopher or a Scholar, far be it from me, but as in my true form, but Still as a man who in the past has had the fortitude of heart to fight all foes, from whence or from where they came. it was all the same. No name no blame. and thank god, I have had the courage of soul to bear . the consequences of every battle fought by me however

DO NOT INTERLINE.—WRITE ONLY ON RULED LINES.

PUT YOUR NAME HERE. PUT FULL ADDRESS OF YOUR LETTER HERE. Give Post-Office, County and State.

Name John W. Hardin Mrs Jane Hardin Sedan, Gonzales County Texas.

Dear Jane I greet you my beloved with a soft sweet good morning my dear

Huntsville Texas June the 24th 1888

—Courtesy Special Collections, Albert B. Alkek Library,
Southwest Texas State University, San Marcos, Texas

dreadful however deathful the result was that to me and mine up to this present time with that resignation and patience of mind and heart which belongs alone to a man that fears the lord and who believes in the Sublimity the Justice of the Statutes of the lord. and who hopes for no greater blessing than to be blessed with Strength to brave the future with equal courage. I shall not reherse any of the tragical Scenes of the past nor dwell on events of those days which are as consecrate to me as life itself, nor indulge in mentioning names the rembrance of which causes my heart to beat with the vim of that day, and impels my head and heart to grasp and reach out into the future with anticipations hopeful of triumph, the Glory of which I may never realize here, but no human agency can Keep me from the embatled escalading walls in yonders citty. "Where neither moth nor rust doth corrup nor thieves brake through and Steal" Jane you Know I am an old warrior, born of battle and the wisest the bravest counselor I ever had except my father was myself why Shall I desert that man now for a Shadow. my reason Say no my common Sense Says nay and my present and eternal welfare Says never. I like advice but when it pertains to me. I must deside the question at isue. I belong to no man or Set of men I belong to my self and god. for all my acts I am responsible to my Self to my god. his laws are right, It has been Said of me before I reached my majority that I had vanquished E.J. Davis's police from the red river to the rio grand from matamoris to Sabine Pass that I had defeated the diabolical Burero agents and U S Soldiers in many contests and that I had invaded a foreign State and released from prison a relative a dear a true friend whoose custodian was Wild Bill the Notorious the redoutable Bill Heycoc of Abaline of whoom no braver man ever drew breath as to the truth or falsity of these assertions I have nothing to Say, except that I have ever been ready to stand tryal on any or all of these charges when a fair and impartial investigation was vouchsafed. but never willing to place my life my liberty in the hands of a mob even if they wore the eupaulets of the State. "The trust thats given guard. to yourself be just but live how we may yet die we must." I had made preparation for this and was not Sculking from any law or hiding from any man when I Shot to death the would be Assassin on the 26the day of may 1874 Who desired attempted to rob me of 'this", call it what you please. I surrender on the Spot and all I claimed was the protection of the law' I demanded justice according to truth, but when mob force Showed itself I Shook of the chimerical protection of the law by the consent of the agent of the law. because it trameled me and threatened me with destruction. and I want to Say that if I never done a brave act a wise act untill then that act alone was Suficient to crown me with imperishable glory. for all time to come (when understood. the con Profundity of which I thourally comprehended. future event proved the wisdom of the act it was my only alternative between to evils this you Know yourself you witnessed with your own eyes to much to mention now, the Spirit that moved me then moves me now. I Stood out for liberty protected by law even against the agents of the law because they were usurpers Subverters impotency to protect was plain even if they wished anomaly reigned Supreme with perfidy an intrigue Staring me in the face I defied the mob and Said I only will Submit to the majesty of the law not to the enemies of law order and good government who blames me no brave man or woman that Knows the facts I Know you dont, for if nothing else Self Preservatioin common Sense and common Justice ordered it. oh Jane you Know as much about those dreadful horrific Scenes and events as I but how true you kno, you remember When I was brought back to this country by main force not alone by the musel of gun and had I Surrendered at the musel of gun I would have deserved nothing but the opprobium of the brave men and fair women of my native State. freely would I have given up my life to have fired one Shot yet that pleasure was forbiden me. well the fact is I was crush by overwhelming no. infact I never have Surrendered nor do I ever expect to. I still wave my colors and will wait my time to plant them on yonders hill. Truth Jane is the mightest batterring ram that this world ever Saw and when Suported by time by a brave heart by a Strong arm with faith in god it is invincible give it Sway and it can and will demolish any lie it is able to uncover the most gigantic fraud, truth when analized is Selfsupporting a lie when analized is Self destructive. it is the peculiar office of truth to uphold the right, let others fear let tremble and falter in this grand battle of right against might I shal make no ignominious compromise, I need never have come here if I had been So inclined. So, one of my brothers conspiritors Seeking to compromise by offering me his protection, hear what I Said to him, in commanchie, and. with a two hundred mob clamoring for my life. Why did you not protect Jo. I need none of your protection nor your Sympathy, all I ask is that Justice and that the majesty of the law be upheld. then pointing to rangers I Said there is my protection. the protection you offer me is the Kind wolves offer to lambs in order to cover then to then devour them begone you Dastard. Jane of course I will have to Suffer greatly to win this battle but if god be with me what care I for those who oppose me I am playing for a big Stake and hope to be able to transmit to you and my lovely children a name untarnished with a Stain. Truth & right backed by hope love pluck and a strong hand and heart can never loose, love to all a Sweet Adieu **J W H**

---

174. J. W. H. to Jane Hardin

Huntsville, Texas, Oct the 7the 1888

Mrs. Jane. HArdin. Sedan Gonzales County Tex

Dear Jane. my devoted my admirable wife. It is not adulation but adoration that impels me to apostrophize you (ad Supra) or above I desire through you once more to make glad the hearts of our precious children by informing them that I by the grace of god Still live. and Still love them with that undying love that belongeth only to a true a devoted brave but oppressed and exiled father and when I tell you that my deep anxious solicitude for your welfare for their prosperity is unabating, and that my love for you for them is So vast that it is boundless So deep that it is unfathomable of that tenacious quality that neither time vicissitudes nor expatriation can impair let alone Sever, that I but faintly outline the love that mellifluently flows from me to them to you that no vocabulary no Symbols can describe no Sum of words define. but you may be partly enableed to measure the length the breadth the depth of that love that Sweetly purls from me to you to them by that mellifluous love that Streams pure and limped from you to me from them to me. Dearest I send each of you my undevided affections with the conventional Kiss of a devoted father and an uxorious husband This is the prelude proem , Dear Jane I have received two letters from you and molley Since I wrote and that they were gladly, welcomely, received and eagarly persued, you need have no doubts, the Sad contents of the former ones as well as the joyful news of the latter ones will not be dwelt on by me to day. but be assured that each was Scaned close-

Wild Bill Hickok
—Courtesy Kansas State Historical Society

ly, and the gist of each weighed justly. I have no apology to offer for not writing Sooner unless it be found in the weak and futile attempt to excuse my Self on the grounds that my conciousness of my inability to alleviate your unhappy condition knowing as I do that words from a fettered man. though they be words of wisdom full of life Shining like pearl or bristling like the dimonds of truth, So often fall dead even at the feet of loved ones, whoom they are intend to bless. but this is not my excuse for it is not appropriate to you. and I frankly acknowledge the coin that I Should have writen ere now. not only a Sympathetic but a loving and encouraging epistle. for I know that if there is any one in this world calculated to encourage you in your virtuous heroine efforts to rear to educate your children to hold them in the paths of rectitude and righteousness it is ,I, your husband. and this my dearest you are justly entitled to at all times under all circumstances, but to "eer is human to forgive devine" I am very 'h u'm'a'n'e'. but how devine you are: and I know that you will be especially So. in this instance when I tell you god willing I will endeavor to be more prompt if not more courteous in the future. and in order to give you Some tangible evidence of this promise I will commence right now for "hope delayed maketh the heart Sick", (and again procrastination is the thief of time" of whoom ,I have no respect for,. dearest Surely you know that I know Some thing of the ways of men and women. The obstacle that Stand in their path and retard their progress and Surely as I write this I know some thing of the means which if properly applied is able to remove every burden every hindrance that Stands in the way of the prosperity and happiness of mankind though they be mountain high. I can only give you a faint Idea of these to day. but honor truth virtue charity temperance and the religion of the bible are able to demolish level them all. this has been So Since the creation of the universe. and when I tell you that these are the only elements of Strength that mankind can rely upon with an intelligent hope to master to conqur the gigantic and numerous foes and difficulties of this life I but mildly express the true Sentiments of my heart. by proclaiming a great truth. I desire to encourage you to day to plant deep in the minds and hearts of your children truth honor and virtue tell them that I say that these are the foundation of manhood and womanhood. tell them that I Say I know that they are brave and that I want them to Show their bravery their Hardin qualities by telling the truth at all times by being honest in every act by practing Self denial and virtue for if the heavens fall they will find them Selves Safe in the omnipotent arms of our blessed Savior If I had Space I would like to dwell upon the beauty the native tallents of each of our beloved children. and have them view with delight the abundant pleasures which is in Store for them for time and eternity if they will only heed my voice 'my council' Now probably the little beauties will Say well mama is papa fortune teller. and I know that the inquisitive little cherubs worry you with questions about me. Oh Jane for your Sake for my Sake for their own welfare tell them all about me. and if you ever Saw any thing good in me or beautiful or virtuous or bravery in me I Say hold it up to them as their paragon. but on the other hand expose condemn my faults and tell them to be aware of them that they ruined or disfigured me and will do them like wise. Tell John W that if a little boy with a father in the penmitenitiary with dark peepers orban hair ruby cheeks with Spendid physical construction will obey his mama love his Sisters, dare, to Speak the truth be honest in all his dealings be industrious in his habits and wait patiently for the return of his endeavors or labor that he will make a man a good citizen and with education he will be fit to be govenor of the great State of Texas, but if he practice not truth nor honor but lead an idle life he will be a miscreant a Taterdemalion Suned detested by all pitied by Some and it would have been better that he never had been born. Teach your children to love one another to Share each others joys to devide each others sorrows by carrying part of each othrs load this will make their lives bright beautiful and prosperous. god bless you all is my peroration hence I bid you a cordial adieu

(There)

Now you See what kind of fortune telling I believe in and it beets all of the gipsies astrologers Seventh Sons wise women and Soothsayers could tell you from the time of the witch of Endor down to the year of 2000 (Anon)

By in-xxxxxxx
xxx, xxxxxxxxx/
xxxxxxxxxx ,xx
xxxxxx/
cobb—xxxxxxx
xxx, xx/x
xxxxxxxxxx , xxx
xxxxxx/

Jane how sweeat
you look with your
bible and your
Song book in your
hand

I come and
you was Gone

from you
friend

By in xxxxxxxx/
Wanted Dominos

L.M.B M.E.H L.A.S
Hardin R.A.D S.L.S J.C.B
B.J.G.J B C J B C
J B C

xxxxxxxxxx , xx
levi txxxxxxx

J-C xxxxxxxxxx, xxxxx
xxxxxxxxxx, xxxxxxxxxx

Meh xxxxxxxxxx, xxxxxxx
xxxx- xxxxxxxxx
x, xxx!

M. E.. H xxxxxxxxxx, xxxx
xxxxxxxxxx , xxxxxxxxxx/
M. E. Hardin
R A Duderstadt xl
J B C xxxxxxxxxx,xxx/
byins -xxxxxxxxxx , xxxxx

Sept ———
W. O,,E
H

Cobb-xxxxxxxxxx, xxxxxxxxxx
xxxxxx

---

175. Mattie Odom to Jane Hardin

Mr ——— [UNDATED]

Dear cosen irevesn you kind leter afue dase i was So glad to here fron you ——— ihave move to mi self at last am So much beter SaDfid than iwas three miles fron Mr ——— Milon anD mat Stes with me tell ant marg to wrie to me iwoD be so glad to see here tell saley iret to here I Dnt neve gt iy ——— some Jane ihave close ——— line close to me you Sa you cant come Don but you ——— kis the chilDren for me give milve to tomey DavD may teel than to ——— giv mi love to ant lue famley frank sin A kiss to you all nd iwil close for this writ as Soon as you get this fron youer tre cosen

Mrs Matie ODom

this was all the paper ihaD

M o

---

176. J. W. H. and ninety-six convicts to lawmakers of Texas

Huntsville Feb the 1st 1889

To the law makers of Texas assembled at Austin Texas. It is with veneration that we the unfortunate inmates of the Huntsville prison whose names are attached to day address you and forward to that august assembly this our petition for the amendment of the Statute that portion that Section and that article which defines and describes the crimes which the Statute Shall run against or be outlawed after a certain limited time has expired and respectfully pray that the crime of Homicide be added thereunto under certain circumstances and conditions. Namely. when a person charged with the crime of murder for which he has not been tried is confined in the penitentiary for any crime and remains in the Said penitentiary for Seven years who bears his true name at the time of entrance to the penitentiary or makes Known his real name within three months after entrance to the penitentiary that all Such persons Shall receive the benefit of this amendment and that Said person or persons Shall Stand acquited of murder because the State has not used due dilligence to bring the Said person or persons to justice: and when any person or persons charged with murder establishes this fact that he has Served in a penitentiary in the State of Texas for Seven years all the time bearing his own true name and that the charge of murder for which he is held was commited Seven years previous to his liberation from the penitentiary and that he has borne his true name during these Seven years in the penitentiary in the State of Texas the establishment of this fact as before mentioned will be ample proof that the State has Slept upon her own time and that She has not used due dilligence and will warrant justify the release of Said person or persons for this amendment is intended for the relief of all Such person or persons. 1st we believe that the Sages and patriots who established endowed and equiped these penal institutions intended that those only who had defied and violated the laws of Texas Should be incarcerated within the walls of her prisons or penitentiaries. the motive being to deter crime by punishing those who dared to break her Statutes, but as Christ has thrown open the doors of heaven to the Sinner. So did these wise men follow his gracious example thus exhibiting their wisdom by declaring that these penitentiaries these punitive laws are intended to reclaim to reform all those who enter her penitentiaries as well as to punish them. 2nd we believe that they did not intend these institutions to be the abode of the wilful malicious or diabolical murderer or assassin but that they intended Such an one to expiate for his attrocious crime upon the gallows or else capital punishment would not grace the Statutes of the State of Texas because these wise law makers graded murder and defined it in each grade So that when a man comes to these prisons tried by and condemned by the courts of the State of Texas it is Self evident that there is Some palliating evidence for the homicide and therefore reformation is the chief desideratum 3rd we believe it is contrary to the constitution to delay the trial of murder for Seven years when Such trial could be proceeded with Sooner for the constitution guarantees to every one a fair Speedy and impartial trial 4th we believe that reformation is one of the cardinal principles of these penal institutes and that the laws governing them prove this and that reformation is possible in every case. and that reformation Should be placed in the reach of all alike and that any other view is narrow minded and fails to do Justice to all alike as the fathers intended and we believe that the law as it Stands now is an impediment insuperable to refomation in all Such cases. to wit. where a man Still has a charge of murder hanging over him. Therefore we respectfully ask that this law be amended. 5th we believe that the laws of the prisons becomes a parody to any one having a case of murder hanging over him when used to admonish him on entering these walls that if he deports himself decorously is obedient industrious &C that he will gain the diminution of Sentence which the State So generously offers for meritorious conduct we donot believe this law has any potent influence for good upon Such a man when he knows that the agent of the State Stands ready at the expiration of his term to lead him back in irons to the Scenes of former deeds at a time when his health is broken without friends money or witness but with the odium of having been a convict which allmost warrants conviction according to the convict view. This idea Seems to obtain, namely that the agent of the State Says obey the rules and gain good time and at the expiration of your Sentence we will take you out try you for murder and hang you or give you a life Sentence, and we believe that it is a prison disorganizer for it is noted fact that one individual evilly inclined often does a great deal of harm and causes trouble untold by inducing inciting leading to mutiny to insubordination to conspiracy his fellow convicts 5,10,20. and even more. to accomplish their designs they often take life. therefore we beseech you with great deference to amend this law. Then trusting in the Justness of our cause, and confiding in your Superior wisdom your patriotism and your love for reform for Justice for mankind and your God we transmit this our petition hopefully to that august assembly for their deliberation with the fervent wish that this law be amended.

.Names.	Mit. Day.	) J.G. Speers.
John. W. Hardin	) Sam, Feagan	(W,H, Kiser
Bill Templeton	(J,B Gough	) Charles. Miller
Jim, Burket	) A,C Barber	(A,J Binford
A,L George	(H,M, Sharp	) H,L Barker
Bob Rierson	) Tom. Riley	(John. Tumblinsom

eighty more names belongs to this as presented. this is the original

---

177. J. W. H. to Molly E. Hardin

Miss Molly. E. HArdin — Sedan Gonzales County Texas

Huntsville, Texas, May the 5th 1889

Miss Molly. E. Hardin

I have again joyfully received, a cordial a Sweet and an interesting missive from you 'my amiable child' be assured that the welcome paraclete was royally received and filled my heart with exultant pride and triumpant joy if for no other reason because I could plainly See in it and easily trace in it. the filial love respect and child like reverence that Silently deftly but mellifluently flows in perennial Stream from a worthy affectionate daughter to a responding loving and reciprocal: but oppressed anathematized and ostracized: but not hopeless neither degenerate father: who will continue to proclaim—with the psalmist the righteousness of the ways. of the lord the justness of his decisions: even if this expatriation Shal go on during my time: and this mephitic tortious lash wielded by an honest but ignorant agency, the inception of which was prompted by blasphemous usurping agents of the law in conjunction with a ribald mob who to accomplish their diabolical designs—halted not at murder or assassination and came at the dead hours of midnight: Subornation bribery and intimidation were free use. I say if this Shall continue untill the last drop of blood is freed from my veins Still I will promulge that the ways the judgments of the lord god allmighty are holy just and true: I hasten with alacrity to avail my Self of this Splendid opportunity to comply with your modest request for an autograph verse: and with my best wishes for your peace happiness and prosperity I bid you a cordial and a fatherly adieu.

John. Wesley. Hardin.

(PS) Now children if there is a word here that you donot know the meaning of go to your dictionary allways use Webster I again Send you a Fathers love (cut these verse out to Suit your selves JWH

Molly. "Keep thy passions down how ever dear: thou Swaying pendulum betwixt a Smile and a tear"

J. W. HArdin.

John W 'John W Hardin Jr'

"The trust thats given guard: to yourself be just: for live how we may yet die we must"

J. W. Hardin

Sweet little Jane -

"Soar not to high to fall: but Stoop to rise: we masters grow of all we despise":

John W. HArdin

Dear jame I have Selected Several poetical verses from my thesarus: their Sentiments are mine. I hope that each of my dear children will adopt them as theirs and learn each verse by heart and as an earnest of this I ask each to inform of this fact at their earliest opportunity asuring you of my unalloyed unwaining love and wishing for you prosperity in the fullest Sense I close by Sending each of our loving children a Kiss and ask you to act as proxy in my behalf

JWH

"To be is far better than not to be though all of ones life may Seem a tragedy" John. W. HArdin

"Live well how long or Short permit to heaven: he that forgives most is most forgiven" J. W. HArdin

178. J. W. H. to Miss Jane M. Hardin

John. W. HArdin Miss.Jane. M. Hardin
Sedan Gonzales County Texas
Huntsville, Texas, July the 14 the 1889

Jane Sweet child and dear daughter Papa received your brief but interesting yes amusing letter,with parental pride and gratification : be assured that it was welcomely received and eagarly perused by your father.Whose Solicitude for your present and future welfare and happiness together with that of your lovely mother your beautiful Sister and your noble brother is my gratest care: and which is only equaled by your fathers love and affection for each of you : and which like the mighty mississippi mellifluently flows in perennial Stream to your mama first. to you last but not least : beloved daughter I cannot let this opportunity pass to commend the Spirit which prompted you to write Such a Sweet letter besides the excellent Style and the 'chirography' 'or' beautiful hand, as exhibeted in you gladinng missive which would of done cred to one of more years than yourself : Therefore your father joyfully embraces this occasion to thank you and he congratulates you on your Splendid Success. as a letter writees. and bids you write often : Jane I happily learn from personal acquaintances of yours that you have a modest a Sweet disposition that you are real Smart and that these are united to a Symmetrical form and a beautiful face Set by pearly teeth and adorned by two bright lovely eyes : and this partly accounts for the pretty consoling letter I received from one whose head and heart are in perfect harmony with each and every other membrane of her whole being : be kind enough dear daughter to accept a fathers hightest commendation and love for your almost unparalleled effort to make light his load.which not only bears down upon him heavy but oppresses you and partly at least enslaves your mother your brother your Sister and which: mankind' at least in your own neighborhood must feel the blighting effects of this mephitic thralldom for "ages ontop of ages" though these Shackles and these bonds which bind me are unjust cruel and inhuman : contrary to the letter and Spirit of our noble instiutions

2nd

yet riveted on by usurpation by Subornation by mob law by anarchy dressed in the royal robes of the of constitution of the laws of the United States : of which the State of Texas is one : yes the grandest one of all for She is first in morals religion education politics,and She is forging to the front in almost every branch of moral and material improvement.and the chivaldry and gallantry of her men are only to be compared to the comeliness and virtue of her women : there are none truer braver nobler than Texians Now my dear child when the whole truth is known. When in after years the facts are all brought out which culminated in the death of a would be assassin who tried to hide himself behind the law to kill to murder your father for filthy lucre for glory : but who in turn was himself Shot to death by your father: and for this act of Self defense your father was forced to become an unwilling refugee not from justice but injustice in the Shape of mob law in its most virulent type: all that he demanded or desired was a fair Speedy and impartial trial before the courts of the land, this was denied and those friends of mine that dared to So proclaim were insulted Silenced and inhumanly treated by a midnight by a ribald mob who drug my brother and counselor and four own cousins away from comfortables homes and tore them from the embrace of loving families at the Silent hour of midnight against the earnest protest of father to let the law take its course: the cries of mother dont wrong dont hurt my boy : the plaintive Sobs of a wife to Spare her husband for justice Sake: but amid the frantic Screams of Sisters and loved ones they were led by a halter barefooted through the Streets of commanchie to a temporary Scaffold in the Shape of an oak tree and there by the light of the moon Swung into eternity: but your father not knowing that this had taken place was still waiting hoping trusting that the hour would Soon arrive when he could have a fair trial by due process: of law: but when this Sad news of the damnable taking off : of Joe.G.HArdin and four own cousins was conveyed to me I was overpowered for a time by amazement and grief inexplicable. which no vocabulary can express no tongue describe : what resourses of justice was left me when I knew that the agents of the law were a party (particeps criminis) to one of the most monstrous crimes ever planed and maliciously perpetrated on a virtuous people or law abiding people

3nd

The attrocity of which excelled that of the commanche indian with his bloody tommyhawk in his palmyest days: the answer is easy: there was none: for the very power that I had looked to.(the agents

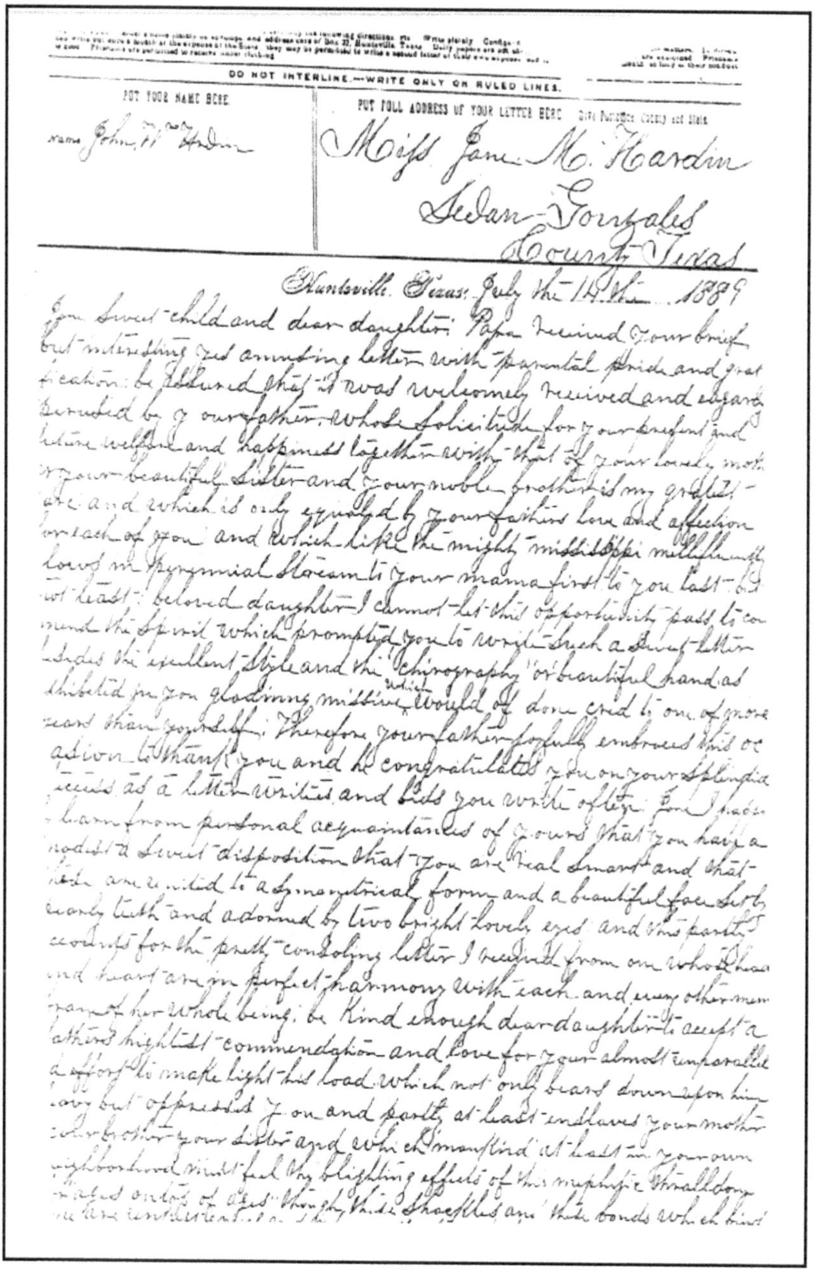
DO NOT INTERLINE.—WRITE ONLY ON RULED LINES.

PUT YOUR NAME HERE. name John W. Hardin

PUT FULL ADDRESS OF YOUR LETTER HERE City, Postoffice, County and State.

Miss Jane M. Hardin
Sedan Gonzales
County Texas

Huntsville. Texas: July the 14th 1889

[Y]ou sweet child and dear daughter: Papa received your brief
but interesting and amusing letter with parental pride and grat
ification: be assured that it was welcomely received and regard
[app]reciated by your father. whose solicitude for your present and
[f]uture welfare and happiness together with that of your lovely moth
[o]r your beautiful sister and your noble brother is my greatest
[c]are and which is only equaled by your fathers love and affection
[f]or each of you and which like the mighty mississippi mellifluently
[f]lows in perennial stream to your mama first to you last but
[n]ot least: beloved daughter I cannot let this opportunity pass to com
[m]end the spirit which prompted you to write such a sweet letter
[be]sides the excellent style and the "chirography" or beautiful hand as
[ex]hibited in yo[ur] gladdening missive which would of done cred[it] to one of more
[y]ears than yourself: Therefore your father joyfully embraces this oc
[c]asion to thank you and he congratulates you on your splendid
[su]ccess as a letter writer and bids you write often. For I hav[e]
[l]earn from personal acquaintances of yours that you have a
[m]odest & sweet disposition that you are real smart and that
[the]se are united to a symmetrical form and a beautiful face set by
[p]early teeth and adorned by two bright lovely eyes and this partly
[a]ccounts for the pretty consoling letter I received from one whose hea[d]
[a]nd heart are in perfect harmony with each and every other mem
[be]r of her whole being: be kind enough dear daughter to accept a
[f]athers highest commendation and love for your almost unparallel
[e]d effort to make light his load which not only bears down upon him
[n]ow but oppresses you and partly at least enslaves your mother
[y]our brother your sister and which mankind at least in your own
[ne]ighborhood must feel the blighting effects of this mephitic thralldom
[...]ages on top of ages through these shackles and these bonds which bind
[...] are unthinkable [illegible]

[illegible] the following directions, viz: Write plainly. Confine yourself strictly to family and business matters. [illegible] care of Box 32, Huntsville, Texas. Daily papers are not admitted. All letters and papers are examined. Prisoners [illegible] they may be permitted to write a second letter at their own expense and to see friends once a month, so long as their conduct [illegible] Prisoners are permitted to receive under clothing.

DO NOT INTERLINE.—WRITE ONLY ON RULED LINES.

2nd PUT ~~YOUR NAME HERE~~ PUT—FULL ~~ADDRESS OF YOUR~~ LETTER HERE. Give Postoffice, County and State.

Name Yet riveted on by usurpation by subornation by mob law
by anarchy dressed in the royal robes of the of the (constitution) laws of the united
States: of which the State of Texas is one yes the grandest one of
all for she is first in morals religion education politics and
she is forging to the Huntsville, Texas, front in almost 188
every branch of moral and material improvement and the
chivalry and gallantry of her men are only to be compared to the come
liness and virtue of her women. There are none truer braver nobler than
Texians: Now my dear child when the whole truth is known when in
after years the facts are all brought out which culminated in the death
of a would be assassin who tried to hide himself behind the law to the
murder your father for filthy lucre for glory: but who in turn was him
self shot to death by your father and for this act of self defense your
father was forced to become an unwilling refugee not from justice but inju
stice in the shape of mob law in its most virulent type; all that he demand
ed or desired was a fair speedy and impartial trial before the courts of the
land this was denied and those friends of mine that dared to so proclaim
were insulted silenced and inhumanly treated by a midnight by a ribald mob
who drug my brother and counselor and four own cousins away from
comfortables homes and tore them from the embrace of loving fam
ilies at the silent hour of midnight against the earnest protests of
fathers to let the law take its course the cries of mothers; dont dont
dont hurt my boy; the plaintive sobs of a wife to spare her husband
for justice sake; but amid the frantic screams of sisters and
loved ones they were led by a halter barefooted through the streets of
comm..anchie to a temporary scaffold in the shape of an oak
tree and there by the light of the moon swung into eternity:- but your
father not knowing that this had taken place was still waiting hoping hop
ing that the hour would soon arrive when he could have a fair trial by due
process of law: but when this sad news of the dammable taking off of Jo. G. Hardin
and four own cousins was conveyed to me I was overpowered for a time by
amazement and grief inexplicable which no vocabulary can express no
tongue describe; what resources of justice was left me when I knew the
the agents of the law were a part (particeps criminis) to one of the most monst
rous cold blooded and maliciously perpetrated on a virtuous people or law abiding [illegible]

...ing letters [illegible] with prisoners must observe carefully the following directions, viz.: Write plainly. Confine yourself strictly to family [illegible] ... and address care of Box 32, Huntsville, Texas. Daily papers are not admitted. All letters and papers are [illegible] ... Prisoners are permitted to receive under clothing. [illegible]

DO NOT INTERLINE.—WRITE ONLY ON RULED LINES.

3rd. PUT YOUR NAME HERE. PUT FULL ADDRESS OF YOUR LETTER HERE. Give Postoffice, County and State.

name The atrocity of which excelled that of the commanche indian with
his bloody tomahawk in his palmyest days: the answer is easy the
was none: for the very power that I had looked to: the agents of the State the agen
cions of the law to protect my life from mob law and to guarantee me a fair
trial had become debauched Huntsville. Texas: and were now after
seeking and threatening my destruction I reluctantly took the only course a
sensible brave man could take and in this I was prompted by the
highest law human or devine the law of self preservation and a man
or woman that fails to obey the mandates of this supreme law is a pol
troon and not worthy to be called an american; and now to save my life
I sought peace and happiness in a foreign State under a nondeplume be
cause mob law disguised in the State of my nativity which had slain my relati
and friends. and was now aiming its venomous blows at my heart: and
when at last after being hounded by the sleuth hounds of injustice being forced
from town to town, city to city: but like the noble elastic stag chased by the
hounds and the hunters from swamp to swamp from hill to valley is at las
brought to bay by the dogs and shot by the hunters. so was I at last brought to
bay and arrested in pensacola: but not until I had exhausted every bit of
the means within my power to free myself and be it said to the discredit
of the officers and to the disgrace of the States interested that they
secured me without warrant or due process of law: and that they
have again perpitrated another cold blooded murder to accomplish their
unlawful purpose no one has ever denied: who had not even a mom
ents warning to prepare for eternity: I believe that there is an intelli
gent righteous conscience in mankind that will condemn the practice that
will detest men that will polute their office and murder innocent parties
without legal process. and use their office and power for a shield
to hide their diabolicism: Dear child whenever the truth is all told dont
dread the result for the common sense and common intelligence of
mankind will vindicate your father: and there will be no stigma
attached to my name for the blood which I have spilt is of that kind whic
can never stain: and the truth will unveil one of the most monstrous
conspiracies. which was wickedly carried out by a wily devilish
people against a brave upright people: I donot fear but in time to
come the treatment I have received will be condemned by all God lov
ing lawabiding men and women.

DO NOT INTERLINE.—WRITE ONLY ON RULED LINES.

4th

~~PUT YOUR NAME HERE~~ ~~PUT FULL ADDRESS OF YOUR LETTER HERE—GIVE NUMBER, COUNTY AND STATE~~

name for the means and manner of my arrest trial and con
viction are contrary to every law of justice human and divine
and are repugnant alike to the highest sentiments of the human
mind and heart: <u>ous. oh: this unjust imprisonment & reputa</u>
tion; amid these Huntsville. Texas; unfurious sorrow JW Hardin
I am happy to say that I am not dismayed; nor hacked; god being
on my side who can prevail against me; for we are taught
not to fear man who can only destroy the body but to fear
god who not only can destroy the body but the soul also;
Daughter I hope to rise from this lethean loom with higher
nobler truer aims and affections than when this lethal life
began; we do not allways get justice here on this earth but
daughter let us remember that we have an advocate christ
Jesus the son of god who when on earth was denied justice
was spit upon was scourged was hooted by the scurrilous
mob that crucified him but he arose again the third day that
was nearly 1900 years ago. but he sitteth to day as of yore
at the right hand of god to make intercessions for us
and you can rest assured that I have put my case in the great
advocate; be a good girl tell the truth obey mama love your
brother and sister and what you learn to do. learn it well and
remember that your books and teachers are but helps. the
work is yours. oh: sweet child let every day be a school
day with you be brave and help papa and mama your brother
and sister fight this battle of right against might. god bless
you sweet child is my prayer. go embrace your mama your
sister your brother in your own sweet way in remembrance
of me I was sorry to learn of your grandpas death
and send my condolence to bereaved ones: but dear child dont
learn to grieve for anything; for god will wipe away all the
tears from their eyes and their shall be no more death neither
sorrow nor crying neither shal their be any more pain;
for the former things have passed away; Hoping that
this will find you prosperous and Happy I bid you a fatherly adieu
John W Hardin

of the State)(the executors of the law)protect my life from mob law and to guarante me a fair trial. had become debaunched and were now openly Seeking and threatning my destruction I reluctantly took the only course a Sensible brave man could take. and in this I was prompted by the hightest law human or devine the law of Self preservation and a man or woman that fails to obey the mandates of this Supreme law is a poltroon and not worthy to be called an american:and now to Save my life I Sought peace and happiness in a foreign State under a (non deplume) because mob law reigned in the State of my nativity. Which had Slew my relatives and friends. and was now aiming its venomous blows at my heart. and when at last after being hounded by the Sluth hounds of iniquity. being forced from town to town,city to city: but like the noble elastic Stag chased by the hounds and the hunters from Swamp to Swamp from hill to valley: is at last brought to bay by the dogs and Shot by the hunters:So was I at last brought to bay and arrested in pensacola but not until I had exhausted every bit of the means within my power to free myself.and be it Said to the discredit of the officers and to the disgrace of the States interested that they Secured me without warrant or due process of law: and thathat they here again perpitrated another cold bloodied murder to accomplish their unlawful purpose no one has ever demed : Who had not even a moments warning to prepare for eternity: I believe that there is an intelligent righteous concience in mankind that will condem the practice.that will detest men that will polute their office.and murder innocent parties without legal process. and use their office and power for a Shield to hide their diabolicism:. Dear child whenever the truth is all told donot dread the result for the common Sense and common intelligence of mankind wil vindicate your father:(and there will be no Stigma attached to my name for the blood which I have Spilt is of that kind which can never Stain): and the truth will unvail one of the most monstrous conspiracies. which was wickedly carried out by a willy devilish people against a brave upright people : I donot fear but in time to come the treatment I have received will be condemned by all god loving godfearing and law abiding men and women

4th

for the means and maner of my arrest trial and conviction are contrary to every law of justice human and devine.and are repugnant alike to the hightest Sentiments of the human mind and heart: but:

Ah: this unjust immurment or expatriation: amid these lethiferous Surrounding I am happy to Say that I am not dismayed : nor hacked : god being on my Side who can prevail against me : for "we are taught not to fear man who can only destroy the body. but to fear god who not only can destroy the body. but the Soul also": Daughter I hope to rise from this lethean toom with higher nobler truer aims and affections than when this lethal life began We do not allways get justice here on this earth but daughter let us remember that we have an advocate Christ Jesus the Son of god who when on earth was denied justice was Spit upon was Scourged was hotted by the Scurrilous mob that crucified him : but he arose again the third day, that was nearly 1900 years ago . but he Still Sitith to day as of yore at the right hand of god to make intercessions for us and you can rest assured that I have put my case in the great advocates hands.be a good girl tell the truth obey mama love your brother and Sister and what you learn to do, learn it well and remember that your books and teachers are but helps. the work is yours. 'Oh: Sweet child let every day be a School day with you. be brave : and help papa and mama your brother and Sister fight this battle of right against might. god bless you Sweet child is my prayer . go embrace your mama your Sister your brother in your own Sweet way in remembrance of me. I was Sorry to learn of your grandpas death and Send my condolence to bereaved ones :but. dear child dont learn to grieve for anything :"for god wil wipe away all the tears from their eyes and their Shall be no more death neither Sorrow. nor crying. neither Shal their be any more pain : for the former things have passed away":Hoping that this will find you prosperous and Happy I bid you a fatherly adieu

John. W.HArdin

---

179. J. W. H. to John W. Hardin Jr.

John. W. HArdin
Sedan Gonzales County
Texas.

Mr John. W. Hardin

Huntsville, Texas, Oct the 20ith 1889

Noble boy brave and beloved Son. I have with delight just received your engrossed letter of the 4th ultimo replete with interesting and

joyful news, and in the outset before greeting your mama and your lovely Sisters throug you. I desire to thank you for reviving my Slumbering but cherished hopes, for thrilling my Soul with delight bordering on the ecstatic. for giving me to understand by your simple modest yet manly epistle that you your mother and two Sisters are quietly yet bravely fighting this battle of life on as high a plane as possible: that you were leading the little band Successfully against the great embattled walls of indolence of poverty. of dissipation of bereavements of vice and crime:
and that having conquered these that you and your little army were quietly Sweetly peaceably marching on down the road of life with higher nobler puer hopes and aims: the natural and legitimate result of honest thrift in every contest with these: Oh my boy if there is anything that makes your papa's heart glad that makes me Strong when I am fatigued with toils and turmoils of my daily labor, that makes me brave in perilous times that makes me kind when others are cross, and that makes me wish to live on when the world on me frowns and that makes me have faith in god and my cause and my ability and will to triumph in the end: It is just such glad tidings as your most excellent letter has imparted to me: and now while in this joyful mood it becomes me to greet your dearly beloved mother with an uxorious Kiss, and to Salute your comely and amiable Sisters with a parental buss: do this in your own filial and brotherly way. Son I would to god that it was in my power to Send you and your lovely Sister to School and to be able to provide for the wants and necessities of each of you as well as your estimable mother. of all duties if it were possible this would be the most delectable, but Son this is out of the question at this present time, but let us hope that the future will render this more practicable: knowledge my boy, education based upon the truth upon the bible is what each of you need now and will need in the future more than all else. now if either of you obtain this you must be brave honest and true. be true to yourselves be true to your god and you will be true to everybody else: you poverty will not permit you to attend school enough to receive a pollished education therefore you must acquire it in some way for you eeach of you must have it for it is necessary to your peace and happiness for time and for eternity. and this and to gloryfy god is or ought to be the aim of all mankind: Now papa has a plan a feasible one and I wish to know which one of you dear chil-

dren will follow it. It Seems to me I hear each of you say papa I will: What is it: Well be patient until I can tell you. well in the first place I wish you to know that your books and teachers are but helps the work is yours any how, and the proper way and most practical way is to let every day be a School day. get some Idea learn Something every day. be inquisitive be modest, be gentle, but be brave, brave enough to Seek to ask information upon any Subject that you donot thoroughly understand Seek honest profitable employment with honorable people. be careful how you promise. and if the promise be lawful fulfill it therefore be careful how you promise make none but legitimate promises. have you a book and every spare moment study your book. You will profit by this in many ways. you will gain Knowledge the most valuable of all wealth and you will acquire the reputation of being studious. donot study your book for pass time. for that will be time throwed away, but study it earnestly and for the purpose spoken of. children each of you if you will be brave and try can acquire in this way erudition or a practical education which will enable you to make better the lives of others as well as your own but bear in mind that an education however polished not based upon the bible is a delusion, is false, is a galvanized tinsel the robes of which the Son of perdition offers to dress mankind in, in order to distroy his Soul; let the ten commandments be the compass to guide you in every Storm: let integrity truthfulness and Virtue capture your minds Soul and body. be rich in good works, love one that is each other, and Share each others prosperity, but in adversity cling to one an other with a tenacious adherence that knows no braking. by alleviating each others burdens, by bearing part your Self you make it light on all. when one triumphs let all Share the Spoils equally, and when one staggers under a heavy weight let each one see which can be the first to give assistance and Stay the fall and lighten the load until all can put your Shoulders under it and then at the word all give one mighty harmonious push and march on triumphantly to a glorious mart, where peace concord and prosperity are the legal tender or medium of exchange. Now I donot want you to over work your Selves, nor to carry to heavy loads you are young dont Strain your nerves and muscles, you will need them by and by. dont try to carry a big load Just Simply to Show what you can do. dont imperil your life or health for money for the destruction of the one and the undermining of the other would be an unprofitable investment for you for

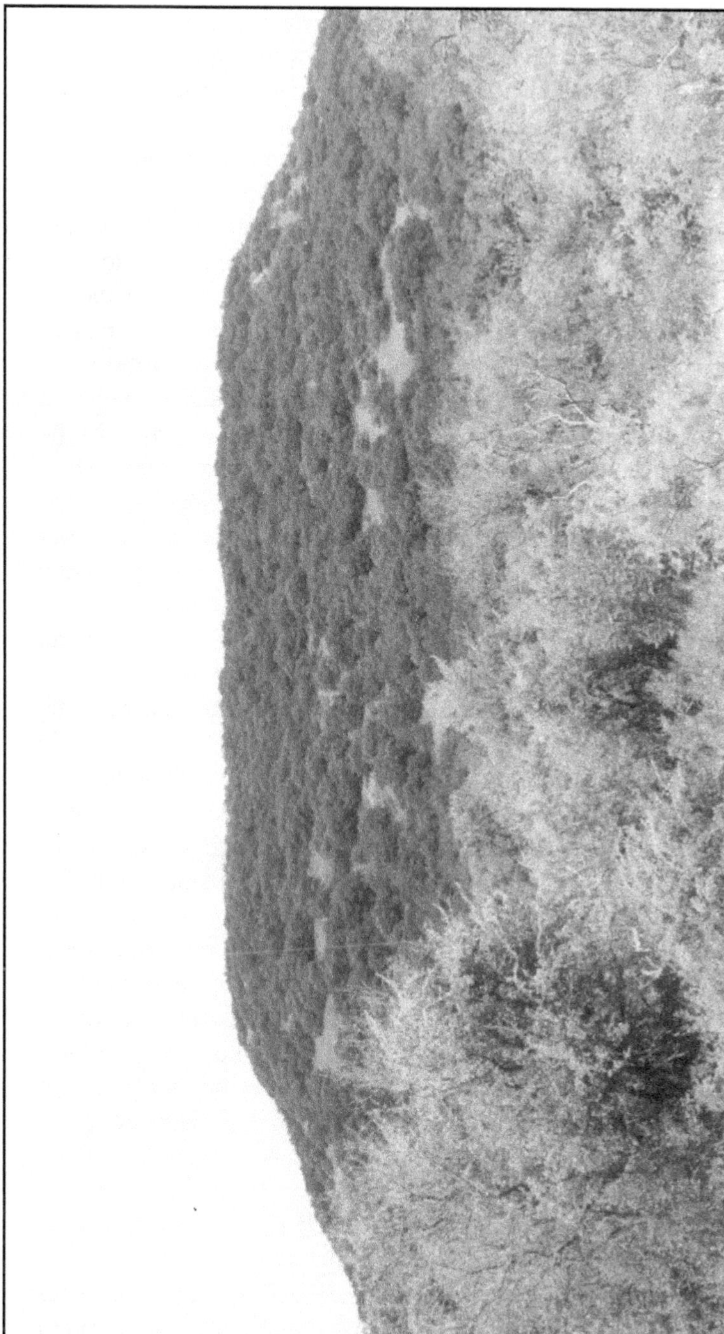

John Wesley Hardin hid out at Round Mountain after Webb was killed.
—Photo by Roy and Jo Ann Stamps

any amount of money "what will it profit a man if he gain the whole world and loose his own Soul or what will a man give in exchange for his soul. The apostle tells us that "the love of money is the root of all evil. then be careful how and from whoom you obtain wealth. I say make all you cam but make it by econemy and honest thrift: but take care of your health "be temperate in all things" dont let your passions control you but control them, this is a prerequisite to manhood or womanhood. and if you Should ever have to resist force or tyranny do it bravely manfully, take a lawful remedy remembering that Self preservation is the first law of nature and the man or woman that does not respect this divine law is not worthy to be called a Texian. who is by nature by education and by rights as brave as the bravest, as high as the hightest and as grand as the grandest. I say if any man assail your rights your life or your character the laws of your country and the laws of god give you a perfect right to arrest to stop him and if need be to preserve these your dearest posessions you have a perfect right to kill. Though I hope you will never have to exercise this inalienable right, but a man that will not fight for his rights and if need be bleed kill and die for them, will never have any possessions worthy of american yeomanry. Son I say encourage your mother = and Sisters by honest means by filial and brotherly counsel to live virtuous lives. So long as they do this be ready to Shed your blood and if need be die in their defence. I hope I belive that they have traveled in the path of rectitude of righteousness So long that there is not devils enough in earth or hell to delude them or Seduce them from their virtuous path: but Son Should any lecherous treacherous Scoundrel no matter what garb he wears or what insignia he boast even it be the ministerial robe, assault the character and try to debaunch the mind and hearts of either of your Sisters or mother, I say Son dont make any threats but just quietly get your gun a double barrel let it be a good gun have no other kind, and go a gunning for the enemy of mankind, and when you find him just deliberately Shoot him down like you would a mad dog or a wild beast. then go and Surrender to the first Sheriff you meet. You need not be afraid of the virdict of a Texas jury in such a case and if you dont come out all right just lay the blame on me. I can Stand it, but god forbid Son that you Should ever be forced to take that which you can not give:but Son if it ever becomes necessary to Shield your body from the assassins blow dont wait to be Struc down, to late then but stay the poisonous dagger in uplifted hand with one mighty death blow

3rd Ah my Son it is a Serious affair to kill a man. but to every man it is more Serious to be killed. live peacable with all men if possible on honorable terms. but the time often comes in every mans life when it is necessary to his peace and hapiness for him to conquer an honorable peac. for peac with all of its blessings looses its charms to an honorable man when purchased by poltroonery. be a gentleman be brave just dare to do right the main thing is to find out what is right and then dare to do it. this is to be a man. I want to lay down a rule for you which if you will only follow will be of great advantage to you through life. in your communion contact and fellowship with man. let it be on your part cordial friendly honest and manly just what it ought to be. and whenever this is not reciprocated brake of your relations at once. have nothing to do with any one that will not deal fair and Square with you, but you Son deal fair and Square with every body let children sincerity be embossed in your minds and hearts let its glittering Sheen adorne your every day lives: donot be afraid to do right even if it cost you Self denial it will only make you brave and Strong and happy in the end. dont be deceived by any body question every thing and every body especially until you find out the truth, and when any one no matter who it is gives you advice consider his motive, there is always a good or bad motive and the motive may be for your ruin and for his agandisement. look out for wolves dressed in Sheeps clothing, look out for devils robed in the garb of angels. (This is Scriptural warning) for when a thief wishes to rob you he dons himself in an honest mans mask: therefore in order to be Secure we must not only watch but pray. "lest we enter into temptation" be temperate" be honest in all things. Dont use tobacco. I thank god and am proud to say that I was taught from my infancy to abstain from its use in any of its many forms and now after many years of personal experience I can truthfully say that I donot believe its use is beneficial to health

4th

or necessary to manhood or womanhood or conducive to beauty or wealth whether chewed Smoked diped or Snuffed especially is this So if the person be of sound mind and body. probably its use might be beneficial to one with a deranged appetite or abnormal constitution: but use it as you may I pronounce it a loathsome noisome uncomely and unprofitable habit, and I hope the day will come when all without regard to sex will abandon the filthy mephitic practice, that they will abandon the use of narcotics and alchoholic Spirits as a beverage and that there eyes may be opened to the truth and their Souls realize that health Strength and beauty do not Spring from these but that to be robust pretty or Sweet one must lend an humble acquiescence to gods divine laws. which are irrevocable and for the violation of which one cannot escape the just penalty. then if you wish to be a man or if you wish to be a woman dont use tobcco. for it is a cachexy without excuse and without compensation. Now Son I wish to Speak to your ma then I am done for this time. Jane in time past I have been tempered by your Smiles and advice as well as comforted by your love which I believe you know was reciprocated by me I have in years gone by planed the destruction of my inveterate and unrelenting enemies but on beholding your face before the contemplated battle I have Set at naught my Scheme. by postponing the battle, for what reason because I believed that I could Serve yous best by procrastination in Such affairs as Spoken of. Since my confinement your wifely letters in the past have been a Solace to me and your ——— love the Sincerity of which I have never ——— has been to me an antalgic an analeptic also; but these of late has almost ceased: Jane is the Oft expressed love of the past dead or doth it Sleep, if the former I will do nothing to revive it, but will bury it with other Idols of the past, and will erect over it with tears the grandest monument of them all. but if it Sleepeth I will be ready to embrace and caress it whien it awakes fron its now Slumbering Siesta even if my future life be confined to this lethiferous tomb: but let us hope that it will 'not be thus' the apostle James tells us that faith without works is dead being alone. Therefore I believe that a love that never exhibits its Self is dead being alone. Jane what are friends for but to cheer to encourage one an other especially in disaster or bereavements and when they fail to do this they pervert their high office and Should be disclaimed or discarded. "Now may the god of hope fill you with all joy and peace in believing that you may abound in hope through the power of the holy ghost. well Son having Spoken to your ma and having written more fully than I intended the application of which I will leave for you your Sisters and your ma but I cannot close this letter without asking you to read this letter over and over again until

you Thoroughly understand What I have Said: I want you to learn to think for yourself. then wishing for each of you (I mean your ma your Sisters and you)rself peac and prosperity
I bid you each an affectionate adieu
your father **John. W. HArdin**
(P S) Molly and Jane papa hopes Soon to write to each of you, a Sweet good by JWH.

---

180. J. W. H. to Miss Jane C. Hardin

John. W. HArdin

Miss. Jane. C. Hardin.
Sedan Gonzales County Texas
Huntsville, Texas, Dec the 8 1889

My dear and amiable daughter. I received your loving and child like letter Some time ago. which was replete with joyful news. I now embrace with pleasure this opportunity to acknowledge its acceptance. Dear child you need not doubt that every word was read with care and contents examined with parental Solicitude: to learn that my children are thrifty godloving and godfearing robust able and willing to earn an honest dollar by honest labor is not one of my least enjoyments. and it Seems to me that it is appropriate that I commend with my praise yours your Sisters and your brothers virtuous valorous and Succesful efforts Spoken of in your modest but Sweet letter. this I assure you I do with my hightest approbation. precious daughter if this is one thing more than an other that I pride myself in it is the love and faithful devotion exhibited by your mother to me during So many years of trials temptations and Sorrows, and her virtuous triumphant endeavors to lead her children in the paths of rectitude and righteousness. and to Know that the virtues She possess' have been transmited to my children in an eminent degree are result worthy of my pride worthy of my commendation and worthy of my everlasting gratitude. Pride my dear child is the foundation of character in man or woman, and when you find a man or woman boy or girl with little or no Self pride you find a being with little or no character. Now I like to See a boy or girl pride in their native country county or town because of the vastness of its territory of its high mountains or beautiful hills its purling rivers its Splendid manufactories its glorious institutions its Salubrious climate and its fertile Soil. but I like especially to See either of them pride in their ancestral name. because of the probity bravery patriotism and general benevolence of the men. and of the virtue beauty patience charity and chastity of the women. for these are Some of the qualities that underlie all manhood or womanhood and are of true value worthy of the pride of the bravst and best but beware there is a false pride: that is puffed up: that boasteth that is a forgery: that would falsely appear to be of Some importance of Some value. when in fact there is no value no importance but a fraud: The peacock will jump upon the fence or Some high dome pearch himself on and clamerously announce: here I am: not seeming to be aware that there are other fowls around him better and far more useful than himself. this is called vanity in the bird: So the boy or girl that will ostentatiously boast of their real or affected possessions exhibit a false pride that finds a counterpart in the beautiful but vain bird: I hope that you will be able to draw the destinction between the pride that is false and the one that is true. the former is like the Sand on the beach Shifted by every wave. like the billows of the ocean that go up then come down. vacillating as the vane that is changed by every Storm, while the latter is the Similitude of the everlasting hills. like yonders mighty oak that defies every Storm around which all the virtues bud Spring and cling to bless mankind but cut down this Sturdy oak and all of its beneficent branches will perish one by one until nothing but the trunk remains. So cut down the pride in man or woman and Naught remains. Now christmas will Soon be here and papa hopes that you your Sister brother and mother will enjoy the festivities of that day and papa dont care if you go to parties or respctable balls but rather desires that you your Sister and brother go. for I believe it is healthful and elevating to the young to enjoy themselves with each other in the dance provided they use good judgement as to time and place and not Keep to late hours. and the Social influence of a well regulated ball room cannot but have a beneficial influence affect on the minds and hearts of the young people that go their for innocent Sport, (this consent is of course allways Subject to mamas approval) thamk Aunt Margret for her Kind and esteemed letter tell her that my love and friendship for her has not been dimed by time or adversity and that I will allways be glad to receive a line from her and to learn of her prosperity give my love to Nannie Sallie Molly and the Cob boys and when you See Mrs

Salley Burnet give her my unfeigned love and tell her that I hope that She may live to enjoy many years of prosperity: as to your mama your Sister and brother I send them a Kiss through you with love unfeigned. tell mama to give my love and regards to whoever She chooses hoping to hear from you often I am affectionately your father

John W. HArdin

(PS) Probably the very presence of this letter will cause tears, but if these are drounded by Smiles that the Sentiments of this letter produce all is well. if you daughter obtain one Idea from this I am a thousand times paid. A tear and a Smile are very close neighbors Separated by a little mound called the cheek I hope your live will abound more in Smiles than tears hence I bid you a cordial adieu

J. W. HArdin

---

181. J. W. H. to Jane Hardin

John. W. HArdin

Mrs. Jane. Hardin
Sedan Gonzales County Texas
(This is off hand I will if god wills write Soon) again)

Apr the 6 .i~~th~~
Huntsville, Texas, ~~March the 30~~ 1890

Dear Jane beloved Wife and my loving interesting intelligent and beloved children. I greet you all topically Speaking with a Soft plain uxorious and fatherly howdy. Then I Kiss and then I embrace each of you chimerically Speaking: of course this is all in the Utopian fashion: but ah loved ones while what I have Said above is only Symbolic of the true Sentiments of my heart yet I hope these words futile and fickle as they are will Serve to point out to to each of you how full my heart is for all of you: full of what I hear each of you Say. I answer you full of love full of hope. full of joy in anticipation. Jane Sweet loving and angelic Jane I received your, longed for and anticipated intermissive and delectable letter with a delight that made me rapturous bordering on the ecstatic. it was the Same true paraclete that has always Stood by me when others run me down: whose Surpressed voice I hope to be able always to reconize without Sound: Whose love labor and Sympathy has all been mine whenever the clouds darkened over me and the world on me frouned: whose counsel of right and faithful love: borne in as pure a heart as chase a mind and as Sweet a Soul as ever Sat or reigned on european throne: I Say just Such comforting cheering messages as that whether oral by pen or pencil has done and is doing more to Keep me in the path of rectitude and righteouness than all the federal Soldiers Bureau agents carpet bagers and Scalawags from Scalewagdom that ever infested Texas Though the E. J Daves' police bokes rangers Hubbards detectives Roberts Knout Irelands torturing rack and Ross' lenity humanity and magnanimity mixed have been active agents to Sap the foundation of my life to assuage my passion to anneal my temper and to make me a more perfect a more Sympathetic a more christian and a Sincer and a braver man

2nd then any man that ever purgered himself to gain poplar approval to please a mob. whether he be Judge Sherriff Juryman or govenor. I tell you to day after 13 years of Slavery Such as few men Survive to Say nothing of 10 years of almost incessant and tragic battle with yankie Soldiers their ilk or agents or abettors I am not conquered am not cowed have not Sold my manhood to any living creature am Square with god. with man. and myself: and I belive with patience pluck and indefatigable effort I will yet be able to rout all the defamers that have ever calumnated me. I am confident that I am right now as to the past it is Secure: but I have learnt a great lesson from it. under the light of which I Shall walk with careful but firm Step to victory or defeat on this earth. I Shall try what ever the result to reach everlasting glory where there is no deformation no treacherous detectives no liars no thieves no murderers into the city which is as light as day where there is no midnight assasins howling around but but where all is pure holy and angelic. I Say that if I am backed by the Strong arm of god who can prevail against me. "Live or die Sink or Swim give me Liberty or give me death" I mean Liberty protected by law: and teach your children that is the only liberty worth having Jane I hope yet to be able to make you happier than you are now and to be able to ameliorate the condition of our children and if when I am free if ever I will be the proudest man on earth if I can only find my family pursuing an honest living by virtuous means that god and all good christian men and woman hail to approve: I want I desire no grater fortune than you an them with pure minds and hearts: on my exit from pen with health: and I hope by gods blessing that I will have: this: though at this time it is very poor. yet better than for years Dont believe any wild tales that you may hear about me and dont be afraid to write me any news or to make any enquiry that you desire Just mark your letter private and ask Capt J.G. Smithers to So handle it himself and he will do it he is a brave gallant man and no enemy of mine I am in perfect harmony with the officers of this institution I Know my Duty and they give me a chance to preform it I was Sorry to hear of John W loosing his plow horse I wish it was So I could Send him a check for $500.00 but tell him to grieve not. but to learn a lesson from the little ant that builds its nest as often as the weary corbies foot crushes it to look at the Spider he wont live without a web: then look at the tinney bee. when the Seasons are bad and the fields Scarce of flowers. he makes a wider circuit and thus by frugality and industry makes up for the unfruitful Season an Scarcity of the flowers in the fields Swamps or gardens. tell him Such is life and I am real Sorry: but tell him all a brave intelligent boy can do is to go to work and make another by honest efforts be careful of going into debt or letting your children go in debt it is ruinous to any body or busines: tell Little Jame and my Sweet Little cousin Sady that their letters were So nice So Sweet So cheering to me that I want them to write again one is jus as good as the other both Superb I close by Sending my love to all with a KissYour Husband **John W HArdin**

---

182. J. W. H. to Jane Hardin

John. W. Hardin

Mrs. Jane. Hardin
Sedan Gonzales County Texas

Huntsville, Texas, Nov the 2nd 1890

Dear jane I received yours and Mollies Some time ago, and avail myself of this opportunity to answer those welcome epistles. Jane I hope in about three years to be a free man So dont loose all of your former good looks even if your averdepoise does deminish: Save them:. Well I meet very often former School mates and acquaintances and they are all agreed in Saying that I hold my own well: nevertheless I am Sick all the time: but jane all things considered I am doing Splendid: with a big hope that no Scales can weigh I am not hacked nor discouraged and hope Yet to enter the arena of life ready to battle for my rights as I understand them: Jane your children are now at that age when their hearts are most Sportive and restless therefore incourage them in hethful Sport: make their home as pleasant as possible: dont scold them or grumble at them in order to govern. them: but rather rule them with Kind words backed by reason and love: Well to make a long Story Short just Keep your children in the pathes of virtue and rectitude and you do well: Tell John,W,H not to be quarrelsome but to be Kind and obliging to every one tell him not to drink Whisky or go with roudies nor gamble but to make an honest living for his ma & Sisters I Send my love to all of our children tell each of them to write no more at present except this will inform you that my affections are the Same for you and yours. Then again I Send my love with a Kiss to you Molley John W H & Sweet little Janie

---

183. J. W. H. to J. Smither

[UNDATED]

J. Smither. (Asst Supt)
—do most respectfully and obediently represent to you that Capt Kelly told me that the result of my act would be to deprive me of all good time gained. he told me to read up on riot that ——— had incited men to riot and would besides being lashed loose all good time gained. capt I believe you to be a just man and I believe you will execute the law impartially. I do not believe you capable of punishing a convict through malice I Know you have no malice towards me for your personal treatment to me Since you came here has ——— Such a nature as to place me under many obligations to you for Kind favors received. I am ——— of these men that care nothing for the past. except to gain Knowledge from it except to gain wisdom from it. it is like Spilt milk to me. "experience is a dear School fools will be taught in no other" I Say from the depths of my heart I hold no malice towards no man and Say to--- as I said to Capt Kelly under the tortuig lash it never ——— my head or heart to do or ofer violence to your ——— or to Capt Kelleys I tried under great excitement and dread to explain my acts I Succeeded So well upon a fair and full presentment by Capt Kelly Several witnesses and myself that you acquited me and told me to go to the Shop. Now Capt you

Surely Know the State cannot in the State of Texas move ——— a new trial or apeal when the virdict is averse to the State in a criminal case Capt Kelly represented the State you upon his motion granted him a new trial and then under Some excitement with Capt Kelly proceeded to the Taylor Shop and their examined witnesses refusing me the privilege of being present to cross question them and examine them in order to be able to explain my language used which Capt Kelly Said was aimed and intended for him. The Constitution and laws of the State of Texas——— that a man Shal in ever criminal case be confronted ——— the witnesses. When you came back you ordered me —ed in the darke cell and Said the evidence was against me: Now capt Let See what the charge was against me. in all truth I will try to Seet it out just as capt Kelly charged and as the proof Showed. Capt Kelly Said that Roland (a negro) had engaged in a fight with Lynch a (white man) that he had bin Sent for to go to the Shoe Shop that he went there and Started ——— negro and Lynch to court that when they got in the Taylor Shop very near me Rowland jumpt upo Lynch and they began to fight that Mr Skelton run up and pulled the niger off of Lynch that a convict helped him to pull him the negro off of Lynch that he Capt Kelly run up jumpt upon the Negro with both feet and Stompt him that after he let the negro up he Saw me (John W Hardin) and Said what have you got to do with it/ Capt Kelly Said that I Said nothing unless it becomes ——— just let him jump on me. that ——— just walked up to me and took hold of me ——— you just hit me if you dare.that I amediately said Capt not you. not you I dont mean you I woun not hit you for nothing in the world I Surrender to your authority—will go anywhere you Say please dont do me violence ——— Capt Kelly was excited. Now capt Let us See what a riot is a——— by the Statutes of the State of Texas.. Title 9 Chap ——— Art 295 of the revised criminal code of the State of Texas Says: Riots: Defned if the persons unlawfully Assembled together do, or attempt to do any illegal act all of those engaged in Such illegal act are guilty of riot. The criminal code refered to above also in chapter 9 Title 1 defines an unlawful assembly:. Article 279 Says an unlawful assembly "is the meeting of three or more persons, with intent to aid each other by violence or in any other maner either to commit an offence or illegally to deprive any person of any right or to disturb him in the enjoyment there of: Now capt I was busily at work at

Edmund J. Davis
—Courtesy Gonzales Library, Gonzales, Texas.
A History of Texas - vol. 5. by Louis J. Wortham, LL.D.

my regular place of imployment anticipating no trouble with any one ploting against no one being allowed by constituted authority the privilege of the Shop for ——— a fight occured in ten feet of me ——— attracted my attention thefirst impression of ——— was to Separate the combatants with fairness ——— parties Just Like I have time and again Separated men here Just as I Separated a negro and a white man in our Shop not long ago when each were using and attempting to use deadly weapons, just as I Some time ago Separated Jim White and Mit. Day when they were fitin—and injuring one another with deadly weapons blood Streaming from each. I did it with fairnes to both parties though one was my avowed enemy. of course ——— I Saw Lynch the white man bleeding my Sympathy my —ion was aroused in his behalf but Capt I S——pose mind to your just judgement Whether ——— imputed to me are of themselves enough to convict me of inciting to riot It is not in evidence nor is it Charged that I assaulted any one or even threatened to but when asked what I had to do with replyed nothing unless it becomes personal let him jum on me it is also in evidence that I never offered resistance to Cap Kelly but amediately Said Capt I Surrender to your authority I dont mean you I would not hit you I would not harm you for anything for god Sake Capt dont do me violence Now this later words are (Res gestae) they are part of my act Showing my intention describing my words Just before when capt Kelly asked me what I had to do with it when I said nothing unless he makes it personal let him jum on me and are admisable in any court of justice in this State my peacible and quiet and humble Submision to the Capt Kelly and Capt Kelly excited mind and condition are equally admisible in any court in this State to Show that that I was not in open revolt any ——— with others a——— lawful authority the unlawful act claimed wo— words to an officer I claimed that my words were misconstrued I am certain that my acts and words amediately a— ——— before any attempt on my part to even assault any one Shows to your just mind that I intended no insult to Capt Kelly. I assure you again that I never intend to assault any one unless he jumpted on me and as to Cap— Kelly my act Surely and certainly prove that I had no intention under any circumstances of resisting or assaulting capt Kelly. - Now The revised criminal code of the State of Texas Defines an (Affray). If any two or ——— persons fight, together in a public place ——— be deemed guilty of Affray and fined not exceeding 100.$ (Title, 9 Chapt 3 Article 313) I am not in my mind guilty of affray for I did not fight I offered no violence to any one but in a round a bout way Said if he the Negro jumped on me it might become personal Capt dont let capt Kelly take my time away from me not forfeited by express and open act I have been here a long time I humbly ask you to closely inspect the charge and See that I get justice acording to law and the facts if you have decided to ——— of my time away from please let me ——— I cant believe that you have but please ——— the Judgement and Sentence at once and——— obediently respectfully and Sincerely.

---

184. J. W. H. to Jane Hardin

John, W. HArdin

Mrs, Jane. Hardin
Sedan Gonzales County Texas
Huntsville, Texas, <u>Apr the 5th</u> 1891

Dear Jane I received your estimable letter a few days ago with a gusto or with a welcome that belongs only to an uxorious husband deprived of the enjoyable company of the happy association of a beautiful a virtuous and devoted wife, and when I Say that there is no man of pluck intelligence and chivaldry. to Say nothing of patriotism who has onced enjoyed the Sweet pure Social company and love of angelic woman. would hesitate to Say that of all earthly joys that of all Solaces. there is none this Side of the grave. to be compaired with that he receives from the lovely long haired Seraph whom he idolizes. I but Speak the truth that millions of men are ready to attest. well I received a letter last Sunday from J.W.H.Jr. and through you wish to thank him for his manly effort and hope at Some future time not very distant to answer the Same. I also received a letter from Sister Nan She Said that She had Sent you a Sample of her fancy needle work with proper description how to use it. So as to make money out of it. and She also Spoke of going out to your country and that She would be pleased to have your or Molly travel with her in connection with Said work. Tell Molly that papa Says that he owes her a letter. but not to let that interfere or hindr her from writing me as I have derive no little pleasure from her correspondence and assure her that I will avail myself of the first opportunity to write my lovely daughter a letter. I wrote Sweet little jane two Sundays ago. I was just recovering from the 'La Grippe' I am not intirely well yet but am on the improve and weigh 170 pounds. tell Molly that her aunt Nan has proved to be a very faithful loving and considerate Sister to me. She is Smart vivacious and a brave christian and that She might do well to form a closer acquaintance with her Jane my hopes are brighter than they have been for many years and they are bound to grow

2

brighter and brighter as the years go by. if I can but regain my health and this Seems possible under the present regime. and god bing on my Side who can down me (nobody) and you can rest assured that the omnipotent the omnipresent and the omniscient god is always on the Side of truth of right and reason, as against falsehood wrong and tyranny. and if need be in the end he will uphold vindicate the former even if he has to do it with his own right arm. which is charged or primed with an explosive more terrible than gun cotton or dynamite. Jane Dearest teach your Children that the fear of the lord is the beginning of wisdom: and teach them that wisdom is the power to use Knowledge correctly teach them to lead honest upright lives: to make good honest citizens Should be their hiest aim: this they cannot do by leading profligate lives: and unless they heed and obey the ten commandments they can never make good citizens: Jane Dearest I take pleasure at this present time to applaud your virtuos and heroine effort. put forth in the past to rear your children right and I ask you as their father and as your husband not to abate those teachings: teach them and dwell upon the Idea that it is cowardly to lie to Steal to rob to tattle to murder or to violate any law civil or devine and that it is inconsistant with good citizenship. and repugnant to gods will. and that the Hardins are a brave people above doing a low down act unbeconing in man or woman. and teach them that their virtue their integrity are their greatest treasure. I mean their man hood and womanhood: not to be parted with at any price: the banker locks his treasure to Save his money from being Stole: then teach those children to guard their character less a thief like Satan Steal from them their greates wealth: and revel in the booty: while they Suffer the consequence of gods violated laws for it is a truth: that though man may Some times and often does ecape punishment for the violation of mans law, but that it is impossible for him to escape the punishment for the violation of the devine or natural or gods law. whether it be by intemperance in eating or drinking or reveling in lust he must pay the penalty with pain Sorrow or death. I bid you a loving adieu and Send the conventional but fatherly Kiss to each of our lovely children as well as to you my Dearest

JW HArdin

---

185. J. W. H. to Jane Hardin

John. W. Hardin

Miss. Jane. Hardin
Sedan Gonzales County Texas
Huntsville, Texas, Oct the 25 th 1891

Dear child I received your nice pretty letter of oct the 12th with fatherly pleasure and gratification and now answer the Same with fatherly pride and love. I have also received one from your Sister of a latter date which I wish to acknowledge through you and wish you to assure her that it was received with equal pleasure and read with equal Joy with yours. I was very proud to learn that J.W.H. had gathered his crop and that he had Suceeded So well as to make 4 bales of cotton and 75 bu of corn. Why Such commendible efforts as that is enough to establish for him the worth reputation or name of being a prosperous farmer. Now tell him that I Say that there is not So much in making as Saving or rather tell him that the latter is of equal importance tell him that he cant Save by Chewing Tobacco and drinking Whisky the one a dirty filthy and expensive habit. the other a debasing dethroning and expensive habit because it debases the mind and heart dethrones reason and depletes the purse without any benefit to the person who imbibes. Tell him not to put that Stuff into his mouth that will Steal away his brain and exasperate his passion and make him a brute for the time being. and tell him not to bet or gamble untill he learns how and probably it will be better if he never learns how for it is an occult Sience that few under Stand that none can practice without endangering their wealth their character and their Soulds: Theirfore "What Shall it profit a man if he gain the Whole World and loose his own Soul: Now I hope and reasonably So that I may be with you all in less than two years: now let me Say to you and loved ones guard your characters as a Soldier does his frotress as a banker does his money for therein lies your wealth do no act or deed nor Speak no word that will bring reproach upon yourselves but live in peac with all men and love one anoth affectionately

John W Hardin

HARDIN WAS ESCORTED TO CUERO FOR SENTENCING FOR THE J.B. MORGAN KILLING. HE WAS THEN TAKEN BACK TO HUNTSVILLE PENITENTIARY.

---

186. J. D. Anderson, indictment for killing of J. B. Morgan

No 1270
The State of Texas
vs
Wes Hardin
Murder
True Bill
J. D.Anderson
Foreman
Witnesses
Neal Bocer
John Sunday
Filed December 21st A.D. 1877
Robt J Kleberg Clerk
D.C. D.W.C
John Blackwell

In the name and by the authority of the State of Texas- The Grand Jurors of the State of Texas duly elected, tried and impanneled, Sworn and Charged to inquire in and for the County of De Witt, at a regular term of the District Court begun and holden Within and for Said County of De Witt on the fourteenth Monday after the first Monday of September in the year of Our Lord one thousand Eight hundred and Seventy Seven upon their Oaths do present that

Wes Harden

late of said County on the tenth day of April in the year of Our Lord one thousand Eight hundred and Seventy three in the said County of DeWitt With force and arms in and upon the body of J. B. Morgan unlawfully feloniously Wilfully and of his Malice aforethought—did. make an assault= and that the said Wes Harden a certain pistol then and there charged with gunpowder and leaden bullets Which said pistol he the said Wes Harden in his hand then and there had and held then and there unlawfully feloniously Wilfully and of his Malice aforethought did discharge and Shoot off—to against and upon the said J.B. Morgan—and that the said Wes Harden with the leaden bullets aforesaid out of the pistol aforesaid then and there by force of the gun powder aforesaid by the Said Wes Harden discharged and shot off as aforesaid then and there unlawfully feloniously Wilfully and of his Malice aforethought did Strike penetrate and Wound him the Said J.B. Morgan in and upon the side back and breast of him the said J.B. Morgan - giving to him the said J.B. Morgan then and there With the leaden bullets aforesaid. so as aforesaid discharged and shot out of the pistol aforesaid—by the said Wes Harden in and upon the side back and breast of him the said J.B. Morgan Several mortal wounds- of Which said mortal wounds he the said J.B. Morgan then and there instantly died. and so the Grand Jurors aforesaid upon their oaths aforesaid do say that the said Wes Harden him the said J.B. Morgan in the Manner and by the means aforesaid unlawfully feloniously wilfully and of his malice aforethought did Kill and murder — Contrary to all law both human and Devine—and against the peace and dignity of the State —

J. D. Anderson
Foreman of the Grand Jury

The State of Texas)
County of DeWitt) I C.C.Hourston clerk of the District Court in and for said County and State, do hereby Certify that the forgoing is a true and correct Copy of the original Bill of Indictment filed in My office on the 21st day of December AD 1891
In testimony Whereof I hereunto set my hand and official seal this the 24th day of December AD 1891

C.C.Hourston clerk
D, C,D, W, C-T

187. J. W. H. to Jane Hardin

Jan the 4th 1892 Smiley Po Gonzales co
Cuero Dewitt County Texas

Dear Jane
This leaves me tolerable well. Buck came in to See me Saturday morning I was very glad to See him though I was Suffering intensely from my wounds he is a Splendid looking fellow and unless my mind deceives me he is brave faithful and Sympathetic of course I have positive proof that he is this and more to I hope you are well and that our lovely little girls are enjoying good health and that their visit to me and our meeting will inspire them to walk in the path of rectitude and righteousness With unfaultering Steps I am certain that their filial devotion to me to you can never be Shaken
2nd
by time vicissitudes or by the torturing cruel and unjust decrees of cruel men rendered many years ago. I hope I believe that they have learned a lesson of virtue of pure devotion that they may carry with them through life and which will Strengthen them to lead virtuous lives to make loving daughters and to make true and affectionate Wivs teach them to be modest to be loving especially to one another to you and to their noble brother" teach them to be true to themselves and to god and rest assured that they will be true to mankind. teach them to be industrious and patient for papa hopes yet to be able to lift them to higher a more prosperous and a more happy State tell John W my unfortunate but brave and manly boy that he has unequivocally a fathers love Sympathy and prayers to Sustain him in his misshap. I hope he will
3rd
learn a profitable lesson from his xmas Sport I hope when he again runs a race a horse that he will agree with his nag and both go on the Same Side of the tree. I hope that he will Soon be well and live to enjoy many christmases in the most approved the most enlightened and in the most delectable maner without anything to mar the Sport of myrthful hearts tell him I hope he will learn wisdom from folly and that he will be a braver a better and a more noble boy when he gets well which I hope will be Soon. That is brave enough to do right against all opposition. Let who will do rong you my Son must do right. better That is love your mama your Sisters andme

with a devotion that nothing can Shake rest assured it will be reciprocated

4th

be Kinder to your associates than ever be polite and respectful to every one no matter their age color or previous condition and you will enable your Self. You will exhibit the Hardin qualities and like your grand Pa JGH you will be a man. recollect that a Hardin never Stoops to do a low a mean a treacherous a cowardly trick ah my Son it is inconsistent with his nature be a Hardin but be an upright man. Now dear my faithful my loving Jane I expect to be here Several days yet I respectfully and lovingly invite you to come down and Sincerly request Buck Cobb to facilitate your coming. I would like for you to be here next Sunday Dearest Kiss each of our lovely children for me and give my love to whom you please and to all inquirers, curious or otherwise. give them my best wishes. Dearest write me at once your Devoted husband

John W HArdin

---

188. W. S. Fly to J. W. H.

W.S. Fly, —OFFICE OF— Thos. McNeal.
FLY * & * McNEAL,

VS.

ATTORNEYS & COUNSELORS AT LAW.
Gonzales, Texas, Jany 8th 1892

Mr. John W. Hardin. Cuero Tex.

Dear Sir: Your very sensible and judicious letter of the 6th instant is to hand. I am so busily engaged in the District Court here that I am not able to write you as I desire, but will say that I believe your plan of presenting each of the cases on its respective merits is doubtless the best plan. I can get a thousand men in Gonzales County to sign an application to the Gov. for a full pardon. My plan is this, to circulate a petition in Dewitt and Gonzales counties at once for a pardon in the Cuero qase and early in February at the close of our Court I can go to Austin and present it to the Governor, with whom I am well acquainted. I have to-night prepared a petition to the governor in the Cuero case and will send it to Mr. Kirk Lynde with the request that he circulate it while people are in from all parts of the county attending Court. I will do all I can to get you a pardon not only in the Cuero case but to get a full and free pardon for you and I believe you will justify my action by living a quiet and useful life. I have faith in your integrity and manhood and I do not believe it is misplaced. I write Mr Lynde to go to see you and if there are any suggestions you have as to changes in the petition make them.

Yours Truly, W.S. Fly

---

189. Fannie C. King to Jane Hardin

[UNDATED]

Mrs Hardin:

I send two dresses for Alma and one for Florence, which I would like for you to make if you have time. The pink one, of Alma's is cut with two ruffles around the bottom, and Babe's with one. Why didn't you come Saturday. I looked for you but thought probably the rain prevented you

I send you a piece of oil calico which perhap's will do to make Jennie a dress. I thought at first there was enough to make Mollie one. but I find there is only about three y'ds. Come soon

Your true friend **Fannie C. King**

---

190. W. S. Fly to J. W. H.

W.S. Fly, — OFFICE OF —Thos. McNeal.
FLY * & * McNEAL,
ATTORNEYS & COUNSELORS AT LAW.
Gonzales, Texas, May 18 1892

Mr. J.W. Hardin Huntsville Tex.

Dear Sir — Your favor to hand. I think the idea of getting the proof about theComanche case is a good one and will be of great benefit with the governor in obtaining a pardon for you. I am still doing what I can for you. When the Sheriff's Convention met a few weeks since I got nearly all of them to sign an application for pardon through our Sheriff who was present. You had better get a lawyer in Huntsville to fix up the papers for affidavits in regard to Comanche case.

Yours Truly, W.S. Fly

---

191. James Anderson to J. W. H.

Richland 7/13/1892

Mr. J.W. Hardin
Sir I received your letter. and the papers this morning and sent the papers on to Mrs. Davis this evening, I will send after the Justice of the Peace to morrow and will have every thing fixed up right away. but will not send papers back untill I hear from Mrs, Davis
I Am Yours &C
Good Bye **James Anderson**
find enclosed 4 envelopes Eight Cents came in This. Kelley

---

192. Jane Hardin to Mollie Hardin (unsigned)

[UNDATED]

Kingbeary the 11
Miss Mollie Hardin
Dear Childron I will try to wrijht you a fue lins this moring to let you all know how I am geting a long I have met with poor Sucksess all thow I have not lost but have just come out even I will go from heare tou Luen [Luling? –eds.] this evenling hope to dow beter thair, you all write to lueing for I am ancious to heare from you all trust you all will get a long well tell J w and Jinnie to be good love to all off the famly you all must write and my from nanie or your papa Send them to me I dont know yet whin I will be at home will try to make Sumthing first I will let you all know whin to meat me if I meeat with Suckses I may Stay weeak or tow longer
Sow good by — Seewit Childon
Johnnie be good and Stay with Mollie and Jannie
your mama

---

193. J. W. H. to Mollie E. Hardin

John.W.HArdin Miss Molley. E. Hardin
Sedan Gonzales County Texas
Huntsville, Texas. Aug the 21st 1892

Molley Dear daughter my precious child and my faithful daughter Your loving father received your brief letter last night with fatherly gratitude and joy. yet I cannot describe or explain on paper my deep and my Sincere solicitude for the health of your most estimable mother, my anxiety in regard to her feeble condition cannot be express. I only wish that it was possible for me to Suffer in her Stead. I do hope ere now. ere this reaches you that my machless wife that my angelic wife will have regained her accoustom or normal health. and being hopeful brave and loving. I Shall look to the god of love of hope off mercy to caress to restore to health that adorable woman that loving and beloved mother that true loyal wife of mine whose heart and mind is free from guile and whose love is as pure as the driven Snow. tell your loving mother and your Sweet Sister and your noble brother that papa Sends them his love with a Kiss. Buck I received your welcome letter about three weeks ago your cousin was glad to hear from you and I wish to Say that my Sensibility would be dense indeed if I did not appreciate your aid and friendship to me and mine and I do hope and believe that the ties that bind you and I in brotherly love are Stronger than Steel more durable than brass more permanent than admant more lasting than granite and will last as long as our lives last. Buck I am not only proud and grateful to you for your friendship. . but I am equally proud and grateful to others of your Section who have Stood up for me and have done all they could for me and mine. I have watched the Houston convention with an interesting and with a critical eye I unqualifiedly approve all the hog (or regular democrat convention) done) I believe and hope they will win easey The Clark faction or boltrcrats lost but would not give the Stakes up but the people will See that they do in november. Yes I expect to be pardoned by the midle of nov for I See with pleasure and hope that the indomitable the Willy and the irrepressible Fly of gonzales is in perfect political harmony with the true democrats I Shall write you next Sunday if nothing hapens. well Molly Donot let your Sweet mama do any work until She gets perfectly well tell her that I Say that She must take care of herself for her children Sake and my Sake and I desire that you your dear Sister and your manly brother Stay with her and See that She does take care of her Self then hoping that you and loved ones will continue to walk in the path of honorable duty and righteousness. for Sucess gained in any other path would at last be an ignominious. Success that all honorable brave and wise people despise Molly when I write to you I mean it for Johny too one of you be Kind enough to write me once a week for a while So write at once good by your loving and your hopeful father and my peroration is "that the god of hope and mercy be with you and Stay with you" Amen your affectionate father

JWH

---

194. J. W. H. to John W. Hardin Jr.

John. W. Hardin

Mr. John. W. Hardin. Jr.
Sedan Gonzales County Tex

Huntsville, Texas, Aug the 28the 1892

John. W. and Jinnie. M.

Your papa through each of you desires to Greet your lovely mama and your amiable Sister with a Kisses of love and tender caresses emblematic of his deep and Sincere affection for each of you and them. Your cousin Buck wrote me the latter part of last month that "your loving and beloved ma was very Sick but that She was better and that he would Keep me posted but he has not writen me Since your Sister Molley wrote me on the 12 of this month "that all was well but mama and that She was doing as well as could be expected." I saw in the Curro Starr of the 18th ult that "Mrs J. W. Hardin had been very Sick for the last three weeks but was able to be up again." I saw in the cuero Buliten of the 26 Ult from a correspondent at C.Dan dating the 21st last that "Mrs Jane. W. Hardin one of the most estimable ladies of our community had been very Sick but that all had been done that could be done by many Kind numerous friends and medical Skill to restore her to health" and "that Mr and Mrs Howel of Runge wer visiting the family of Mrs Hardin." So you dear children can plainly See that I have just heard enough to make it direful. for any Serious mishap to your worthy and lovable mama would to each of you my dear children as well as to myself be a calamity irretrievable and irreparable. and being hopefu and brave always endeavoring to look at things in their proper light "as they are" or as the evidence Show them to me to be." I cannot and will not contemplate at this time any Serious results but hope pray and trust ere this reaches you that your devote mama and my loyal machless and angelic wife will be on the high road to perfect health. and your papa desires through each of you to tender his heart felt thanks to those Kind friends and relatives and especial to those medical advisers who have by untiring labor and endeavors done So much to restore to health your Sweet mama and my true and Superb wife. Johnny I am glad to Know that you have a nice crop of corn and cotton I am So proud of you. Your Sisters and your mother because each is virtuous and honorable and Know how to make an honest living by hones toil I hope you will Keep away from bar rooms race traces or any Species of gambling or crime or vice Just be brave enough and honorable enough to labor in honorable employment for your ma and Sisters and I promise you the good will and praise of all good people the thanks of your father which he hopes to return and the love and gratitude of your mother and Sisters:

adieu

---

195. J. W. H. to J. B. Cobb

John, W. HArdin Mr J. B. Cobb.

Sedan Gonzales County Texas

Huntsville, Texas, Sep the 11the 1892

(PS) Barnett Young is a cousin of mine So is Bishop Send me their letters or any others of note)

Mr Cobb. Dear cousin, I received your welcome letter of the 2nd ultimo. for which I desire to thank you from the deepest deapths of my heart, and although your estimable letter did not bring to me that news I most craved to hear, the thorough recovery of my devoted my loyal, my true. my Sincere my loving, and beloved, and my angelic wife. Yet the news it conveyed to me was cheering. and bing of a hopeful nature. I can only hope and pray that moving my beloved, from place to place and the wise care and attention bestowed upon her by her friends relatives and medical advisers together with her courage prudence and patience will Soon restore her. to her accustom health. Buck cheer her up, and tell her. that I believe that I will get out in november. and while it is my ambition to be free. that is to gain my liberty by lawful means, that is to have my liberty based upon lawful endeavor. not that liberty that plays hide and Seek with the officers of the law, for that is the liberty of Tiger, and not the liberty of intelligent man in this day of progress improvment and enlightenment and peace and (political bolts) but you tell my loving and beloved wife, that then when I am free. that my hightest object aim and ambition will be to do Some act Say Some word. that will cheer heer. and make her happy. You can Say to her Softly that all that I am or ever will be is dedicated to her and our lovely Children. caution her about taking to much excersise. Tell Johny to be brave, brave to work for the Support of his worthy mama and Sister and thereby gain the love and esteem of every-body, (his papa's thanks) Tell M&J. that they have a Splendid oppor-tunity to prove their virtue to prove that they are little ladies by fol-lowing their mama's Teaching. my love to all my thanks to you adieu **JWH**

---

196. J. W. H. to J. B. Cobb

John. W. Hardin

Mr. J. B. Cobb.
Sedan. Gonzales County Texas
Huntsville, Texas, Nov the 6th 1892

Dear cousin. Buck.
I received a letter from you last night and have answered it and will inclose it. You can see I had Some hopes, but your wel— letter of the 4th Ultimo, blasts my hopes of the recovery of my beloved my faithful Wife. and the restoring to health one who in my estimation was the possessor of those qualities that make woman So lovely So beautiful the worthy companion of man his compeer and his best friend. and for whom an honest intelligent a brave and chivalrous man is always ready and willing to Suffer for, to bleed for and even to die for. whether he be Strange to her or related to her, or whether he be father Brother or husband. Such a perfect woman was your cousin Jane that to Know her was to love her and (JWH) he who Knew her best loved her most, at least with all his heart and no one Knew this better than She and no one Knew better than he that his love was reciprocated my highest object and aim was to be able yet to prove to her by my every act and word that her loyal love and faithfulness to me was appreciated. to Say nothing of the debt of gratitude and love I owed her and hoped to bestow upon her for her matchles conduct as a mother to those She loved dearer than life. my children listen to the last words your beautiful and beloved

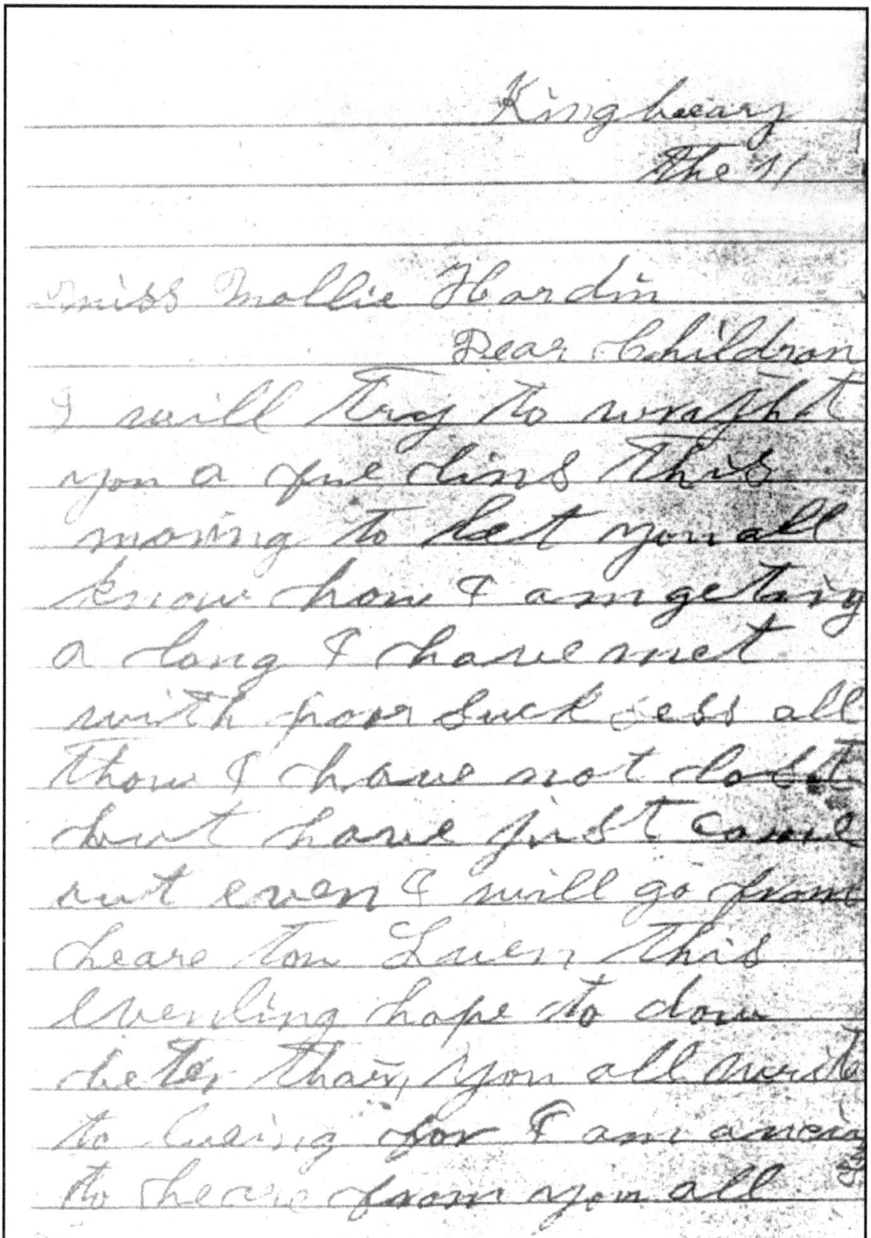

Kingsbury
the 11

Miss Mollie Hardin
Dear Children
I will try to wright
you a few lines this
morning to let you all
know how I am geting
a long I have met
with poor succsess all
thow I have not lost
but have jist come
out even I will go from
heare to Luling this
evening hope to dow
better thair you all write
to Luling for I am anxious
to heare from you all

Jane Bowen Hardin
—Courtesy Special Collections Albert B. Alkek Library, Southwest Texas State University, San Marcos, Texas; restoration work by Phil Kolbe and Alex Crane

mother had to Say about you and your father in a letter to me just before She taken down in the latter part of ——— from Kingsburry while virtuously earnestly and motherly laboring for ——— —mans for your and her Support and Know that as a mother as a wife She was a most beautiful paragon. She Says "John it Seems So hard that we must be apart, but that cannot be helped now, but to be away from my children is harder still under the circumstances and I am going to try to avoid this in the future. your loving your true wife until death Jane Hardin". Buck I Shal not try to console the children or you or our relatives and friends for I Know your tears your anguish your deep Sorrow like mine is Spontaneous but god alone, and time alone, can wash away the tears of grief perenially flowing from our eyes and heart. I Say tell the ——— god can wipe away their tears (their Sorrow) "and their Shall be n— —re deat— ——— —w nor cryin- —ither Shall their be any more pain, for the former _______ pas

---

197. J. B. Cobb to [John Sr. or Jr.?]

[UNDATED]

Cortez Nevada April 15 **Mr Jno Hardin**

Dear Cousin

answer your kind and most welcome letter received yesterday was glad to hear from you and Lillie we are all sick or has been Eunice is up Maggie is very sick with Lagript I am taking it. I sent to Doctor for medicent for Mag---Man havent got in yet dont think her dangirous Jno Man have taken place I mention or place I was to take and if I had of taking this place would of been Vacated I dont thing Ill stay here longer than Sept this is said to be the harest Man in nevada to get a long with he has treated me all right so far I Judge way he talks to his hands you or me Could not stand it Seems to be plenty work here at present not many $40^{\underline{00}}$ Jobs I am sure if you come you can get plenty work Tom has been over looking for him now they are gathering Horses Jnoy Ive been air gating it the hardest work I ever done Ill be up with it in few days not be so hard then Jno if I can find you place let you Know at once as all s— I think have some few Ill close Maggie said tell Lillie She would write her soon — as got up. Love to all write

Your Cousin **J B Cobb**

Jno I fail to get chance to mail this Ill write few lines let you Know why I did not write sooner. Eunice been sick since I began this letter Magie and Eunice up. and. eat like pigs I am still air gating think Ill get through Monday No special news you and Lillie write I wrote al and Mollie. havent heard from them

good night

Your Cousin **J.B.C.**

PS Johny if you come Take train at Gonzales. think you can do better there if I can find you Job Ill do so seems to be great demand for hands dont think you would have any trouble getting Job **J.B C**

---

198. J. F. Smith to J. M. Bockins

J.F. Smith, Clerk. Stuart Scott, Deputy Clerk.
GEO.D.BARNARD & CO.ST.LOUIS
OFFICE OF COUNTY CLERK
BROWN COUNTY. Brownwood, Texas. **May 29"189**3
J M Bockins Sedan

Dear Sir: —

Replying to yours of the 27", will say that it is not usual for me to recomend one Law firm in preference to another, but in this instance will deviate from. my usual policy by saying that Jenkins and Mc Cartney are the leading Lawyers in that line.

Respectfully

J. F. Smith

"

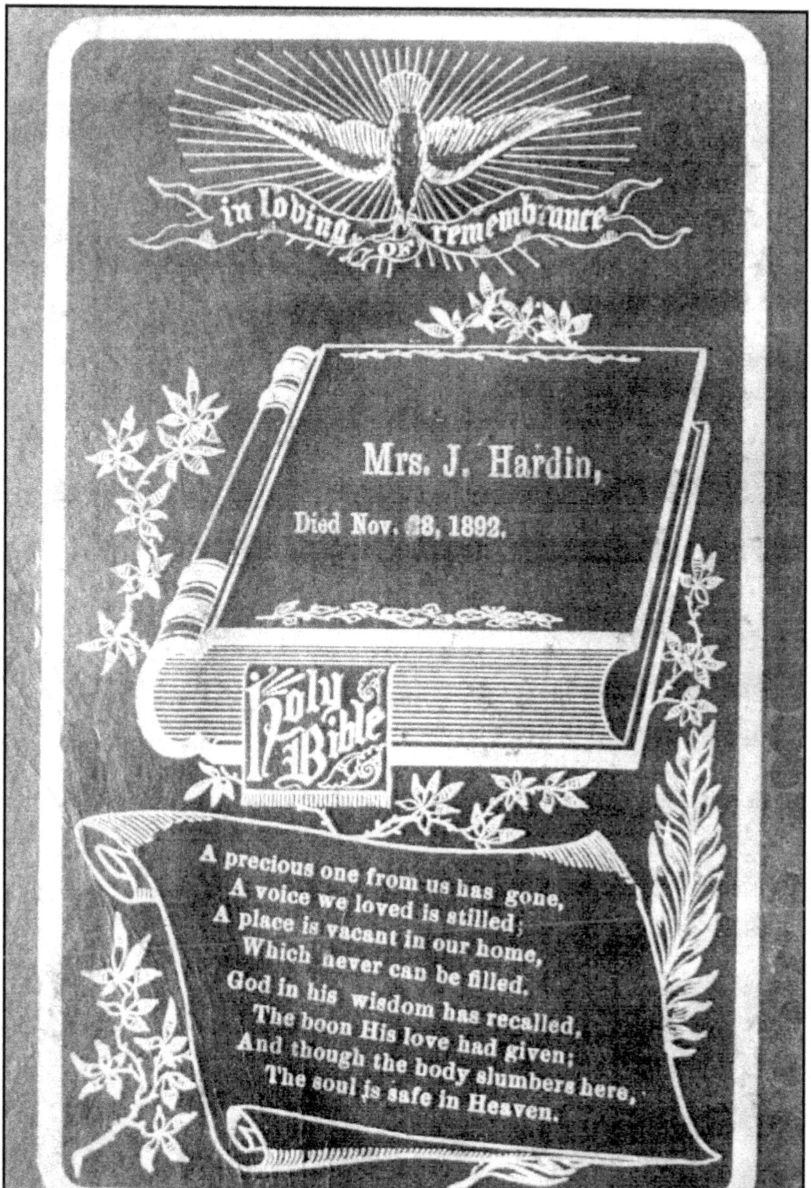

Jane's bereavement card.

—Photo by Roy and Jo Ann Stamps;
Courtesy Special Collections, Albert B. Alkek Library,
Southwest Texas State University, San Marcos, Texas

LETTERS, PHASE 4

June 29, 1893–July 28, 1895

"We heard that you[r] papa was out and I want to know if it is true?"

HARDIN IS RELEASED FROM PRISON WITH A FULL PARDON FROM THE GOVERNOR OF TEXAS. HE THEN PASSES THE BAR EXAM AND BECOMES A LAWYER. NOW BEGIN HIS FINAL YEARS.

199. M. E. Howell to Mollie and Jennie

Runge Tex., June 29, 1893.

Dear Mollie and Jennie.

I will try to write you a few lines to let you know that we are all well, hoping these few lines will find you the same. Mollie come down and attend the normal, and you can stay here. We heard that your papa was out and I want to know if it is true? There is going to be a camp—meeting in July and if you all will come down, I will come after you.

Mollie the normal commences the eleventh of July. Why didn't you all come down to the exhibition, I looked for you? Write and tell me how Nute Sunday is getting along. I give you all my love.

I will close for this time

Your affectionate Aunt. **M. E. Howell.**

---

200. K. R. Blackshear to J. W. H.

1 OFFICE OF H. J. MANGUM,

Dealer in Groceries, Hardware, Fancy and Staple Dry Goods,

DRUGS AND GENERAL MERCHANDISE.

ELI SUBSCRIBER

Pennington, Tex., July 14th 1893.

John W. Hardin Esq.

Dear Sir: In 1861 Congress levied a direct tax on lands in the South but owing to the war Federal Officers could not collect this tax. and did not until 1865—6. This was known as the direct land tax. In 1891 congress passed an act Refunding said Tax as same was unconstitutional. This last act. provided only for the refunding of such tax to the States Territories and the Dist of Columbia as was collected of the people of each. leaving to the Various Legislatures of the States and Territories to provide for its refunding to the individuals who paid. This our last or 23rd Legislature did by act approved March 15th 1893, but the

Page 2 Mode provided for proving up the claim is in many cases cost more than the amount of Tax refunded. I have a list of all those who paid such tax in this Trinity county and I find that J.G. Hardin who, if I mistake not was your father, was your father paid $\$2^{\underline{80}}$ If I am correct in this I can collect this amount for you less $\$1^{\underline{00}}$ which it will take to pay co Judge his fee 25c allowed by law and for notarial work in proving up claim. The law requires affidavit, certificate and seal of two witnesses other than claimants to certain facts, I can get these two witnesses. here among the old men acquaintences of your father. I will make no charge save for these affidavits cert— and seal &.. My father & Judge Rogers or Bill Divas all live near here and can make the affidavits I am doing about all of this work for these tax payers free of charge

3 save for notarial work. cert & seal and pay all postage on letters to co Judge & the auditing Board at Austin If you desire me to collect this little sum for you let me know and be sure to give me the following information. Have you a brother living. If so give name and Post office address. Have you a sister living?. If so her husbands name and P.o. address, if married. If a widow her name.. Your mother & father I believe are both dead. My recollection is Joe was your only brother & he is dead. That you have only one sister married &c, but I am not sure. Nor do I remember her name- It has been a long while you know since we went to school in old Sumpter

4 page This amt is small and the law states same shall be divided among the legal heirs equally. but if proof is not made—on demand or claim filed same will remain in the State Treasurery- I will write your sister or both and a brother If one as will as you again in closing proper parpers for each to sign and when I get same duly executed will get up the necessary proof here to get the co Judge, cert, which if approved by the auditing Board will authorize a Draft on State Treasurer. Which I will cash and send you a Postal note for $\$1^{\underline{80}}$being all but the $\$1^{\underline{00}}$ necessary to pay cost of proof &c,, That is provided you so wish and will write me to that effect, I send this to my old friend col AT McKinney to get to you. He will reply and in close your reply - I will ask him to send you paper to reply on. I would send it but would have to fold it and I know he will cheerfully comply with my request—I will in close stamps to him—Yours Truly
K. R. Blackshear

---

201. K. P. Blackshear to A. T. McKinney

OFFICE OF H. J. MANGUM,

Dealer in Groceries, Hardware, Fancy and Staple Dry Goods,
DRUGS AND GENERAL MERCHANDISE.
ELI SUBSCRIBER

Pennington,Tex., July 14th 1893

Hon A. T. McKinney Huntsville Texas
Dear Sir: and Friend: Inclosed
I hand you a letter to John W Hardin which Explains its self. Will you Kindly, as once before get same to him and a sheet of paper to reply on. and send me his reply at your Earliest convenience and ablige
Yours Truly, **K.R. Blackshear**

When Ever I can serve you don't fail to Call on me. I have gotten nearly well. and am a N.P. working up these matters simply for the Natinal fees while I can't do anything Else.
Yours **H.K.R.B.**

---

202. J. W. H. to Gov. James Hogg

Oct the 29/93
The State of Texas
County of Walker

To. James. S. Hogg. Esq
Gov of the State of Texas

I do most respectfully. represent to you that I was tried and convicted of manslaughter and penalty assessed at two years in the penitentiary in the district court at cuero Dewit county Texas. on the 1St day of Jan AD 1892. I do also represent to you that I was tried upon an indictment for murder: which indictment is attached to this petition and made by me part of the petition which I present for your perusal: by an examination of said certified indictment you will perseive that the homicide which resulted in the death of James. B. Morgan occured on the 10th of Apr.AD.1873. and that the indictment upon which I was tried was not presented until Dec.AD.1877. four years and nine months after the Killing. Manslaughter being barred by the Statute of limitation in three years from the time of its commission: although the indictment charges murder: See White V.S. 4. app.4—8 S-S- 1028. Wilsons criminal Statutes CC See also Articl 199 and notes by the author. Wilsons criminal Statutes C C.P. Title 4. chap 1. Sub article 6 of article 420 of the C C P. which pre-

John W. Hardin the lawyer;j surface embellishment with pen and ink.
—Courtesy Robin Campbell

scribes the requisites of indictments Says "The time mentioned must be Some date anterior to the presentment of the indictment and not So remot that the prosecution of the offense is barred by limitation". Now with the greatest deference I Submit to your judicial mind whether or not the virdict of the jury acquitting me of murder in the 1St and 2nd degree and finding me guilty of manslaughter did not virtually and legally Acquit me of any crime. the crime of manslaughter being barred before presentment: was not the Sentence

and judgement absolutely void under the circumstances. If you So think please be Kind enough to grant me a pardon
John W. Hardin in propria persona

HARDIN DESCRIBES GUNFIGHT WITH J. B. MORGAN AS FOLLOWS:

"I remained in town, finished my business, and went to a bar room on the southwest corner of the square. I took a drink with some friends and then went into a back room where a poker game was going on and joined the play. It was a freeze out for $5 and I won the pot. We all went to the bar, and a man named J. B. Morgan rushed up to me and wanted me to treat him to a bottle of champagne. I declined to do this. He got furious and wanted to fight, starting to draw a pistol on me. Some friends of mine caught him, and I walked out, saying that I wished no row. I walked outside and was talking to a friend. I had forgotten all about Morgan when he came up again; told me I had insulted him and had to fight. He asked me if I was armed. I told him I was. He pulled his pistol halfway out, remarking, 'Well, it is time you were defending yourself.

I pulled my pistol and fired, the ball striking him just above the left eye. He fell dead. I went to the stable, got my horse, and left town unmolested."

---

203. J. W. H. to Capt. J. G. Smither

10/29/93 Capt. J.G. Smither.(Asst Supt)

Please be Kind enough to inform me when my time will be out providing my conduct remains excellent. as I wish to make application for pardon and as every body wants to Know just when I will be turned loose I have been asked a hundred times in the last month. John when you going out. not only by convicts but by men with dark clothes on. of course you are aware that my relatives are anxious to Know. So please give me the information at once as it is the desiderat now. Obediently and respectfully
John W HArdin

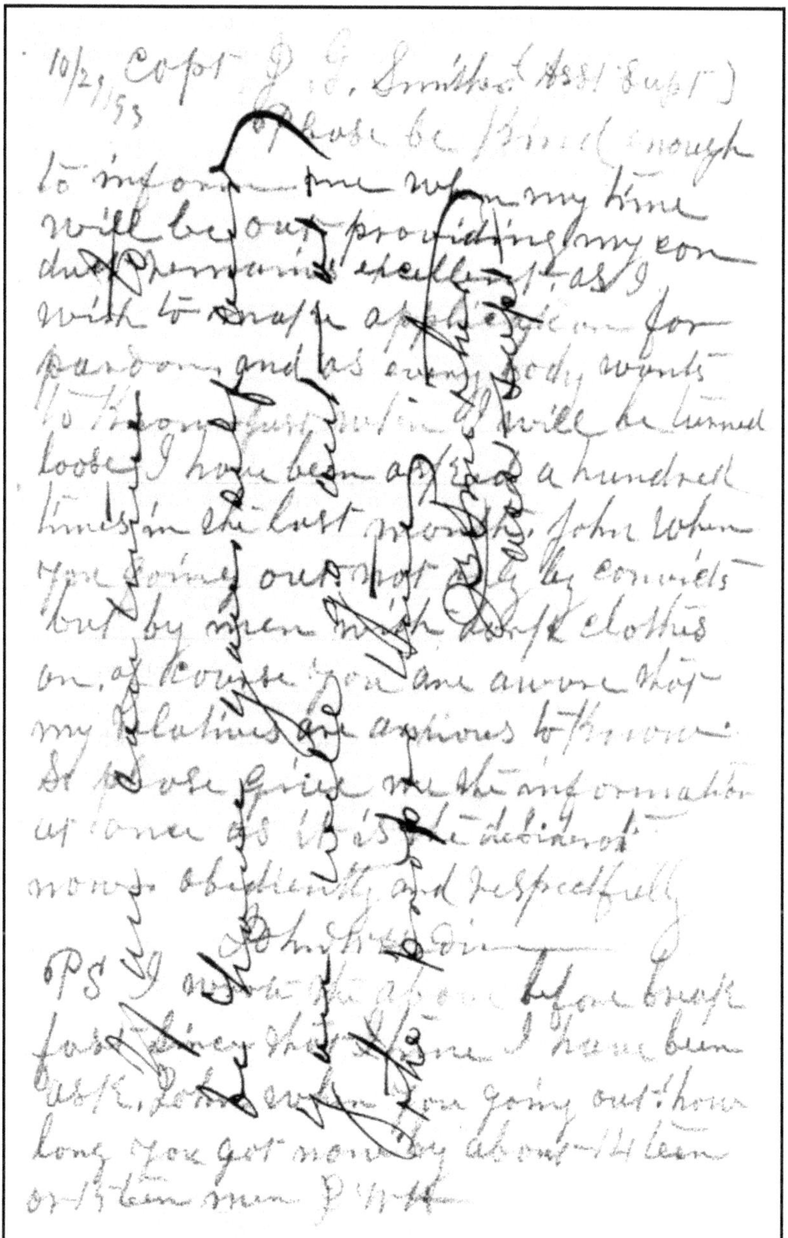
10/2/93 Capt J. G. Smither (Asst Supt)
Please be kind enough
to inform me when my time
will be out providing my con
duct remains excellent as I
wish to snap application for
pardon and as everybody wants
to know just when I will be turned
loose I have been asked a hundred
times in the last month, John when
you going out not only by convicts
but by men with citizen clothes
on. of course you are aware that
my relatives are anxious to know.
So please give me the information
at once as to the date of
same. obediently and respectfully
John W Hardin
PS I wrote the above before break
fast since then I have been
asked, John when you going out how
long you got now by about 14 keen
or 15 keen men J W H

—Courtesy Special Collections, Albert B. Alkek Library,
Southwest Texas State University, San Marcos, Texas

PS I wrote the above before break fast Since that time I have been Ask. John when you going out! how long you got now by about 14 teen or 15 teen men **JWH**

You continue to be have your self and you will go out at the proper time.
JG Smither
Asst Supt

---

204. J. W. H. to W. S. Fly

John W HArdin Judge. W. S. Fly
Sanantonio Bexar County Texas
Huntsville, Texas, Nov the 5th 1893

Dear Sir.
I Send you an application for a pardon drawn by myself on the hon James Stephen Hogg (gov) of the State of Tex I apprehend the legal point raised by me is irrefragable, I hope you will loose no time in forwarding the Same to the gov either with or without your endorsement at your option: under the circumstances I felt it my duty to Send the petition to the gov through you of course all I wish is my citizenship. do you think you could prevail upon the gov to pardon me on the commanchie case at the expiration of my term of course I think we have a cinch on the cuero case it Seems to me to be free without political liberty is no freedom you can ascertain when my time is out by writing to the Supt or the Asst Supt.Now whatever you do will be Satisfactory to me in the mean time let me hear from you at once and be Sure of my confidence of my respect and of my gratitu— ——— deference **John W HArdin**

---

205. J. W. H. to Gov. James Hogg

Jan the 1St 1894
The State of Texas (To the hon James. S. Hogg.
county of Walker (gov of the State of Texas
I do respectfully represent to your excellency that I was tried and convicted in the town of commanchie county of commanchie and

State of Texas at the fall term of the district court for commanchie county in the year AD 1877. for the murder of charles Webb on or about the 26th day of may AD 1874. the punishment assessed being 25 years in the penitentiary from which conviction I appealed to the court of appeals. and which was affirmed by the court of Appeals Sitting at Austin in the year AD 1878. (See Texas court of Appeals reports vol 4. page 355) And I do respectfully request and beg you as governor of the rich and poor alike of the great State of Texas to grant me a full pardon from Said conviction before mentioned, that is if you can find any valid reason at law in moral justice or righteousness to So do that will Satisfy your conscience to a moral certainty that you are doing right, and for this purpose you are respectfully refered to all papers accompaning this petition as well as to the law applicable. the case to the Sound reason pertinent to the case which your the judicial mind may comprehend or apprehend: Now at the time I was tried the defendant was not a competent witness in his own behalf hence I did not testify. but Since that time the legislature has removed the disability of a defendant in a criminal prosecution See the acts of 21st leg, Page 37. Chap 43. 1887 Therefore I avail my Self of this humane and progressive right and have prepaired an affidavit which I hope to have certified but if the Affidavit or Statemen comes to you without being properly

2nd. certified according to law please give it Such consideration as your just and judicial mind may apprehend it deserves. hence I respectfully and confidingly refer you to each and every word it contains and request that you peruse and view it in conjunction with the evidence of William cunningham James, Carnes and others as reported in the 4th Vol. App. page 355. John. W. HArdin V.S. the State relied upon a conspiracy and all the testimony introduced upon that Subject was William cunninghams Who was one of the party who accompanied my brother Jo. G HArdin and Sheriffs party to Brown county after the cattle except one other Who Swore that just before the tragedy I remarked to jim Taylor that I never Seen anything coming up finer as we were going up the Street, and that charles Webb was on the other Side of the Street &C. Yet it was not in proof that I Saw him the deceased at that time. Now I wish to Say that these very witnesses Cunningham carnes and Talbot were Suspected by my Brothers friends and relatives as being principles in his Jo G HArdins murder. I deem the Affidavit of Mattie. Smith establishes the fact that my brother Jo. G. Hardin and my cousins William Dixson and Tom Dixson were cruelly deliberately and unlawfully murdered in cominanchie by a mob in June AD 1874. I have been told that there was at that time 50. or a 100, rangers Stationed at commanchie. I refer you to the proper records at Austin. I am certain that Capt Waller was there with his company of rangers and it is a notorious fact that my brother Jo. G. Hardin. William Dixson and Tom Dixson my own cousins were cruelly wilfully deliberately and unlawfully put to death without any protest from the authorities of commanchie county or from the authorities of the State of Texas neither have they the mob been proceeded against by indictment or otherwise. I ask you to draw you own conclusion, "but let it be just if the heavens fall"

3rd Now Judge J. R. Fleming the trial judge in the court below Knew that my brother and relatives had been Surrendered to a mob on or about the 5the of june AD 1874 in the town of commanchie — and county of commanchie who placed ropes around their necks in the court house and drug them bareheaded and barefooted a Short distance from town and there hung them until they were dead. because J. G. HArdin ——— he had the temerity to demand a fair Speedy and impartial trial for his brother and client. from the officers of the law and that Tom Dixson was put to death because he was a relative of mine and an eye witness to the homicide of Charles Webb: and he knew that the prejudice in the county of commanchie was So Strong and violent against me at the very time of my trial in commanchie that the governor of the State of Texas had deemed it advisable to Send with me from Austin Texas a company of Rangers numbering 30 or 35 to escort me to commanchie to guard me while there at trial to Keep me from being mobed as my brother and relatives were and then to escort me back again to Austin for he the Said Judge J.R. Fleming. resided and practiced law in the town of commanchie in the year AD 1874 and was judge of the district court of Said county in the year AD 1877. Article 576 of the C.C.P. of the State of Texas Says "Whenever. in any case of felony. the district judge presiding Shall be Satisfied that a trial, alike fair and impartial to the accused and to the State, cannot from any cause be had in the county in which the case is pending, he may upon his own motion order a change of venue to any county in his own or in an adjoining district, Stating in his order the grounds for Such change of venue." See a case where the judge Should have ordered a change of venue on his own motion. Steagold V.S. 22. App. 464, Now by recapitulation and by close inspection of all the

4th material facts and circumstances connected with the case your grasping judicial mind can easily determine the grade of homicide I commited when I Shot to death charles Webb whether or not I had a fair and impartial trial or whether or not it was possible under all the circumstances for me to have a fair and impartial trial in commanchie at the time of my trial. The jury by their virdict Said their was no conspiracy to Kill deceased they heard the evidence and it is evident that they (the jury) did not believe the States witnesses and the States theory upon the Subject of conspiracy for their virdict was "we the jury find the defendant guilty of murder in the 2nd degree as charged in the indictment and assess his punishment at 25 years hard labor in the penitentiary at Huntsville" having disposed of the theory of conspiracy your judicial mind will readily grasp and investigate the facts and circumstances more approximately connected with the tragedy and you will view charles Webb a deptuty Sheriff of Brown county in the town of commanchie threatening to Kill John W. HArdin at the race tracks Then after the races he the Said charles Webb telling the reason why he never killed John. W. Hardin at the Said race tracks that he had too many friends around him but that he charles Webb intended to Kill him the Said John. W. HArdin before Sundown or die in the attempt and that I was informed of these threats and was prepairing to go to my Fathers to avoid him the Said charles Webb that he came to where I was at Jack Wrights Saloon and that I Spoke to him not with any intention of bringing on or provoking a difficulty with him but if possible to avoid a difficulty. he came up from the back way he had on a big pistol he stoped near me he eyed me closely he had been announced to me as the man who but a few moments before Seriously and earnestly threatened to Kill me before Sun down or die in the attempt and he had

5th his hand behind him, did I not under the circumstances have a right to ask him if he had any papers for my arrest. and when he Said that he did not Know me. did I not act manly and fair with him in telling him who I was, and when he Said <u>now</u> <u>I</u> <u>know</u> <u>you</u> <u>but</u> <u>have</u> <u>no</u> <u>papers</u> <u>for</u> <u>your</u> <u>arrest</u>. did I not have the legal and moral right under the peculiar circumstances to ask him what he had in his hand behind him. and when he Showed a Stump of a cigar. did I not have the right all things considered to tell him that I had heard that the Sheriff of Brown county had Said that John Carnes the Sheriff of commanchie was no man and no Sheriff because he was harboring the Notorious John W HArdin. and that he the Sheriff of Brown county had come over to attend to John Carnes business that he intended to Kill John W Hardin before Sun down or die in the attempt, and when he Said I am not the Sheriff of Brown county I am only a dept, my name is charles Webb. and am not responsible for what the Sheriff does, or Says. besides I think John Carnes a brave officer and a jentleman. all things considered did I not have the right to Say as I did Say that Settles it, there is no difference between us (in other words let us be friends) and when we were introduced to each other did I not evidently exhibit a desire a willingness to be friendly with charles Webb when I cordially Sincerely and in good faith invited him to join me in a Social cigar or drink did I not Show my confidence in his assent by innocently and peacefully turning my back to him to go ito the Saloon but ah: my confidence was

6th betrayed almost at the Sacrifice of my life, for he (charles webb had came to where I was. with murder hid deep in his heart. for the purpose of murdering me. and he had herald his malicious purpose on the Streets of commanchie. on the race tracks. in the Stores. and in the Saloons. that he (charles Webb) would Kill John W HArdin before Sundown, or die in the attempt. So while my back was to him. he like a Sneaking cowardly assassin perceived the opportunity he was watching for. and now attempts to execute it with dispatch (with a vim) by instantly without a words notice drawing a big pistol (a deadly weapon) and firing its contents at my back (or vitals) but at this juncture there came a voice (like the voice of god) look out Jack and his game was up and he himself died before Sundown. I ask in the name of truth of the eternal principles of justice if I did not have a legal and moral and inalienable right under the circumstances to Shoot down. to death. the wood be assassin. though clad in a Sheriffs armor, though plated with the Shield of State:

Let your brave pen dictate the answer, By a close inspection of the records in the court below as well as the case reported in vol 4 page

355 of the court of Appeals Reports. you will find that considerable attention has been paid to the point that if I "provoked the deceased into the contest. or produced the occasion, in order to have a pretext for Killing him, or doing him great bodily harm. the Killing would be murder, no matter to what extremity I may have been reduced." in Selfridgis case it was held that. no words nor libellious publication, however aggravating. will compromit his right of Self defense. if in consiquence of the Same he is attacked: for no words, of whatsoever nature will justify assult.Now while the 1st proposition is true—

7th. the Second is equally true: See White V.S. 23.App,154. where the rule is qualified and extended to its legitimate purpose: Hurt, J. Says. "But if he provokes the combat or produces the occasion. without any felonious intent —intending for instance. an ordinary battery merely—the final killing will be manslaughter only". The Same Judge Says in delivering the opinion in the above case cited. "It will be observed that the intent with which the contest. or occasion was Sought. or produced. is of the hightest importance. Suppose a defendant provokes a combat. or produces an occasion without intending to do So: or let us Suppose his acts or language did in fact provoke the contest. but were not intended to have that effect. nor were they Such as would usually and naturally lead to a contest. If under these circumstances. he kill to Save him Self. or to prevent Serious bodily harm. Will he thereby be deprived of full and perfect right of Self defense": And then he Says. "The rule laid down in the notes to Staffers case, "Which we take to be the correct one. clearly indicates that there must be a purpose behind the provocation and impelling to it." "It is also evident that. notwithstanding the defendant may have provoked the combat or produced the occasion by his own wrongful act. yet. if these were not clearly calculated or Intended to have Such effect. his right of Self defense is not thereby compromited. It is not ever wrongful act that will deprive the doer of his right of Self defense." And Hurt. J. Says again in "Peter V.S. 23. App. 684." Cases may and do arise in which the original trespasser. or one who provokes or furnishes the occasion for a difficulty. becomes entitled to the full and perfect benefit of Self defense But this right being forfeited or abridged by his own act. it must be revived by his own act: as where one condones his trespass or wrong by retiring from the difficulty in an unequivocal maner. and his adversary then renews the combat." There remains an other legal question which I respectfully call your attention. Our Statutes provide that. "Where a defendant accused of murder. Seeks to justify himself on the grounds of threats against his own life. he may be

---

8th. not be regarded as affording a justification for the offense unless it be Shown that. at the time of the homicide the person Killed—by Some act then done manifested an intention to execute the threat So made: Penal code. Art.608. Now White. J. in Howard V.S. 23. App. 265. Says. "From all the authorities we are of the opinion the true doctrine is that threats are admissible ordinaryley per Se as independent evidence in cases of this character." "But as to how far they will justify or mitigate a crime. we believe the correct rule is that announced by Moor. J. in Johnson V.S. 27. Tex.757. He Says. "If at the time of the homicide there is any act from which the accused may reasonably infer an Intention to carry them into effect. he is justified in resorting to Such means as may be in his power. to defend and protect himself against their execution.: "If death ensues. it is justifiable homicide." I again respectfully ask you to apply the law to the facts. See. Art.570.571.573.574. of the criminal code. Another fact pertinent to the case all things considered to which I call your attention is that the Legislature next in Session after the homicide of charles. Webb and the mobing of my brother and relatives empowered the governor (probably and evidently through the influence of the mobs emissaries) to offer four thousand dollars for my arrest. But no money was then nor has there ever been a dollar appropriated for the Special purpose of bringing the mob to justice who with express malice aforethout put to death Jo. G. Hardin. William and Tom Dixson in the town of commanche AD. 1874. Besides I was Kidnaped in Pensacola Florida and my Kidnapers Shot to death at the time of ——— without excuse and without warrant of law. Will any sane ——— mind acquainted with all the facts and circumstances in the case. Say that I am less worthy of citizenship than the individual members of the mob Spoken of above. than the Judge who tried me or the Kidnapers. I hope you will take a favorable view of this matter and grant me a pardon. Now while I have writen plainly I have writen truely not in malice to any one but in vindication of myself. Now in conclusion I will Say that my high-

Governor James Stephen Hogg
—Courtesy Gonzales Library, Gonzales, Texas
(*A History of Texas*, vol. 5, by Louis J Wortham, LL.D.)

test hopes object aim and ambition is to yet lead a life of usefulness of peace in the path of rectitude and righteousness respectfully

John W HArdin (in propria persona)

Jan the 1st 1894

The State of Texas (To the hon James. S. Hogg.
County of Walker (Gov of the State of Texas

CALLIE LEWIS WOULD BECOME JOHN WESLEY HARDIN'S SECOND WIFE.

---

206. Callie Lewis to Mr. Rogers

London Texas
Jan 2nd 1894
Mr Rogers Junction

Dear friend
I received your note and was sorrow That you could not come new year I went to a dance last night. miss Nora Ivy is with me! They are going To have that party friday night at uncle Ely Boyce's aunt palestine Told me to besure and write to you to come she is going to look for you and I will be disapointed if you dont come.
besure and come
Excuse bad writing as I am in a hurry
Your Cousin **Callie**
P.S don't let any one see this **C L.**

---

207. John D. McCall to K. R. Blackshear

Form No. 76.

EXECUTIVE DEPARTMENT.

OFFICE OF COMPTROLLER,

AUSTIN , 1 / 9 1894

JNO. D. McCALL, COMPTROLLER.
STEPH. H. DARDEN, CHIEF CLERK.
Mr. K. R. Blackshear

Pennington TEXAS.
DEAR SIR:
Enclosed find Treasury Warrant No. 15116 for $5.88, covering the amount of Direct Tax paid by J. G. Hardin in Trinity Co
Please acknowledge receipt.
Very respectfully,
Jno D McCall
Comptroller.

---

208. K. R. Blackshear to J. W. Hardin

Pennington Texas Jany 11th 1894

J. W. Hardin.
Dear Sir:
After some unavoidable delay I have received your check which I inclose for your signature to the Indorsement Which you will note I have written on back of same—It is necessary that the Indorsement be same as in face of the Check hence I worded it for you. Sign your name before the words Et als and sign it J. W Hardin. Just as the Competroller wrote it &C and return to me in enclosed envellope and I will send you a Postal Money order for same less fees for Collecting &C—I have been unable to find out if your father paid any of this Direct Tax in Polk Co. but suspect he did not. I will hower satisfy myself on this point soon & let you Know.
Yours. as ever. **K.R. Blackshear**

---

209. J. G. Hardin to J. W. H.

Perry, Ok. Ter. Jan. 28th 1894.
Mr. John W. Hardin, Huntsville Texas.

Dear Brother:
Not very long ago I wrote you a letter while I was at Gainesville Texas. I have received no answer but of course am not kicking because I know how it is but if you can answer this soon and let me know how you are making it. I understood that your time would be out last Nov., how about That? I intend to write W. S. Fly a letter

about you some time This week. Write to me and tell me how this matter stands. I left Gainesville last Thursday week. Bud wanted me to come up here. and so I came. He gave me a good lot. He has a Saloon, Wagon yard and feed store and is going to start up a meat market Monday. His business place is on the 1st two lots of the fourth block from the square on C street. I think he will do well. In a year or two his lots will be worth a good deal. Nannie is in Witt, Texas now. She wanted me to come there but there's nothing but grass hoppers and dead grass out there. I like this place fine. Hoping to hear from you soon. I will close. Bud wants to hear from you He thinks the is no one like you. He told me to write to you two or three days ago. And when I was at Gainesville, every letter he wrote he asked about you. Your Bro.

J. G. Hardin.

---

210. J. G. Hardin to J. W. H. (fragment)

Ennis Ellis Co. ———
Mr. John W. Hardin,
Cuero, Texas.

Dear brother:
I received your most welcomed letter yesterday. I was greatly supprised to hear that you are at Cuero. I wrote to you about a month ago. but received no answer. From your last letter it seems that you understand that I know all ———, ——— says she is going to ——— a treat before long.——— be supprised indeed ——— of the course you are —ing. Just as soon as the —al is over you must write —d tell me the results and the particulars about the case, in full. I would give any thing to be present, but it is impossible.
Wishing you success,
I remain
Your brother,
Jas. G. Hardin.

---

211. K. R. Blackshear to J. G. Smither

Ack. receipt

2/11/94

Pennington Texas. 2/7/1894

J. G. Smither Esq

Dear Sir:

Yours with Hardins Check and also an Express Money order. To hand, I return the Hardin Check. Any merchant will Cash same for him. The Ex. M.O. Order is for $1^{\underline{25}}$ Which Hardin Says is my fee, I wrote Hardin that for him I would Collect for about Cost and supposed $1^{\underline{00}}$ would Cover same. and in Ordinary Cases it would, but in this Case some of the heirs at first objected. Not fully understanding the matter and as a Consequence I had to get a Power of Attorney from All the heirs thus running up expenses to fully one half of the Check ie $5^{\underline{88}}$ or, $2.94 I think he will readily Consent to let you send me another Ex. Money order for $\$1.^{\underline{50}}$ and you to deduct same from Check. I will say that all parties for whom I have made these Collection voluntarily give me half. I dont Care to make anything in the Case but of Course prefer not to lose by it. Kindly explain to him and oblige

Yours Truly

K. R. Blackshear,

P.S. If I can ever return the favor dont hesitate to Call on Me,

yours **K.R.B,**

---

212. R. M. Glover to J. W. Hardin

Gonzales Febuary 28th 1894

J.W. Hardin Sedan

Dear Sir & Friend:

Yours of 26th inst

Just received and was very glad to hear from you. though very sorry to have disappointed you on Saturday. My business was shaped that day (as is frequently the Case) so that it was impossible for me to leave town. I have seen aunt Elvira since you was over, and can assure you that your visit did her a wonderful lot of good.

I also have Just received a letter from Mr walton in which he expresses warmest friendship and pledges "all assistance possible for him to render at any time." No news of interest in Town. everything quiet. when you come in, if in day time come direct to office. and if at

night come to my house. any one can tell you where I live and I have plenty of good course but substantial grubb. with kindest regards to all and hoping to see you again soon and again soliciting pardon for disappointment Saturday, I remain as ever
Truly Your friend
R. M. Glover

---

213. Barnett Gibbs to J. W. H.

[UNDATED]

LAW OFFICE OR BARNETT GIBBS, MAIN. & LAMAR STS.

Dallas, Texas, F 1894

John Wesley Hardin — Texas —

Dear Sir —
I see from the News that you have been pardoned and I am glad of it for however great your offense I feel sure that you have in you the making of a useful man — I hope you will adhere to your good resolutions and many a man has started in life and in law at your present age and made a success — you have my best wishes in your new life and I will at any time be glad to serve you — Lawyers as a rule are generous and liberal in their views, and I dont think any of them will fail to appreciate your desire to make up the time you have lost in atoning for your offense against society — If you should come to Dallas call upon me —
Yours Respt — Barnett Gibbs

---

214. John B. Ashe to J. W. H.

Houston, March 6th, 1894.

John W. Hardin, Esq. Gonzales, Texas.

Dear Sir:
After a careful search of all the records in the office I fail to find the indictments against William Kelly or Milt. Day. The record of their conviction is in the office however, and I can furnish you with a certified recore of that if it will be of any service to youl. If you wish this, please notify me at once and I can make it and send it to you by Saturday or Monday at the latest.

Respectfully, **John B. Ashe.**

---

215. J. D. Long to J. W. H.

Schulenburg. Texas March 8 = 1894
Mr John W. Hardin Sedan Tex

Friend John
I saw recently In the Galveston News that you was Once more a free man allow me sir to congratulate you also your wife and Children and believe me that I am truly glad to live to know that you are a free man and want you to come and see me I have been living In San Antonio since I saw you most of the time I married there have been living here this year with Dr Clark as rusher on his stock farm one mile from Town John let me know If you will come and about what time I am the same Jim Long as when you saw me last Yours Respectfully. **J D. Long**
write soon

FORM 29*
TEXAS STATE PENITENTIARIES.

CERTIFICATE OF PRISON CONDUCT.

To Gov. J.S. Hogg

This is to Certify, that Convict No. 7109 John Wesley Hardin who was an inmate of the TEXAS STATE PENITENTIARY at Huntsville and who was heretofore by the District Court of Comanche County, at the Spring Term thereof, convicted of a felony in One case, to wit: Murder 2nd Degree after a plea of Not guilty, and sentence Affirmed on the 5 day of June A.D. 1878 to 25 years confinement in the Penitentiary, was received here the 5 day of October A.D. 1878,and has now served 15 years 8 months 12 days.
The Prison Records show that when received his Age was 26 years, Height 5 ft. 9 in.,Weight 160 lbs. Color White Marital Relations Married Habits Temperate Education Common Occupation Labourer Nativity Texas Residence Gonzales County Health when

received Fair Health when dischgd Fair Escapes None Time lost by escapes None Charges of misconduct ~~to date~~ Eleven Character of offense Mutinous conduct — Conspiring to incite Impudence — Throwing food on floor—Laziness—Gambling—Trying to incite convicts to Impudence
Punishments to date. Jan-1879 -Jan.9"1880 -May 6-'81 -Feb-'83 - July 28"83 -Oct-'83(3) -July 31-'85 -aug. 6-"85 -Aug 26"85 -May 12.'93 -May 26" '93.
Commutation gained to date, _____ yrs. ______ mos. ____ days,
out of possible commutation, _____ yrs. _____ mos. _____ days.
Expiration of sentence, full time June 5" 1903 with full commutation Oct 2" 1893 Date of discharge Feby 17" 1894
~~Conduct~~: Note: Concurrent with above is a 2Yr term from Dewitt Co: Manslaughter: Sentenced Jany 1st 1892.

Given under my hand and official seal, at
Huntsville Texas, on this 15" day
of March A.D.1894
LAWhatley
// Superintendent.
8

Request of
Gov. J. S. Hogg

No. 15075
John Wesley
Hardin
Received and Filed
MAR 16 1894
B F Green
Private secretary

216. Tom Bell to R. M. Glover

OFFICE OF TOM BELL,
*Sheriff, * Hill * County, * Texas. *
Hillsboro, Texas, 3/27 1894
R. M. Glover Sheriff Gonzales

Dear Sir
In ans to yours of the 26th will state there is an Idictment against J. Wesley Hardin for murder committed in this County over 20 years ago and I have no Idia that a Conviction Could be had on the Case. I knowned Hardin while here, and supose there has been considerable change in him since that time I Know all his Relations In this County and they are all fine people and the citizens Thinks generaly that John Wesley Hardin has been punished enough and had I not thouth so I would have went after him before he was released from the pen, But It might Be Best to hold this case on the Dockett untill he thoroughly proves by His conduct that he intends to keep out of trouble and not any one else trouble However If you Insist on it I will get the case Dismissed
yours to command
Tom Bell Shff.

HARDIN DESCRIBES THE KILLING IN HILL COUNTY AS FOLLOWS:

"The game was composed of Jim Bradly, Hamp Davis, Judge Moore, and myself. I knew afterwards that these three stood in against me, but did not know this at the time. One thing, however, I did know, and that was how to protect myself pretty well from such fellows in a game of draw poker. I placed about $350 in gold in front of me and about $10 in silver. Bradly, on my left, placed in front of himself about $5 in silver and $20 in gold; Davis, on Bradly's left, about $10 in silver and $40 in gold, and Moore about $30 in gold. The game proceeded quietly until about 12 o'clock at night, about which time I had won all the money. We were playing on a blanket in a small box house without a door but with a place open for a chimney in the north end. The house was about 13x14 feet and was situated about a quarter of a mile from the grocery. The moon was shining brightly and the night was clear and cold. I had won all the money on the blanket, as I said before, and all the players owed me. I had pulled off my boots and thrown them in the corner to my left next to Bradly, not suspecting that robbery was the intention of the game. I was quietly fixing to quit the game unknown to the others and had put all the gold in my pocket, only having about $25 or $30 in front of me. Moore remarked that everybody owed Hardin. I said,

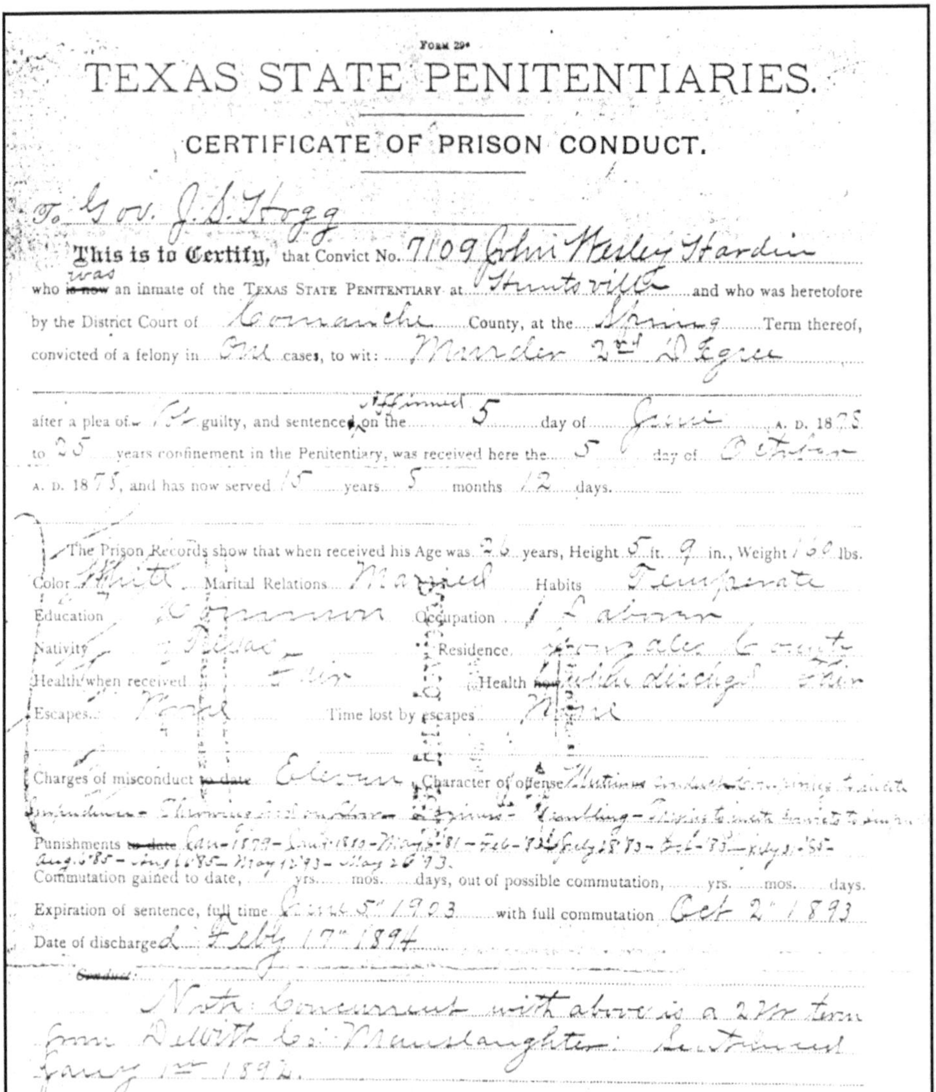

FORM 29a

TEXAS STATE PENITENTIARIES.

CERTIFICATE OF PRISON CONDUCT.

To Gov. J. S. Hogg

This is to Certify, that Convict No. 7109 John Wesley Hardin who ~~is now~~ was an inmate of the Texas State Penitentiary at Huntsville and who was heretofore by the District Court of Comanche County, at the Spring Term thereof, convicted of a felony in One cases, to wit: Murder 2nd Degree

after a plea of Not guilty, and sentenced, Affirmed on the 5 day of June A. D. 1875 to 25 years confinement in the Penitentiary, was received here the 5 day of October A. D. 1878, and has now served 15 years 5 months 12 days.

The Prison Records show that when received his Age was 26 years, Height 5 ft. 9 in., Weight 160 lbs.

Color White Marital Relations Married Habits Temperate

Education Common Occupation Labor

Nativity Texas Residence Gonzales County

Health when received Fair Health ~~now~~ when discharged Fair

Escapes None Time lost by escapes None

Charges of misconduct ~~to date~~ Eleven Character of offense Mutinous conduct ... Impudence ... Gambling ...

Punishments ~~to date~~ Jan-1879 - Jan-1880 - May 5-81 - Feb-83 - July 28-83 - Feb-83 - July 31-85 - Aug 5-85 - Aug 16-85 - May 12-93 - May 26-93.

Commutation gained to date, yrs. mos. days, out of possible commutation, yrs. mos. days.

Expiration of sentence, full time June 5th 1903 with full commutation Oct 2nd 1893

Date of discharged Feby 17th 1894

~~Conduct~~:

Note: Concurrent with above is a 2 yr term from DeWitt Co: Manslaughter: Sentenced Jany 1st 1892.

Certificate of prison conduct.

—Courtesy Archives and Information Services Division, Texas State Library and Archives Commission, Austin, Texas

"yes," but Jim Bradly said no, and we left it to Moore and Davis to decide. They said, "yes, you owe Hardin $5." About this time we both got good hands and I bet him $5 on three aces. He made me put up the money but "called" me without putting up a cent. I said to him: "Now you owe me $10, let us settle up or quit. "He said: "You are a g— d— liar and a coward," drew a big knife, and quick as a cat could wink made a grab for me, while Davis got my six-shooter in the corner. Collins then threw himself between Bradly and me and kept him from stabbing me to death. This gave me a chance to get up, and when I did Bradly drew his six-shooter and threatened to kill me if I did not give up my money. "Give me $500 or I will kill you, g— d— you," he said. Collins came to my rescue again and grabbed him, crying to me to jump out of the chimney opening or I would be killed. Out I went, barefooted on the frosty ground, and ran out to our horses. Davis gave me a fearful cursing, calling me a murderer, a coward, a robber, and saying he would get me before day. Collins came out to where I was standing behind a tree and said: "John, let us go home; we are in a hell of a scrape." I said: "Where is your pistol?" He said: "Bradly borrowed it in the early part of the night." "No," I said, "I am not going home to face my father in this condition; I want my boots, my money, and my pistol. Don't be a fool, but take things coolly," Collins went back to get my boots, which Bradly finally gave him permission to do. Bradly continued to abuse me and went to the grocery with his crowd, who by this time were all cursing me as a man who had been posing as a brave man, but who in fact was a coward and a damned rascal. As soon as I got my boots on, I told Collins I wanted to go and see Moore, who had my money and pistol. He said he would go with me to his boarding house, as he knew the proprietor. We left our horses where they were and found Moore at the boarding house. He refused to give up either the pistol or the money without Bradly's consent. He agreed to go with Collins to see Bradly at the grocery about 100 yards off across the road in an easterly direction. When they got to the grocery and saw Bradly, he was still cursing. He threatened Collins and swore he would kill me if he saw me. Moore told him I was at his boarding house after my pistol and money. Bradly said, "well, I'll go over there and fill him full of lead." Meantime Collins had borrowed a pistol and persuaded Bradly to exchange, telling him he was going home and wanted his own. John Collins bade him good-bye and came back to the boarding house where I was. He wanted me to go home, but by this time Bradly had started over to where I was, swearing to kill me. The proprietor was trying to get me to leave, when I asked him for a pistol to defend myself with from robbery and death. He refused to do this, but Collins gave me his and said, "Now let us go to our horses." I said, "All O.K.," and we started to go out of the gate and into the public road that led to where our horses were. Just as we got out of the gate we saw Bradly with six or seven others, including Hamp Davis, coming toward us, threatening to kill me, his crowd urging him on by shouting, "Go for him! We are with you," etc. I told John Collins to go in the lead. The gin was on the right, about fifty yards away, with a store about fifty yards from where we were standing. Bradly saw me and tried to cut me off, getting in front of me with a pistol in one hand and a Bowie knife in the other. He commenced to fire on me, firing once, then snapping, and then firing again. By this time we were within five or six feet of each other, and I fired with a Remington .45 at his heart and right after that at his head. As he staggered and fell, he said, "O, Lordy, don't shoot me any more." I could not stop. I was shooting because I did not want to take chances on a reaction. The crowd ran, and I stood there and cursed them loud and long as cowardly devils who had urged a man to fight and when he did and fell, to desert him like cowards and traitors."

---

217. R. M. Glover to J. W. H.

Gonzales March 28th 1894

Jno. W. Hardin Sedan

Dear Friend:

Enclosed find letter from Sheriff Bell of Hill Co. in regard to your Case. He seems to have a loose screw, in wanting to hold a Case that he acknoledeges there is nothing in over you, as a kind of prize pole to make you do right. However we all have our peculiurauties and I am glad to have his good wishes as expressed in the letter. I wrote him annother strong letter which I think will Completely knock his theory of holding this Case as a prize, out. I think when we hear from him again the Case will be dissmissed. no news, all quiet and family well. with regards to all

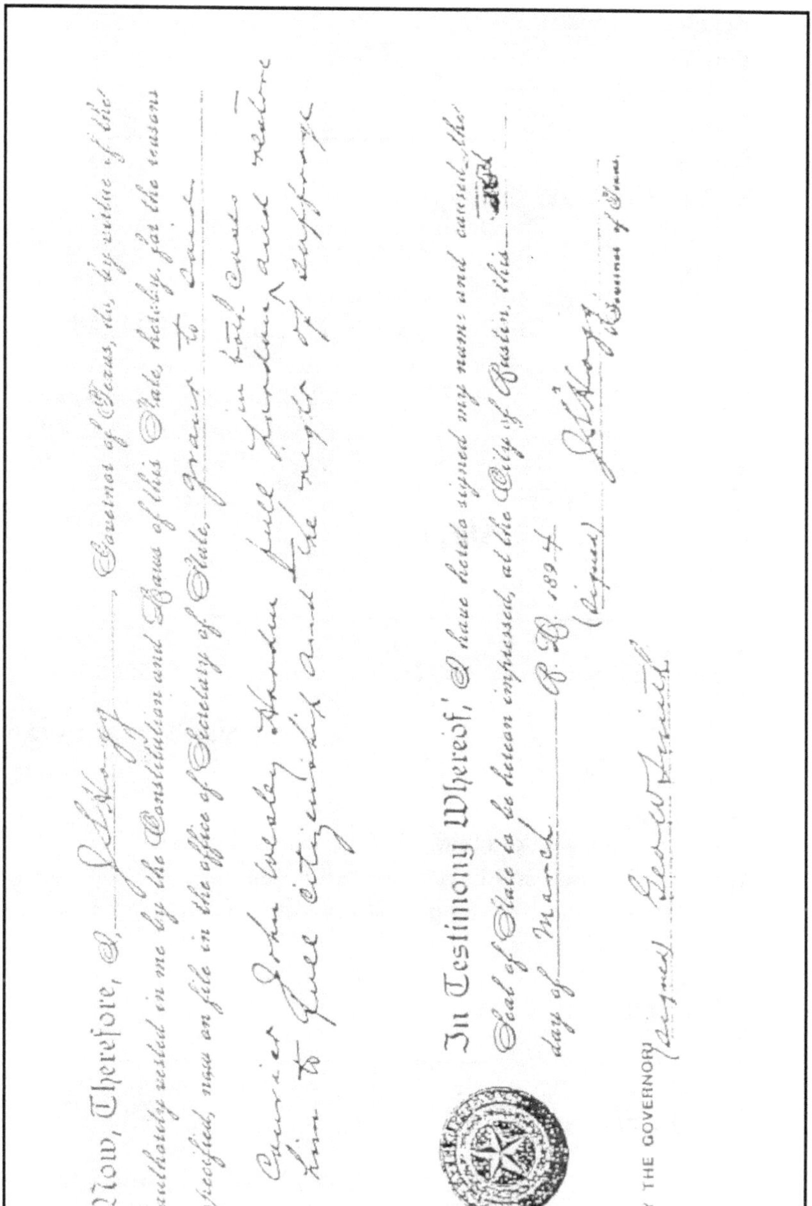

Now, Therefore, I, J S Hogg Governor of Texas, do, by virtue of the authority vested in me by the Constitution and Laws of this State, hereby, for the reasons specified, now on file in the office of Secretary of State, grant to convict John Wesley Hardin in toto full pardon and restore him to full citizenship and the right of suffrage

In Testimony Whereof, I have hereto signed my name and caused the Seal of State to be hereon impressed, at the City of Austin, this [illegible] day of March A.D. 1894

(Signed) J S Hogg Governor of Texas.

BY THE GOVERNOR (Signed) Geo W Smith

Full pardon, restoration to full citizenship, and the right of suffrage.
—Courtesy Archives and Information Services Division,
Texas State Library and Archives Commission, Austin, Texas

I remain
Yours Truly
R.M. Glover

---

218. Tom Bell to R. M. Glover

OFFICE OF TOM BELL,
Sheriff, Hill County, Texas.
Hillsboro, Texas, March. 30. 1894. 189_

R. M. Glover, Sheriff, Gonzales, Texas.
Dear Sir:— Replying to your favor of the 28th, will say the county attorney has agreed when the case of Wesley Hardin is reached to have it dismissed. Trusting in his reformation and that he may yet be a useful citizen, I remain
Yours truly, **Tom Bell, Sheriff.**
Per T.

---

219. R. M. Glvoer to J. W. H.

Gonzales March 31st 1894
J.W. Hardin Esq. Sedn

Dear sir & Friend:
I infer from above letter that their Court is now in session, and that the case will be dismissed when reached in its regular order on the Docket at this term. Did you get the other letter from Bell? I mailed it to you several days ago
Yours &C.
R.M. Glover

---

220. R. W. Finley to J. W. H.

HUNTSVILLE, TEXAS Apr, 1894.
Jno. W. Hardin Smiley

Dear Sir:
I shall be a candidate, before the State Democratic Convention, for nomination to the office of Comptroller of Public Accounts.

That office is purely a business one, and my experience in that character of service for the State has inspired me with what I trust is a laudable ambition to fill the office.

I was appointed to a clerkship in the Comptroller's office by the Hon. Win. J. Swain; served during his administration; was promoted by the Hon. Jno. D. McCall to be Chief Bookkeeper, and filled that position four years, when I was appointed by Governor Hogg, Financial Agent of the Texas State Penitentiaries. The management of the financial affairs of the Penitentiaries, during my administration, is a matter of public record, and to which I confidently refer.

I was born, and have lived, a Democrat, and believe that the prosperity, happiness and progress of the great State of Texas and her people are inseparably linked and interwoven with the continuance of Democratic supremacy.

I respectfully and earnestly solicit your support; and promise, if nominated and elected, my best efforts in the administration of the affirs of that department of the State government, in the direction of wholesome economy and to the best interests of the taxpayers of Texas.

Respectfully,

R. W. FINLEY.

---

221. R. M. Glover to J. W. Hardin

Gonzales april 13th 1894

Jno. W. Hardin

Friend John:

Yours of the 11th inst. Just received and contents noted. I received your other one the next day after I wrote to Buck. I am very glad to hear you are still improving in health and to soon see you completely restored and ready for business and would like very much to be with you on some of your hunting and fishing trips. I will watch the Hill Co. Case Closely. We are going to have a big Democratic rally here on the 21st Inst with Hogg & Clark as speakers and I want you to be sure and come in then and see the Governor

Yours &C,

R. M. Glover.

---

222. Ferdy Bishop to J. W. H.

OFFICE OF Sheriff of Polk County.
T.J. EPPERSON, Sheriff.
Livingstone, Texas, April 14 1894
Jno W Hardin

Dear John
Yrs of the 13th to hand—Was glad to hear from you—but Sorry to hear that you had been Sick. hope You are All O.K by this time—Would be gladest in the World to See you. Come over here before Setling down. maybe this would be a. good place for you to practice Law. Come & see—Dist Ct opens here on 21 of May. & holds 5 Weeks— J. I dont think you Could sell any Horses at this place for a While. not before fall People Have no
(2)
money—And Crops are very backward—there have been a great many Small ponies sold in here—try & come over by the 4th of June at any rate the people in this Co would like to See You — And you also have a great many Friends here—Write me often. I like to hear from you whether I can See you or not. Love to Children And All send Love to you with best wishes for prosperity in the future I remain yours to serve at any time & Cousin F. D.. Bishop
NB. Have you heard from P. or J lately write soon
Ferdy

---

223. Tom Bell to R. M. Glover

OFFICE OF TOM BELL,
Sheriff, * Hill * County, * Texas.
Hilisboro, Texas, April 14 1894

R M Glover sheriff
Gonzales Tex

Dear Sir
Our District Court adJourned last evening. will meet no more until sept. The Case against John Wesly Hardin was dismissed So there is nothing in Hill Co against Wes. Tell wes to be a good man And Keep out of trouble
Yours Truly

Tom Bell Shff

---

224. R. M. Glover to J. W. Hardin

Gonzales april 16th 1894
Jno. N. Hardin Belmont

Dear Sir & Friend
I received annother letter from our mutual friend Tom Bell of Hill Co. in which he states."Our District Court adjourned on the 13th inst. and will meet no more untill sept. The case against John Wesley Hardin was dismissed so there is nothing in Hill Co. against him". The above is a qotation from Bells letter and he Continues by assuring you of his friendship and interest in your wellfare and says that you have a host of friends in the Co. who would be glad to see you at anytime. I will keep his letter untill you come to town. I wrote you several days ago at Belmont in Care Derrick Mc. Gee. If you can possibly do so be sure and come down on the 21st inst.
Your true friend
R. M. Glover

---

225. J. M. Taylor to J. W. H.

Yorktown, Texas. April 28, 1894.
Mr John W. Hardin,
Sedan. Texas.

My dear friend.
Your letter was a surprise never the less a pleasant one. I was so sorry I didn't get your letter in time for I would have gone to Gonzales a purpose to see you if I ever get time I am coming to see you I am the same old John I always was and am always glad to see my old friends, so if you ever come down here be shure and come to see me. I would like So much to see you and talk to you it would remind me of olden times,
Crops are fine in this part of the country, and so is grass, and cattle are mending rite along I would write more this morning but am in a hurry so please excuse me this time. hoping to see or hear from you soon With my best wishes for your future,
Your friend

J. M. Taylor

---

226. J. P. Randle to J. W. H.

Folio.__________ **Gonzales, Texas, May 9th 1894**

Mr J W Hardin

BOUGHT OF J. P RANDLE,
DEALER IN
Dry Goods, Notions, Ladies' wear,***
**** Clothing, Gents' Furnishings and Hats.
—— FINE SHOES A SPECIALTY ——.

Terms. __________

3	Pr Blk ½hos^{75} 2Pr Scrim Draws 2^{00} 3 C Bander Sheets 1^{50}	4^{25}
1	Parasol 1^{20} 2PrBlk Hose^{50} 1 Comb^{35} 6 HKfs50 1 Bot Cologn^{50}	3^{10}
1	Paper^{10} 1 Pa Needs^{5} 1 BoxHairPins^{15} Fan^{15} thimble^{5}	50
2	sp Silk thred^{20} 6sp thred^{25} l4yds Scrim. 1^{40} 20 yd Scrim2^{00}	3^{85}
12	yds Dontic1^{00} 5yds Pillow Case Lace^{50} 4 yds lace 50	1^{80}
9	" Embrdryl^{18}/1^{62} l0yds embery 1-1^{25} 2yds luy L———50	3^{37}
20	" Crepine2^{00} 4yds Cor— — 50	2^{50}
9	" Challie1^{80} 5yds Pink Ribbin^{75} 5yds ----- 75	3^{30}
9	" Calico^{55} 9yds Calico^{45} 6yds Calico 30	1^{30}
3	" Calico^{20} 4yds losi dale Cau—^{40}	60
20	" Dotted 5wiss5^{00} 2-1- 6yds Val — 1^{80}/30	6^{80}
3	" Val — 45 6 yds Muslum^{75}	1^{20}
6	" ze— Silk 18= 1^{08} 2 ----- 2^{00}	3^{08}
		35^{75}

---

227. Tom Lay to J. W. H.

Seguin May 20.oth 1894

Mr John. W. Hardin

Dear Friend
As I have a fieu moments to spare I take pleasure in writing you a fieu lines have bin very busy since you was here I am wriding all day long and have a very rough cuntry to wride over the most of my paster land is hilly and awfuly thick I sometimes hunt all day before I find the Horses I want am geting along fine breeding the last rains has made the grass prety good have breed bout 75 mares up to date do not Know how many more I will breede but think I will get in all 100—I find it very hard to Collect money the last three years has played the wild with our Cuntry but hope it will all be well in the future the prospects for a good crop is very. very faivorable now but still its too early to cont on any thing yet I here a great many Say we have a show thing in corn but I differ with thin surpose we do not get any more rain what will be the average corn crop I say bout ten bush. ———. acre I have the best Crop I have had for years say I had bout 30 acres of cotton to plant over from the big raim we had the night you was here. but it looks fiene now. after I left you I taken supper at the same Hotell we ate dinner. at the table Mr Johnston asked me who you was after I told him he seem to be very much hurt because I did not make him acqinted with you. I was in Seguin once since I saw you and a great may of my acqintances talked to me bout you and I Cam say you have a great many friends in Seguin evry one wants to get acqinte with you so you must come up to my House and we will go up a gain I will meet you in Seguin Kingsbury or Luling any time you will let me Know have not seen Dunk or Martine since you left herd some of my Negrows say he planted over some of his Cotton my sadle is over there yet but will sind over after it write soon.
Heffhin is a funney boy dont you think so. I will Close by asking you to excuse this badly written letter write to me soon I am anxious to here from. you. your sincere friend.

Tom. Lay

---

228. P. Levyson to J. W. H.

Prompt Payment secures confidence and credit.
NEW YORK Office: 75 Franklin St.

Gonzales, Texas, May 23, 1894.

Mr John Westly Harden

Bought of P.LEVYSON,
DEALER IN
Dry Goods, Clothing, Hats, Boots, Shoes.
* Millinery Parlor Up-Stairs.*

To 1 Damask Table Cloth	1 75
"4 1/2 Yds Table Cloth 70	3 15
	4 90

Received Payment
P. Levyson.

---

229. Thom Lay to J. W. H.

Seguin Texas June 22.sd 1894
Mr John. W. Hardin Gonzales

Dear friend
I received a lettle from you some three weeks. ago but have delayed answering untill now. was glad to here from you and to here you had gonn to house Keeping I have no news to write that will interest you more than we have had lots of rain I am satisfied I will make 40 or 45 bushels of Come pr acre on and average this is a big corn crop for Texas. The Corn Crop as a general thing. is very sorry in this Cuntry that is all west of me a great many had to cut their Corn for Sodden. west of me to Seguin will make bout 15 bushel pr acre. I have not bin able to plow for twenty days on accont of rain but my crop is in good fix. I am still breeding mares yet have five or Six that is giving me lots of trouble but think I will get thim off in a fiew more days. I am geting awfully tiared of working thim I would not mind it so much if I cowld Collect any momey but times are very hard in regard to money matters I was at Leesville rancho. Belmont and Luling, last week trying to Collect and was not able to get ome cent so you Know this is discourage day. but still I will do the best I can at it I saw our friend Hefflin Saturday he has a fine crop. the man mosley that lives on his place is very low. and I have herd that the Doctors have givin him out to die. there is a great deal of sickness in this county but mostly are Children I have lost one on my ranch. I

will close for This time I wrote to you at Sedan reckon you did not get it.
wishing you much Success I reman yours true friend
Thom. Lay.
write to me soon **T.H.L.**

---

230. J. P. Randle to J. W. H.

J. P. R A N D L E, ***DRY GOODS****

GONZALES, TEXAS, Aug 4" 1894

Mr J. W. Hardin Gonzales

Dear Sir
I will go to market to buy grrces on the 8" or 9" inst, and have to call on my patrons, for at least some payment on their acts, any payment you can make on your act. at this Time, will be duly appreciated.
At the same time I must call your attention to the fact that Mr Glover does not feel that he can be responsible for the future increase of your act. which amounts to this day $114^{12} And under the circumstances, if you wish to still increase the act. you will do me the favor of making Some other arrangement of securing it — I am sure, you will readily see the justice of this—
Very Truly **J P Randle**

---

231. E. F. Schlickeisen to State of Texas and J. W. H.

The State of Texas Know all
County of Gonzales Men by these
presents that I the undersigned for And in Consiliations of Legal services rendered and to be rendered to the value of Twenty five $25^{00} Dollars have this Day bargained Sold and delivared to J W Harden One Bay Horse about 14½ hands high about 8 Years Old And branded thus Ssp on left thigh Given under My hand This 10th day of Auguist 1894 E.F. Schlickeisen
Witness J N Beain

C.C. Britton

232. E. F. Schlickeisen statement

The State of Texas — Know all men
County of Gonzales — by these presents:

That I, the undersigned for and in consideration of Legal services rendered and to be rendered to the value of Twenty - five(25\underline{00}$) Dollars, have this day bargained sold and delivered to J. W. Hardin, one gray horse about 15 hands high, about 8 years old and branded thus J on left shoulder. Given under my hand This 10th day of August 1894 E.F. Schickeisen

Witness J N Blain

,C, C, Britton

---

233. John B. Ashe to J. W. H.

Sour Lake Hotel

FOR PARTICULARS APPLY TO J.E. NEWTON PROP.

FOR PARTICULARS APPLY TO J.E. NEWTON PROP.

ORDERS FOR WATER TAR & MUD PROMPTLY ATTENDED TO

R E O P E N E D .UNDER A NEW PROPRIETORSHIP

UNDER NEW AUSPICES AND NEW MANAGEMENT

Sour Lake, Texas, August 16th 1894

(HARDIN COUNTY.) John W. Hardin, Esq. Gonzales, Texas.

Dear Sir:

Your letter of the 10th Inst has just come to hand. If you will reread it, I think you will find that I states that the papers in that case were missing. I have hunted the office over, but without result. Nevertheless, I will search again on my return to the City, which will be either Monday or Tuesday, when you will hear from me again.

Respectfully,

John B. Ashe, Deputy Clerk

---

234. John Buchannan to J. W. H.

Office of R. M. CLOVER,
SHERIFF GONZALES COUNTY.
GONZALES, TEXAS,_

Aug the 22 1894

Mr John. Buckhannan Halletsville Texas
Dear. Sir Please be Kind enough to inform me of the financial Standing of W. A. Dixson and whether property if any is incumbered and confer a lasting favor respectfully

John W HArdin

W A Dickson paid taxes for 1893 on following property
86.½ acres A ------ League
41.½ " J Hughes. survey
72 " P. Guthrie "
7 Horses & mules
20. Cattle
I find the following incumbrance on the 81½ acre survey Deed of Trust to secure
J D. Neimyer for $250.00 due 3 yrs after date dated Jany 16/93 with 10% — from date.
said D.T. Recorded in Book E D/T. page 201. this County Records.
yours &C **Jno Buchanan**
Clk ccie

---

235. Harris A. Crim to J. W. H.

Sour Lake Hotel
For Particulars Apply to J.E. Newton Prop.
FOR PARTICULARS APPLY TO J.E. NEWTON PROP.
Orders for Water Tar & Mud Promptly Attended To
R E O P E N E D .Under a New Proprietorship
Under New Auspices and New Management

Sour Lake, Texas, August 23d 1894

(HARDIN COUNTY.) Mr John Wesley Hardin, Gonzales Texas.
Dear Sir,
Your favor of the 12th inst was opened, and I suppose answered by my Son and Deputy Clerk, during my absence in North Texas. We have had several Communications within the last 12 months from Mr Day and others at Huntsville, asking for a certified Copy of the records in his case, but as you have been informed, could never discover, among the papers & archives of the Clerks office any records other than such as were contained in the Minutes of the Court: I will however, today drop a letter to Mr Henry Brashew, my

predecessor, asking him to call at the office and perhaps he may be able to direct my son, in an other Effort to find the papers for you — If successful he will communicate with you at once.
Hoping you success I am Sir Very Respectfully Y'r ob't s'vt

SSAslu

Clerk Harris A. Crim. Dis. Court

** This Wonderful Sanitarium **

Is now opened to the world. It is located near the Texas & New Orleans Railroad, with an elevation of fifteen feet above the surrounding country. Malaria is unknown here, its poisons being destroyed by the gases arising from the earth and from the waters of the

I R O N, S U L P H U R and A C I D L A K E

near which the Hotel property is situated. THE BATHING ACCOMMODATIONS ARE UNSURPASSED; the two swimming pools in the bosom of the Lake will accommodate fifty persons of either sex. The exhilerating effects of the iron and of the sulphur baths, and the curative properties of same, are unequaled. The wonderful freak of nature, placing THIRTEEN MINERAL SPRINGS in such close proximity, and all possessing the highest degree of curative properties, is a phenomena unaccounted for by scientists.

Persons suffering from cutaneous affections, eczema, scrofula, tetter, scald head, rheumatism, dropsy, dyspepsia, paralysis, chronic diarrhoea, as well also constipation and GENERAL DEBILITY, find relief and restoration at Sour Lake.

The remarkable cures of female diseases which have resulted from bathing in the sulphur and acid baths and from the application of the sulphur and acid earth surrounding this wonderful spot, deserve special notice. The petroleum oil, reaching the surface through a tube inserted sixty feet under the ground, when used externally, is a certain and speedy remedy for long standing sores, carbuncles, piles and like affections.

The water from the mineral wells of Sour Lake, the mineral mud and tar, are shipped to every section of the country, giving entire satisfaction.

236. Carl Reuter to J. W. H.

Gonzales, Texas, Sept 1 1894.

Mr Wes Harden.

BOUGHT GONZALES ICE WORKS, OF CHARLES REUTER, Machinist AND Proprietor.

	Ice Delivered from Aug 1 to Sept 1 included			
30	"	"	@ 10.	3. 00.
1	"	"	@ 20.	_ 20.
			Paid	3. 20.

Carl Reuter

---

237. Gilbert Book Co. to D. Cobb

A.E.Gilbert, Sec'y. W.J.Gilbert, Pres't. M.J.Gilbert. Treas.

TEXAS

Myer On Vested Rights.
Webb On Record of Title.
Murfree On Sheriffs.
Mills On Eminent Domain.

THE GILBERT BOOK CO.

"The Greatest Legal Publication of The Century."

Publishers of Law Books

Myer's Federal Decisions Containing Decisions of All U.S.Courts For 100 Years 30 Vols. Art Catalogue Free.

Especially For Texas and Missouri.

205 N.Fourth Street. St. Louis

Warehouse Ewing Ave.& Caroline St. Compton Co. St Louis

Sept. 15th, 1894.

Mr. D. Cobb, Gonzales, Tex.

Dear Sir:

In answer to yours of Sept. 13th, would reply that the books you wish come to the following figures:

2 willson's Criminal Form Books at $6---------------------------$12.
2 Sayles' Civil Form Book at $6------------- 12.
Sayles' Civil Statutes, with Supplement bringing
it down to date, and Constitutional History -- 31.
Supplement to Willson's Criminal Statutes--------- 3.50
Total---------- $58.50

In consideration of the present dull times, we will agree, for a special cash order to send you the complete lot prepaid on receipt of $50. You can then keep the two Form Books for the county and turn the balance over to Mr. Hardin.

Yours truly,

Gilbert Book Co.

---

238. John B. Ashe to J. W. H.

Houston, Texas, Sept.20th,1894.

John W. Hardin, Gonzales, Texas.

Dear Sir:

you letter of the 5th inst to hand some time since and I would have replied at once but that I wanted to see the Sheriff of our County who was out of the City. He has returned and after getting some information from him in regard to the case I had another good search which resulted in finding the supposed missing papers. I have just unearthed them and can furnish you with a complete transcript in all the cases should you so desire. My fee for making the transcripts in all four cases will be $20.00. If you want them notify me at once and I can have them ready in a week from now. Our Court begins on the 1st and I would have to do the work before it convenes. So kindly let me hear from you at once.

Respectfully,

John B. Ashe, Deputy Clerk

---

239. Gilbert Book Co. to J. W. H.

A.E.GILBERT, SEC'Y. W.J.GILBERT, PRES'T. M.J.GILBERT. TREAS.

TEXAS

MYER ON VESTED RIGHTS.
WEBB ON RECORD OF TITLE.
MURFREE ON SHERIFFS.
MILLS ON EMINENT DOMAIN.

THE GILBERT BOOK CO.

"THE GREATEST LEGAL PUBLICATION OF THE CENTURY."

PUBLISHERS OF LAW BOOKS

Myer's FEDERAL DECISIONS CONTAINING DECISIONS OF ALL U.S.COURTS FOR 100 YEARS 30 VOLS. ART CATALOGUE FREE.

ESPECIALLY FOR TEXAS AND MISSOURI.

205 N.FOURTH STREET. ST. LOUIS

WAREHOUSE EWING AVE.& CAROLINE ST. COMPTON CO. ST LOUIS

Sept. 28th, 1894.

Mr. Jno. N. Hardin, Gonzales, Tex.

Dear Sir:

In answer to yours of Sept. 26th, would reply by enclosing our full catalogue, also sending you some sample pages and descriptive circulars by mail in separate bag. In addition, we enclose you slip giving prices on Texas Reports. We do not ordinarily, as you will see by another slip enclosed in regard to our terms, give time on amounts under $50; but, to accommodate you, if your references prove satisfactory, we will sell you a bill of that amount for $20 or $25 cash, dividing the balance into three or four monthly payments, the notes of course to draw 10 per ct. interest and be secured on the books.

Yours truly,

Gilbert Book Co.

---

240. J. W. Hardin to Jim Clements.

Gonzales County Texas Oct the 4th 1894

Mr Jim Clements Sterling city and county. Texas

Dear cousin

Bill Jones by his treacherous conduct toward me has forced me to oppose him for the office of Sheriff and to favor R R Coalman and I have exposed part of his transaction with me while he was Sheriff in 72 now I look upon him as a trator a back number and a corrupt man for he Secretely Solicited me the other day to Sigm a libell for his political advancement and to deceive the people of this county but I did not Sign and I read the riot act to him now he has forced me to oppose him by trying to turn John Lackey against me &c and if you Know anything that will refflect upon his Character as an officer please write me plainly, how about that trip of yours and his below if any &c: I will not use your name in conjunction with the exposure but I am after him to defeat him for office and in case I fail will move I send my Love to all your cousin

John W HArdin

(PS)he expects to be elected by the negro vote but I think he is badly beaten

---

241. Mary Barnett to J. W. and Jinnie Hardin

Neville Tex., Oct 4, 1894.
Mr. J. W. and Miss Jennie Hardin. Gonzales Tex.

Dear Cousins:
As I have gotten a home in this region, I'll. let you all know where, so you will visit me.
School has been going on successfully four days.
Have 29 students. They seem, so far, to be very good. I have a very pleasant boarding place at Mr. Minears. But must acknowledge I have been very homesick. Off among strangers this way never seems like home or at your home.
Really (I ought to be ashamed I know but,) I have taken a good cry. Cousin Wes, I know you will say, "She didnt go down there to be satisfied". But I cant help it.
Had a very sweet letter from home today. Not from Johnnie but Marguerite and Ettie.
I cant come to Gonzales this week. Am going to let you all rest.
But would be so glad you would come down here. Do come. Havn't anything to write so good night.
Your Cousin **Mary Barnett.**

---

242. M. N. Blackburn to J. W. H.

Killeen Oct 6 1894
J. W. Hardin Gonzales Co

Dear Sir
I wrote to you in July giveing you all of the Particulars concerning the Land. I suppose you did not get My Letter, My case was continued till Jan Turm Please Let Me heare fron you at once, & also what will you charge Me. If you did not get My Letter I will write you all of the Particulars concerninge the Case
Yours Truley
M N Blackburn

---

243. Luis Aguero and Ramon Aguero (statement)

Office of R. M. GLOVER, SHERIFF GONZALES COUNTY.
GONZALES, TEXAS,__________189__
Gonzales Texas oct the 7th 94

Know all men by these presents that we Luis Aguero Ramon Aguero have this day bargained and Sold to John W HArdin the following property to wit one thimble Skein Wagon and two mares or horses one Brown mare 13½ hands high, and one Dun mare 13½ hands high for value received the consideration being that he will rendr us Luis Auguro & Ramon Auguro his Legal Services as a lawyer in cases pending against us in the town and county of Gonzales in the Justices Court and that we authorise the Said John W Hardin to represent us in Said Suits and we do this and Sign our names of our own free will and accord and freely Attest our names

Luis Aguero Ramon Aguero

Witnesses .C. C. Britton
E. R. Robles

---

244. Ramon Aguero to Matinna Mendosa

Office of R. M. GLOVER, SHERIFF GONZALES COUNTY.
GONZALES, TEXAS,__________189__
Gonzales Texas Oct 7th 94

Mrs Matinna Mendosa
Dear wife please Deliver the new wagon and two mares & harness to J.W hardin and oblige me I am in Jail he is my att I hope to be out Soon

Ramon Aguero

---

245. Luis Aguero, Ramon Aguero (statement)

Office of R. M. GLOVER, SHERIFF GONZALES COUNTY.
GONZALES, TEXAS, Oct the 8th 1894

Know all men by these presence that we Ramond and Louis Augero have this day bargained and Sold delivered to John W HArdin one bay mare about 12½ hands high for value receive (The

consideration being that John W HArdin will render the aforesad parties his legal Services in cases pending in the Justicies court in the town of gonzales and we Say that we do this with our own free will and accord **Luis Aguero Ramon Aguero**
Witnesses C. C. Britton E R Robles

---

246. M. C. West to J. W. H.

WILSON COUNTY TEXAS

A.D. Evans, County Judge.
E.D. Mayes, County Clerk.
A.R. Stevenson, Co. Attorney.
M.J. Ximenes, Sheriff.
R.R. Creech, Tax Collector.
J.J. Cope, Tax Assessor.

E.Y. Seale, County Treasurer.
W.J. Sutherland, Co. Surveyor.
Thos. H. Spooner, Dist. Judge.
John E. McMullen, Dist. Clerk.
S.L. Green, Dist. Attorney.

CLARKE & COURTS. GALV.
WILSON COUNTY COURT HOUSE.

Floresville, Texas, Oct 15th 1894
Mr. John W. Hardin Gonzales Texas

Dear Sir

Your favor of 12 inst. is at hand and Contents carefully noted.

In reply I beg to say that I can not fill J.J. Bratton's bond here. When we were jointly indicted here last Dec. for murder I failed to get him bond then on account of his being a transeient man.

All my property is under Mortg. which bars me from being responsible as a bondsman.

I am sorry to hear of Bratton's trouble and hope that he is innocent of the Charge.

Respectfully

M. C. West

---

247. J. W. H. (unsigned) to people of Gonzales Co.

[UNDATED]

Turn on The .Light.

To the people of Gonzales county greetings. There Seems to be a desire among many of you to Know how I Stand upon the contest or election for Sheriff. Well I am for: R. E Coalman first last and all the time, first because he is my friend and because he is a brave honest capable man worthy to be our Sheriff a man if elected will execute the Law will do his whole duty as he understands it, regardless of Clicks & Clans & ring whether in the town of gonzales or the county I desire R.E elected Sherif because Lif Liberty and property will be Safe in his hands. and because they will not be Safe in ——— his hands if elected I look upon him as a back number as far as the Sheriffs office is concerned he was Sheriff here in 72 by appointment of. E. J Davis our Republlcan gov of that day and if I am properly informed he conducted the office in Such a manner that it failed to even meet the approval of E.J. Davis hence he resigned in ignominy. and went to galveston for his health. Now there is a few old people here now that was here in the 70ties and Know whether this is true Substantially Speaking or not. You all Know that he is called a Slick a wire pulling man do we want a Slick wire pulling man for Sheriff I say no give us an honest brave Sensible and capable man like R.E.C. Now it has come to my ears that Some of my best friends and I congratulate myself that I have as many as I have have Said well I understand Wes Hardin is against ——— and that he has Squealed on ——— him &C and if this be So I am done with Wess and I am going to vote for for ——— regardless of his past official corruption i wish to Say to just Such friends joy go with you but beware that the Viper you take to your bosom Stingeth you not. Wess HArdin is here to Stay regardless of foes within or enemies without or either and he is going to Support R E C in this race for Sheriff because he believes the peace the Happiness and the prosperity of Gonzales county greatly depends upon the election Bob and because he believes the Scenes of the 70ties when this and adjoining counties was over run with mob Law will be renacted if ——— is elected Sheriff—I am going to vote for R E C because I wish to Se peace and Harmony prevail and Spread her beautiful wings over the entire county for if ——— is elected there will be no peace but contention and Strife and probably bloodshed will mark the era of his induction into office: The democrat party made a mistake when they nominated. ——— for Sheriff he ——— come to me the other day and requested me to write a letter or Sign one he had wrttten exhonerating him from any corrupt conduct in his dealings with me in the past as an officer I politely declined to Sign because the contents of the letter he wished me to Sign were wholely false and he new it I ask you fellows that are going to quit me because I am against ——— if you blame me for not Signing an infamous Libell and I wish to Say to those erring friends of mine if they knew ——— as well as I do they would vote for R.E.C. and I believe the most of them will. you all Know that among the Knowing ones it has been understood for many years that if one is in trouble and ——— is on his Side he is is all right that the Law can not reach him however inculpating the evidence may be: but that if ____ is on the other Side or against you there is trouble for you however innocent the evidence proves you to be. I Say that no man Should possess Such power I Say it is a dangerous power for one man to possess and it is a Standing menace to the lives Liberty and Happiness of ever law abiding god loving & god-fearing man in Gonzales county hence I ask you to join with me to throttle tyranny and bossism in gonzales by casting your vote for R E C Now I hear Some one Say Wess you ought to Keep Still. I wish to Say that when the peace the wellfare of Hapiness the people Gonzales depends upon what I Know my Knowledge my tongue my pen and my lifes blood if need be are at their command. I Say I have a natural loathing for a coward a liar a misouthrope and above all deliver me from Such men as Benedic Arnold and Judias is coriot whether they be in public or private life now I Know Some of you will vote for him because you fear him and dread his power: here my friend do you Know you are free: if So assert your manhood by voting for R.E.C. yes I am going to work for his election and then after all I Shall vote for: R E C Believing that he is the right man for the right place

---

248. Frank Kelso to R. R. Coleman

Leesville Texas Oct the 20th 94

Mr. R. R. Coleman
Dear Friend
thinking you Would like to hear from this Section I take pleasure In riteing you a few Dots I read Mr Hardins letter it is a daisy with out paint and I glory in his Spunk I think it Will have good affect all over the County it has in this part any way Lump & my Self is going

2
to Wrightsborrow in a few days we are going to take B. B. with us as we want to Work on that Mexican Dem if we can handle him we will pin a feather in our hat and I think 20 or 30 will do it we ar fixed for him any way I sent little John McCoy to you when he lost his Horse and I tell you — you hit the Key note by going with him for he is doing all he can for you he was a Jones man but I heard him Say the other day in a
3
Big crowd boys if you want to vote for a man that never quits vote for Coleman—now Bob I have this to Say for God Sake do ant have any trouble if you can avoid it but I Say this old Boy be Carefull you had better Keep your eyes open also Caution Mr Hardin to Keep Out I have a warm place in my heart for that man and I would certainly
4
hate to hear of his Being in Trouble a gain I have no harm to Say of Mr Jones to his back but my private opinon is he would use foul means to win if you are forced to Bulletts try and win & if it is left to Ballott you will win
with Loev & Best Wishes to you and yours
I am Very Truly
Your Friend
Frank Kelso

---

249. May Hardin to J. W. H.

[UNDATED]
oct the 20

Mr John Hardin
Dear Little Old Johnnie I will This sad eavning ans your Letter which I received this eave Johnnie I have ask and Lookig all time sence sence my Poor Boys death you canot mageine of my truble Just think he was Killed in my such way. wasent give no show Poor Boy thought this Coward was his Best freind Just eat dinner at our house three days be fer that he has Made his Brags how he Killed him some one herd him beg fer his Life oh he Just Mured him Poor Boy dident eaven have his Pistol Killed him first shot and then Shot him 5 or six times Johnnie I would give my thing if you could come thaie

is Sevrel interfering with my Poor Little Boys Stuff which is what thae Poor father has Left them do come if can I have wrote home so meny Times haven Received no ans I dont think they have ever bin sent off are Jim would of bin here do come if so you can and

herry and come

your true auint

May. Hardin

See you can
tell you more

ans soon
come

---

250. Frank Howell to Robert Coleman

Cheap Side Gonzales Tex October 21. 18.94

Mr. Robert. Colman I see John. Preston with a copey of the inquirey showing a letter riten by W. E. Jones I wish you would send me the drag net one month send me the copy with Wes. Hardens reply to Jones letter I hay had severl men to ask me to let them read the paper you & Mr. Harden ceap cool & dont rite any thing but what is true I dont think that you will Write any thing falce so I will close When you read this tair it up I will vote for you and a friend to Wes. send by first mail as I am anches to read the letter your friend **Frank. Howell**

---

251. J. F. Wingate to J. W. H.

Big Foot Frio Co
Oct the 21st 1894 Tex

Mr J W. Harden

Dear Friend

I now try to write you a fewlines to let you know that I am still in the land of the living I have been studying about you so much of late I concluded to write to you I reckon you remember the last time we met it was at the Panitentiary and bad enough I hated to leave you there in that dreadful place I have had some hard troble since I saw you Brother Ned has been killed since I saw you I disremember whether I told you about Brother Jack being killed when I saw you and my Mother died several years ago and I feel very lonely in this world Abe Smith was waylaid and killed in Jasper Co Cap McGee was killed at Trinty station I have been living in this country 12 or 15 years Old John Gates still lives at Trinity Old Dr Hastings is living here by me he tells me that you are liable to get into Some trouble about the sheriff election there he used to live at Knicka—t he is a good friend of yours and mine too I hope you will take no part and get into no trouble for sheriffs never did a great deal for you or myself either I have often thought of the escape you made at Trinity when you was wonded there I learn that you are now practicing Law I am glad to hear it I hope you are doing well I dont know of any other Location you could get that would suit you any better than there I want you to write at once and let me know how you are getting along and have your photo taken if you please and send it to me maybe that will help my feelings some I live 6 or 8 miles from the International R.R. near a little Town by the name of Devine if you ever have the opportunity I want you to come out and see us I shall expect to hear from you soon Your Friend as ever;

J. F. Wingate Big Foot Frio Co Tex

---

252. Ben Bratton to J. W. H.

Leesville Texas Oct 22nd 94

Mr J W Hardin
Gonzales

Friend Wess

I write to you in regard to the piece Bill Jones published about you and denying Killing the nigro. I was Talking with Ed Martin yesterday and he says he knows a man that Jones told that he did go to Columbus and Kill a nigro. so if you want more evidense about the nigro Killing write to Ed Martin at this place and he will tell who it was The man says he slept with Jones after he come back from Killing the nigro and he told him all about it — you have a great many friends out here but we are all uneasy about you for feare Jones will have some of his curs kill you some night So as the mexican says look a little out be verry careful for you are dealing. with a verry cunning rascal So I will say again if you want more evidense about the nigro killing write or see Ed Martin

I remain Verry Rsp
Your friend
Ben Bratton

---

253. George Anderson to J. W. H.

F. B. HOUSTON'S SCALES.
Gonzales, Texas, Oct 27 1894

Load of Corn
From Geo Anderson — To J. W. Hardin
Gross 1500 Pounds.
No.________ Tare 710 Pounds.
Net . 790 Pounds.
Fees 10cts — Swift Weigher.

---

254. Jo Denson (statement)

The State of Texas
County of Gonzale

before me personaly appeared
Jo Denson

Who upon oath being duly sworn deposes and says that he was stopping at N. C. Densons in the year of 74 when one Manning Clements came there and Staid all night and I Slept with him Clements and he told me that he had been on the colorado River with W. E. Jones or Bill Jones to kill a negro because the negro had killed Bill Jones brotherinlaw and that he and Bill Jones hed killed a negro. Now I was well and intamately accuinted with Manning Clements and had his confidence and believed what ever he told me

J. Denson

given under my hand and Seal This the **27th day of Oct 1894**
Subscribed and sworn to by. J. Denson
before me this the 27 day of October 1894
W. W. Glass—Notary public in and for Gonzales County Texas

---

255. Nannie Witt to brother

Bowie, Montague, Co Oct 28 / .94

Dear Brother: —

I will write you a few lines again. We wrote you about two months ago—Just after we left greer Co. & told you to write to Gaines N—but have not heard a word from you. We have been canvassing in this Co a month. The Co is very thickly settled & people have made plenty. but most of them are complaining of the "four C cotton" & say "Old Clevland" is the cause of such hard times. They have raised more cotton than any thing, Have raised Just enough, most of th— of corn & to do them—and have only cotton to bring money. I have not any patience with their talk (The Populist Party)" Johnnie are you a strong Dem.c Well the people are not so pressed but what they will hand out the $.½ for my needles. We have been at work about seven weeks and it is wonderful the success we have in the Country

Page 3

as well as in towns. We lack about 20.$ of being out of debt. I took in $40. above expenses the last week. We hope to make some money clear <u>for our use</u> after this month. I beleive we could canvas most of the winter down in your County. I want us to work until about Christmas spent Xmas at Matts then make our way towards your County. What do you think about it? It looks like a little thing to travel with, but we can average $5,00 a day & I think we had better never settle down while we can make so much canvassing. Camping out agrees with us. Mr Witt does all the work, except Sundays, I get dinner that day. We live fine too. You ought to see me trading my needles & patterns which costs about 16c for several glass Jars of caned & preserve fruit! I thought I would not go to the Fair, as I

5

Want to make all I can before cold weather, Johnie write me & tell Mollie & Jennie to write, this is to them too. I got a letter from Gip sometime ago he was making his 9.$ a week, I was so glad to know it. I should rather see him do well than myself. & Johnnie I hope to hear of you prosperity too for I love you & clip better than any one. I want to make you all a christmas present. How is little old Johnnie getting along? I

hope to have a happy visit when I see you all. The other time I could not hardly look at the children without thinking of you & crying. hopeing to hear from you soon I remain Your sister **Nannie Witt**
Write right soon to Chics, Wise Co.
We heard from home a mo— ago. They had good rains, and our. renters were doing finely, putting in their wheat, some wheat up then.

---

256. Fred Diedrich to A. M. Kotzebue

Gonzals 10/29 1894
Druggist A. M. Kotzebue Moulton Tx

send fourty Dollars at once
By Post Office money Order.
By mail Answer if you send
it.
Fred Diedrich

---

257. John Taylor to J. W. H.

Oct 31,1894
Mr John W Hardin

Dear Frinend
I reseved your letter and was glad to here from you and to here that you and famley was wel this leavs us all well you rote to me fore some money Where do you want me to send the money are you comeing after it I never go back on a frind you write and tell me Where to Send the money and I will Send you a check I wish you would come to See me when you get time I Will close Write Soon to your friend
John Taylor

---

258. R. B. Hudson (statement)

The State of Texas /
county of Gonzales / Before (me)———

appeared. R. B Hudson this ——— who upon oath being duly Sworn by me deposes and Says that he was Sheriff of Dewitt county in the year of 1871,2,3 and was well acquainted with the disturbed condition of Gonzales & Dewitt counties and Know that there was a feud and that Jo Tomlonson belonged to one side and that J. W. HArdin & the Clements brothers belonged to the other Side I had papers for J. W HArdin and made Several futile attempts to find ——— arrest him and became convinced that He was posted as to my movements So that he ——— eluded me. It was my understanding and I bel— is that Bill Jones Belonged to John W HArdins party and Kept him posted as to me and other officers movements who wished to arrest Hardin and it was my understanding that Bill Jones the Sheriff of Gonzale couty Turned John W HArdin out of Jail & was a party to it in the year of 1872. I remember ——— Bill Jones was Sheriff by appointment of E.J Davis the republican Governor in 1872 and that —vious to that he was a ——— police man by appointment from the Same republican governor and belonged to Jack Helms company. He Helms being the Captian of the State police in Gonzales & Dewitt counties

,R.B Hudson

Subscribed and Sworn to by R.B Hudson. before me this the 1- day of november 1894 **W.W.Glass**
notary public in
and for Gonzales County
Texas

---

259. S. H. Cresap (statement)

The State of Texas) County of Gonzales)
(Before me personally

appeared S. H. Cresap this day Who upon. oath being duly Sworn / deposes and Says that he was residing in Dewit county in the year of 72 at Jo Tumlinsons ranch near Yorktown and about 10 or 12 miles from where John W HArdin and the Clements Brothers lived and Knew them well and Know that when John W HArdin got out of the Gonzales Jail in the year of 1872 that it was commonly and currently reported that the Sheriff of Gonzales county had turned him out or had been a party to his escape I also Know that there was a feud in counties of Gonzales and Dewit in year of 72 3 4 and. that Jo Tumlinson belonged to one Side and that Hardin and the Clernents brothers belonged to the other, and I heard Jo Tumlinson Say on his death bed that Bill Jones belonged to the party composed of HArdin Clements & others and that at certan time Bill Jones made an abortive attempt to assassinate his Son John Tumlinson in the Town of Gonzales while he was under the protection of a ranger

S. H Cresap

Subscribd and Sworn to by S. H. Cresup. before me this the 1-day of november 1894

W.W.Glass notay
public, in and for Gonzales County Texas

---

260. N. G. Denson and W. J. Denson (testimony)

[UNDATED]

Cheapside
To whom it may consern
I was a close observer of all the proceedings at that day and time, and I had good reasons to beleave that Hardin and Clements were all posted in regard to the movements of the Gonzales officers.
I Know from hearsay that Hardin was in jail in 1872, and that he escaped with the assistance of the officers.

N G Denson

I Know that M. Clements visited my fathers' house in 1872,'73, 74,. I was about 20 old at the time.

W. J. Denson

4
I, N. G. Denson, do certify that M. Clements and Jo Denson did stay with me on the night mentioned above, and they slept, togather, and I know they were intimate friends. M. Clements did tell me that he had been on a tour or rip in the lower country with Bill Jones. Clements was well armed and showed that he was on the alert. I lived in the section in which the outlaws, and officers were scouting to and fro. I often advised Clements to leave off his bad habits, and I did not indorse his actions. I know he and Hardin were cousins and

bosom friends. I Know that Hardin was an outlaw, and he did not visit me.

---

261. Unknown writer and recipient

[UNDATED]

The State of Texas county of Gonzales

Before me personally appeared

this day who upon oath being duly Sworn deposes and Says that he was residing in gonzales county in the year of 1872 and 1873 and 1874 and remember that when J W HArdin got out of the gonzales county Jail it was currently and commonly reported that Bil Jones or W E Jones had turned HArdin out of Jail or had been a party to his HArdins escape from Jail I Knew from hersay and otherwise that Bil Jones the then Sheriff of gonzales was a friend to J W HArdin and his friends and Kept him HArdin posted as to the movements of him Self and other officers So that HArdin could elude the officers I also heard Soon after HArdin escaped from Jail that he HArdin rode Berry Andersons Horse out of gonzales the night he got out

---

262. R. R. Coleman to J. W. H.

[UNDATED]

Gonzales Nov 2nd

J. W. Hardin

If you have finished your letter let me see it before you put it in print. Come over this morning

R.R. Coleman

---

263. (?) to citizens of Gonzales

[UNDATED]

To The Citizens of Gonzales county.

When R.R Coalman and W. E. Jones Became the nominees of their respective parties for Sheriff they mutually agreed to carry on their campaign against each other without Slinging mud that is each was to let the character of the other alone and ask the votes of the people Strictly upon their merits. But, W.E Jones Soon Secetely began a war of crimination against R.R Coalman the Populist nominee for that office hence Mr Coleman began to investigate Mr Jones character as an officer when he was Sheriff and found that Bill Jones was Sheriff in the year of our lord 1872 by appointment of E.J Davis the republican governor of that day and he found that he had beaten a negro up unmercifully and unlawfully in his charge in Jail in the town of gonzales while he was Sheriff and that he had the Notorious John W HArdin in Jail for Killing a negro and Shooting an other and He Hardin having ben arrested by Dick Reagan in cherokee co Texas) that he Bill Jones turned the Notorious HArdin out without Lawfu authority the consideration being. that HArdin would go with him (Bill Jones) to columbus and Kill a negro for him who had Killed Bill Jones Brotherinlaw Now when he come to Wess HArdin After he had turned HArdin loose to get him to Kill the negro HArdin told him that he was not in the negro Killing business and he would have to See the party that made the bargain with him that he would Kill a negro to get his liberty from the Gonzales Jail Now the other day Bill Jones tried to get Hardin to State by Letter that Bill Jones carachter as a man and officer was good above reproach for his Bill jones political and personal advancement to injure R R Coalman Rap and deceive the people of Gonzales county: but the Notorious Hardin refused to be his tool refused to Sign his liebil: Well we do not want a man for Sheriff that has been a tool that will turn a man out of jail to Kill a negro or that will try to get one of gonzales best citizens to Sign a liebil. No My country men 'no' . we want a man that is in Sympathy with us. incorruptible one who will dare to do his duty as he understands it. regardless of the consequences, and Such a man is Bob Coalman and the populist rest assured he Solicits your vote and rest assured that your life Liberty and property will be Safe in his hands Wide Awake.

R. R. Coleman did not win the election.

---

264. Otto P. Kroeger to Joe Barbish

Mahncke Hotel.
L. MAHNCKE, , Proprietor.
San Antonio, Texas, Nov 20th 1894
Mr Joe Barbisch:— Austin Tex

Dear Sir:—
This will introduce to you Mr. Wesley Hardin of Frontier days fame He is getting estimates on having some books published.
You may rely on him as a thoroughly reformed & reliable gentleman
Your friend **Otto. P. Kroeger**

---

265. R. M. Glover to J. W. H.

Gonzales Dec. 1 st 1894
J. W. Hardin Junction City

Friend Wes:
You probably think by this time that I have Completely forgotten you but be assured this is not so I have been so very busy winding up my business that I have not had time to write or even think I have been very unwell for several days and fear that I. am going to be Confined to ——— I have systoms of Slow fever I ——— in a worse fix generally than I ever ——— before, physically financialy and —aly but hope to be on feet soon ——— able to look the world squarely ——— face. I have heard nothing of any Contemplated trouble in store for you from W. E. J. nor do I believe that he will attempt to work up any of ——— old Cases against you for he knows to well there is nothing in them save a little trouble for yourself and friends Johnnie & Jennie moved out all ——— and seemed to be all right Giv ——— my regards to all inquiring friends and write me soon. I will go to S— tomorrow and try to get a Job under Dick Ware.
Your true friend **R.M. Glover**
Later was in San Antonio for several days this week: **Dick**

---

266. Callie Lewis to J. W. H.

London Texas
Sunday Eve. Dec. 30 / 94

Mr Hardin
I guess you will be a little bit surprised to receive a note from me. Either that or think me Cheeky to address you first. but you told me if I wanted to see you to let you know so I will tell you I will Expect you new years Come and I will be glad To see you / your friend

Callie Lewis

---

267. P. N. Hawkins to J. W. H.

SMITH & HAWKINS,
STAPLE AND FANY GROCERIES.
FRUITS & VEGETABLES. CROCKERY AND GLASSWARE.
Gonzales, Texas, Jan 11th, 1895

Friend Wes
I am hard up and appeal to you for help I will be out of a job in a few days—and am in debt now—been traiding Some and got flat Cant you help me Some— Court going on.—think you are out of danger have heard nothing to the Contrary—All well & doing well—money Matters Close & weather dry R R Coleman has moved to Waelder will assess for Hopkins—Dr Karnes was shot out at Tom Boothes—took for a Turkey yours

P M Hawkins

---

268. A. G. Weston to J. W. H.

Kerrville
1/18/95 TX
J W Hardin
Junction TX

Kind Sir and friend Know Nuse of interest only two Letters Has arrived to Date one to you and one to Gip of No importance and will Hold them
untill you arrive
Resp

A. G. Weston

---

269. Capt. Len L. Lewis to J. W. H.

London Tex
Jan 23rd 95
J. W. Hardin Kerrvill Tex

Dear Sir and friend
We arived Hom all OK — found the House all Rite = London is shore Dead = It Seemes that way to me and will be until Rain = comes = tell Callie to Send me a order for Her male their is a letter in the office for He from Her antie = Mrs Susie Westerman — thats my Sister — and I will Reed It and send it on = if she says So = ailso tell Her to tell mr Brewer to Turn Callies Letter Box over to me = tell Callie the Pigg is 0. Ok. the Colt is geting Gentle = Rite at once Bettie Wants to Hear from you and Callie = tell us How you air plesed with the Trip.

over

We Do Hope you air both Well plesed tell Callie for God Sak to Not Think of coming to see London until times changes = or She will Take the Blues in .3. ours = Let us Hear from you Ever chance
Best Wishes to Both
I am as Ever your Friend
Capt Len. L. Lewis

---

270. Sallie Clements Miller to J. W. H.

1- 26-95
Mr J W Hardin

Dear cousin I will Write you a few lines as Mr Miller is away. Received your Telegram & sent it to him. So you Will hear from him Soon he has gone away for a little While until he Recovers entirely. Were will you be in the corse of a few weeks say 3 weeks. We want you by that time Sure. we want you to visit us Any how. We are living now in Pecos city Mama is with us & joins us. me & My Little Son Claude in Much love & best wishes for your Future. as ever
Your affectionate cousin

Sallie Clements Miller

P.S. where & how is your 3 little ones. give them my love

S C M

---

271. J. B. Miller and Mart Hardin to J. W. H.

[UNDATED]

OFFICE OF
T. J. COGGIN,
DEALER IN
General Merchandise, Staple and Fancy Groceries.
C.M.COGGIN, SPECIALTIES: HAY AND GRAIN.
Manager.
(2)

Lordsburg., N. M.,____189

I guess you know that I have had so mutch trouble that I am intirely broken but considering all of that I have got lots of friend in Pecos. the best citizens of Pecos said they would make up a reasonable fee for you if you would come and Prosicute him.

—am here with one of our cousins Martin Hardin he was the one that was in the consperìcy case with me: Let me hear from you regular and at once

as ever yours

J.B. Miller

Cousin Johne

I would be glad to hear from you although I never saw you but I would like to see you and hear from you. it may be I can help you some time but am inhopes you will never need my assistance.

your Cousin

Mart Hardin

---

272. Annie Lewis to J. W. H.

London Tex Feb 5th 95

Mr Hardin and friend I felt Like I Wanted to Write you a few Lines— as = Paw was Writing = I am allways = glad to Hear from you —

and Would Kiss you if you Weair Hear = Hoping to hear from you Soon — No moore this time = But Will Write moore Next time—

Miss annie Lewis

---

273. A. G. Weston to J. W. H.

Kerr ville 2/5/95 Tx

J W Hardin Austin Texas

Kind Sir and friend Yours Recieved and was glad to here from you Will Have your Mail Sent you at once Bill Holman is en from London and ever thing is all ok you must write me and tell me How you are Geting a lon with your Book Would like So much to Be with you your friend Deel arrives En ——— All ok Am still on trade with thos Parties if Close out will write you will As ther is Know nuse of Intrest will close By wishing you all the good luck with your New under taking as evr you true friend

A. G. Weston

---

274. Bettie Lewis to J. W. H.

London kimble Co

Mr. J W Hardon March 4th 1895

Dear Son

I resceved your kind letter was glad to hire from you I have bin in bed sick 6 days. To day is is the first day I have set up I am so weak I cant hardly rite. The rest of the flamily air all well. Callie is washing to day. Callie seame to be dow heairted. I cant tell wother she has change eny or not. I let here go to one danc with green Denson but she did not dance eny That is the oinly time that she has evor went with eny one She stayes home with me all the time Callie is needing some cloth vrry bad and if you want to you can send

2

hire some money I would of bought cloth for her but I thought best not She would think that she was Just the same at home as she evor was / and I want to make her think that I wold not get hire eny thing. She is so yong and and so motch like a baby that I think think maby if you send her mone or her clolothing that she would see and think that you was the best friend that she has got if you send her eny money send it in my naim for you know as I do. that we dont no what she wold do She might leavle for she seames like she is wild all of the yong peapel air mad withe me becose I wont let Calie go to dances and go like she did befor she was mairred I alwys tell them she a maird woman and at hom with her mama is the place for her while hire husbond is gone I wil do evry thing for you. that I can you may rest assured that I am a true friend to you and that Callie will not have eny thing to do with eny oter men more than Just politness I would be glad to see you and Some day in the neaire future that I may see you and Callie liveing hapy with ech yoter.

I am so weake I will hopeing to hire frome you soone I am as evor your true friend and mother

Bettie Lewis

---

275. Capt. Len L. Lewis to J. S. H.

London Texas March 4th 95

J W Hardin Pecos Tex

Dear Sr and friend

I Reseved your Letter glad to Hear from you = Callie is just as you Left Her—She is full of Hell = We Have Keept Her at Home = But the Devil is in Hear What—and How She Will Com out is moor than I Can tell = I—Would Like to See you the = Town is improving and a Good Seson in the Ground = I — Sopose Green Denson = Can tell you moore News = than I Can = as He Has Ben around moore than I = I am geting along all Rite With male Contract = Denson Will moove Neear Junction City on the (6)th March Mager Spencers Son Comited Suside on—26th Day of Feb = Bad on the famly = old man Spencer Was a good friend to me Hoping to Hear from you Soon

I am as Ever your friend

Capt Len: L: Lewis

---

276. Captain Len L. Lewis to J. W. H.

London Texas March 23rd 95

J.W. Hardin Pacos Texas

Dear Sir

and Friend = I Reseved a Letter Some time ago But wating to see if thir was Eney change in Callie I See No change in Her She = Seems Just as you Left Her = you Said in your Letter you wanted me to Be plain in the matter I Dont think she will Become Satisfied with you = altho she may change Eney Day = Green Denson Has Not Ben since He come Back from the Pacos = Green can tell you moore and can Do moore with Callie than all of us Put to gether = I Hope she will Becom satisfied and make you a first clase wife = But I am at my End = = if Green Denson can't fix the matter Betewen you and Her we mite as well Let the matter sleep a while— Let me Hear from you I would Be Glad to meet you and Have along Talk = with you

Hoping to Hear from Soon—

Capt: Len. L. Lewis

P S Callie Has Just come in She tells me to Rite you = that she will Rite to you Next male

Hoping to Hear fromfrom yous Soon

Capt L L

---

277. R. M. Glover to J. W. H.

Smiley 5/18/95

Jno. W. Hardin El Paso

Dear Wes:

I have just seen your letter to the "Times" as copied by the Gonzales "Inquire" My Friend: let. me once more enjoin you to be cautious and guard well your ever act and word. your many friends here that know you and are acquainted with your honorable aim in life very mutch regret that you have found it necessary to again return to your old gaming life as they think that it will throw temptations in your way which could be avoided in the quiet practice of of your chosen profession. Write me a long letter and let me know how you are getting along. I hope you will not deem this piece of free advise presumptive on my part as you must know that I am prompted by oft expressed motives only. I am not one to "turn loose" because some one else dose and can only say that I entertain now all the

feelings of friendship heretofore expressed and have the utmost confidence in your honorable and manly aim, as expressed to me, and as evidenced by your acts while here. I believe however that you are more susceptible to temptation under certain influences than the ordinary man viz: whiskey cards & bad men (Claimed to be fighters &c) hence this unasked for advice. Remember: that wherever we be that there is a God, Whether it be in a Saloon Gaming room or elsewhere and that He holds us accountable for all our acts and is ready and willing to remove all difficulties and troubles, with kindest regards and love from wife & children to you I am as ever
sincerely your friend

R. M. Glover

---

278. J. B. Miller to J. W. H.

OFFICE OF BUCHHOLZ & COMPARET,
Cash Merchants THE TEXAS HOUSE, GALVESTON
Pecos, Texas, Jun th 2 1895
Mr. Joh. W. Hardin El Paso Tx

Dear Cousn
I write you in regad to the Red Fox
I wish you would find out whin He is comeing down this away
an let me no when He takes the train. an in case He intento
staye at at El Paso or not Write me at once an in case he
staertes on the train wair me then my mony will be on train
I will under stand it all ar well an join in love to you
as yor Bulia my regardes as—your cousin **J B Miller**

---

279. W. D. Allison to J. W. H.

OFFICE OF
W.D.ALLISON, SHERIFF & TAX COLLECTOR.
MIDLAND COUNTY.
JNO ALLISON, Deputy.

Midland, Texas, June 16 1895
J.W Hardin Esq El Paso Tex.

Dear Sir: Yours of recent date received. It being relation to John

Denson. and the Bail Bond Yourself and others are Sureties thereon. and while I would take pleasure in doing for you Gentlemen all that is in my power, yet I have to inform you that I Cannot do anything with our County Judge and County Attorney in this matter. Densons Case together with others was passed until next Friday the 19th at Which time they will be Called, and Unless Denson is here in person on a plea of guilty with guarantee of payment of fine and Costs is entered, a forfeiture will be taken. So the best instruction and information I can give, Is. that in the event it is certain to you gentlemen, that John will not appear, then you had better send me $50.00 to pay $25.00 fine and all Costs.and I will get someone to appear and plead guilty for him. Manning Clements is at my home this evening, wounded in right hip. "Flesh" Wound" from an accidental discharge of his pistol, While it is painful, yet it is not dangerous. and he shall have good Care. and attention, He Sat down on a cott. and pitched his pistol on a palate on The floor. and the hammer being on a cartridge, it was discharged.

Yours Truly. **W.D.Allison**
Sheriff

---

280. A. G. Weston to J. W. H.

(OFFICE OF)
TWO BROTHERS' SALOON A.G. WESTON, Proprieter
G.W. PARTON'S Private Stock.
SARATOGA, Belle of Bourdon.
Fine Imported and Domestic Wines, Liquors, Cigars, etc.

Kerrville, Texas, __**7/27**__ **189**__**5**__

Mr John Wesly Hardin Elpaso Tex

Kind Sir and friend. As I Have Not Heard from you En som time Will Write you No News of interest Ever thing very quiet John Taylor Got in som Serious trouble I am a witness a Ganst him and they Have Som Plain surcumstanteal Evidence Let Me Here how your Getting a long Seen En the paper where you Had Goten En som trouble Hoping you are out of it think I will Go to London soon and I will likly Call and See Mrs Callie Hardin and will Write you a Gain and tell you the Nuse Will close Hoping to Here from you soon Resp

A.G. Weston

281. J. D. Hargis to J. W. H.

OFFICE OF
J. H. Muenster.
Luling, Texas. July 28 1895

Dear Wes.
I rec'd your most kind and welcome letter this morning which found me all right
Was glad to know you were well I have no news to write this time as I have not Saw any of the folks since you left
We are getting dry here but had plenty of rain in the Spring Would like to see you very much
The P.P.s are all right here had a picnic on the 4th at Orang. about 2000 there the thing is beginning to warhi up again Wes when you get your life out I want you to give me all the Territory down here that I can possibly work I believe I could sell 2000 in Gonz Co. If you don't have any thing to do with the selling of the books I wish you would get me the agency any way there is no one that would take as much pleasure in Selling them amongst these folks as I would Wes I know you are very busy now but write to me when ever you can and let me know how you are getting along hoping to hear from you soon I remain as ever your Friend
J. D. Hargis
Dont forget me in regard to the above matter Jeff

El Paso Daily Times, Thursday, May 2, 1895.

CRUSHED TO DEATH

M BROWN MEETS A SUDDEN AND HORRIBLE DEATH.

Accident Which Resulted Fatally—His riends Deny That the Deceased Was runk—A High Tribute to the Dead.

...n the ex city jailor, met a ...rrible death yesterday ...nt of the city hall on ...et. Brown's term ...terday morning,

AROUND TOWN.

Mrs. Dr. Nellie Mayo has been granted a divorce from H. B. Mayo.

The vigilants were out last night looking after the morals of the city, and will, it is stated, seek some advertising in the courts today.

The bull fight next Sunday in Juarez will be for the benefit of the Mexican Mutual Protection Society of El Paso, Texas, and deserves a full house.

J. T. Gentry, who shot and killed one of two Mexicans who assaulted him at Plateau station, a few nights ago, gave bail yesterday in th... of $500.

... worth of ...fam- ...nd

HAS LOST HER NERVE.

El Paso is no Longer Bad Medicine as it Were

Last night a quiet game was opened up in the Gem building and the game was moving along smoothly when a visitor to the city dropped into the game and commenced losing and was behind a nice little sum when a dispute arose between the dealer and the stranger. The stranger with the remark: "Since you are trying to be so cute, just hand over the money I have lost here," placed the muzzle of a ferocious looking pistol in the dealer's face. This created a stampede at the table which was promptly deserted by every one except the two principals in the little play. The dealer winked his other eye t the muzzle of the savage looking ... and remarked:

...hy, yes, sir, you can get just ... want."

...

EL PASO DAILY H

Second Edition

El PASO, TEXAS, TUESDAY AUGUST 20, 1895.

V. FLOURNOY, VICE PRESIDENT
…LLIAMS, ASST. CASHIER.

BANK

WES HARDIN IS KILLED.

This Noted Character Dies by John Selman's Pistol.

THE FATE OF ALL BAD KILLERS.

The First Bullet Hit Him in the Eye and Passed Through his Brain.—A Sketch of Hardin's Life in Brief by one who has Known Him Since Boyhood.

Last night between 11 and 12 o'clock San Antonio street was thrown into an intense state of excitement by the sound of four pistol shots that occured …the Acme saloon. Soon the crowd … against the door and there, lay the body of John Wes… …'s blood flowing over the … oozing out a pistol … though his …

What Met…
Silver……
Lead……
Copper……
Mexican pesos, El Pas…
" " Juarez

Some shots were f…
down.
Mr. E. L. Shack…
follows:
My name is E. L. …
in the general b…
When I came dow…
evening I had und…
parties that Mr. Ha…
threats against Mr…
formerly been in …
a friend of mine an…
Acme saloon when…
man. At the time …
he was in the saloon…
er parties and was d…
I told him I…
was occasion for hi…
and having heard t…
man with whom he…
I advised him as a f…
der the influence of…
out on the sidewalk…
to the saloon, I bel…
ahead of Mr. Selma…
the back of the sal…
shots fired. I can't…
shots as I did not se…
around but left imm…
…as full of powder s…
have seen anyth…

5-2-1895

HAS LOST HER NERVE.

El Paso is no Longer Bad Medicine as it Were

Last night a quiet game was opened up in the Gem building and the game was moving along smoothly when a visitor to the city dropped into the game and commenced losing and was behind a nice little sum when a dispute arose between the dealer and the stranger. The stranger with the remark: "Since you are trying to be so cute, just hand over the money I have lost here," placed the muzzle of a ferocious looking pistol in the dealer's face. This created a stampede at the table which was promptly deserted by every one except the two principals in the little play. The dealer winked his other eye at the muzzle of the savage looking gun and remarked:

"Why, yes, sir, you can get just what you want."

A venturesome bystander, who had remained on the scene, and who furnished the reporter with the particulars, said:

"And the dealer proceeded to count out money. When he had counted $95 the stranger raked it into his pocket and strolled leisurely out of the room. I tell you El Paso has lost her nerve and she can't try to play tough any more. Two years ago no man on earth could have walked into a house in this city and held up a game in that style and got out of the house alive. No, sir, El Paso is no good any more. She is cornered, and I wouldn't be at all surprised to see the stranger hold up the entire police force. Why the other night he took charge of a jack pot in a social game of poker in the same manner, and there was not grit enough in the crowd to make a kick, and I guess if I had been there I would have broke the door down getting out."

—These two pages courtesy *El Paso Times Daily Herald*

El Paso Daily Times, Saturday, May 4, 1895.

THEY DID IT.

THE CITY COUNCIL ACCEPTS THE TIMES' BID

Without the Consent of the Dying Herald—A Very Busy Session of the Council Last Night—The Lighting of the City Receives a Passing Notice.

The city council met in regular session last night at the appointed hour with Mayor Ca— presiding and the fol— present: — Messr—

Alderman Davis thought it was a good idea to have the bills read.

Mrs. M. Taylor's claim for $750 damages on account of the overflow of the acequia was referred to the acequia committee.

A report from the city board of health was approved.

The bill of the American Fire Engine company for $1,415.15 was referred to the finance committee.

Leave of absence was granted to Alderman Stewart for two weeks.

THE CITY PRINTING

The sealed bids for — were opened and rea—

We agree to p—

—siderable kicking — to what — should be sprinkled, and his motion the matter be referred to the fir— water committee carried.

The council then adjourned.

John Wesley Hardin's Say.

To the people of El Paso, a— everyone to whom it may conce— have noticed several articles in Times and Tribune refl— c— character as a man. I wish to ann— —ight now that in the past my onl— — has been to be a —

—quisi— —mittee.

A report from the city board of health was approved.

The bill of the American Fire Engine company for $1,415.15 was referred to the finance committee.

Leave of absence was granted to Alderman Stewart for two weeks.

THE CITY PRINTING.

The sealed bids for city printing were opened and read as follows:

We agree to print and publish in the El Paso Daily Times, the leading newspaper of this city, issued every morning except Monday, all your ordinances, notices, proclamations and tax lists at a rate equal to one fifth of the wholesale rate charged to merchants and business men whose liberal patronage we enjoy—that is at one cent per line for each insertion in Brevier or reading matter type. When merchants contract with us for 1000 lines they receive a wholesale rate of five cents per line. We ask one fifth of that price. We have had the city printing at that price twice in the past few years. Yours respectfully,

TIMES PUBLISHING CO
THOS. O'KEEFFE.

The EVENING TIMES makes the following bid for city printing for one year as per your call:

Reading matter in Brevier per line, each insertion, one cent; in Nonpariel per line, each insertion two cents.

Table matter in Brevier per inch, each insertion, 12 cents; in Nonpariel per inch, each insertion, 15 cents.

A complete bound file of papers furnished the city at the expiration of contract.

MCKIE & LAMB,
EVENING TIMES.

The Tribune's bid on printing is as follows: Brevier three cents an inch on each insertion; Nonpariel four cents an inch each insertion; table work double price. All Nonpariel new and never been used. Respectfully,

E. P. LOWE.

A recess of five minutes was taken to consider the bids and when the time had expired the mayor called the council to order.

Alderman Shutz moved that the TIMES' bid be accepted.

Alderman Whitmore moved to amend by referring the matter to a special committee. The motion was lost.

The motion of Alderman Schutz declaring the TIMES the official paper of the city was carried and a resolution to that effect adopted.

A requisition from the city clerk was referred to the finance committee with power to act.

The official bonds of Chief Fink, Captain Frank Carr, J. B. Chipman, J. M. —kinne, I. E. Archer and T. D. Feath— — were approved.

John Wesley Hardin's Say.

To the people of El Paso and to everyone to whom it may concern: I have noticed several articles in the TIMES and Tribune reflecting on my character as a man. I wish to announce right now that in the past my only ambition has been to be a man and you bet I draw my own idea, and while I have not always come up to my standard, yet I have no kick to make against myself for default. My present and my future ambition is no higher than it has been in the past and I wish to say right now that whether in a gambling house or a saloon, and El Paso seems to be crowded with these places, my only aim is to acquit myself manly and bravely. And as to the Acme jack pot, I would not stand a hold out and got the pot without even threatening violence or drawing a gun. As to the Gem hold-up on craps, after I had lost a considerable sum I was grossly insulted by the dealer in a hurrah manner, hence I told him he could not win my money and hurrah me too, and that as he had undertook to hurrah me he could deliver me the money I had played and you bet he did it. And when he had counted out the $95 I said that is all I want, just my money and no more. He said all right Mr. Hardin, and when I left the room and had gotten half way down stairs I returned, hearing words of condemnation of my play. I said to every one in the house and connected with the play, I understand from the reflective remarks that some of you disapprove my play. Now if this be so be men and get in line and show your manhood, to which no one made any reply, but others nodded that I was right and that they approved my play. Now some one has asked for my pedigree. Well, he is to gross too notice, but I wish to say right here, once and for all, that I admire pluck, push and virtue where ever found. Yet I contempt and despise a coward and assassin of character, whether he be a reporter, a journalist or a gambler. And while I came to El Paso to prosecute Bud Frazier and did do it on as high a plane as possible, I am here now to stay. I have bought an interest in the Wigwam saloon and you, who, whether in El Paso or elsewhere, that admire pluck, that desire fairplay, are cordially invited to call at the Wigmam where you will have everything done to make it pleasant for you. All are especially invited to our blowout on the evening of the 4th.

Now I have no apology to make to any one for my acts over a jack pot or a crap game, but solicit everybody's custom and guarantee fair play.

JOHN [illegible]. HARDIN.

At the Wigwam

(may 4–1895)

Twelve pounds of Sugar,
Six packages Rolled Oats,
for One D—

Six Cans Eagle Milk,
for One I—

Seven Cakes White Star So—
One can Price's 12 oz.
1 can 10lb Pure Leaf Lard,
5 packages Rolled Oats
for Two D—

Everything else from a — stock of Staple and Fanc— —ceries in same proportion.

White House Gro—

213 El Paso street.

MANY MEN of MANY MINDS

MOUNT MONARCH—

Easy to Bu—

Easy to Ri—

The Clark-Whitson-—
MUSIC COMPAN—
119 San Francisco S—

Money Loa—
—ON—
ECQUITABLE T—

Do you desire to pay off a — and reborrow the money at 5 — interest annually? Would yo— buy your family a home? If — write

F. J. WIL—
218 Myrtle street, El Pas—

MEXICAN

OPAL—

—Courtesy *El Paso Times Daily Herald*

Index

Chronological Calendar of Letters

PHASE 1

Year 1876

LETTER NO. PAGE

1. Sept. 8, 1876 3

From J. W. H. to Jane

He tells her that he is well and is looking for a place for them, and to be cautious.

2. Sept. 8, 1876 3

From Jn Smith, J. W. H. to A True Friend, John

About Jane and family's care, and the fever panic in Jacksonville. Writes, "No use to try to talk you with Black and White."

Year 1877

3. May 6, 1877. 5

From Joshua Bowen to Jane Swain (Hardin)

Discusses who was killed in the Sutton-Taylor feud, and who is in jail. Tells of destroying the letter.

4a. & b. May 9, 1877 5

From R. E. Barnett and Mattie to J. H. Swain and Jane Hardin

He speaks of family affairs. Says there is a lot of "Murdering stealing & mobbing going on in the state."

5. June 6, 1877 7

From JWH Swain [Hardin] to Mrs Jane Swain (Hardin)

The only money he has is "Scrip;" discusses family concerns. Says he "does see an opening."

6. Aug. 25, 1877. 8

From J. H. Swain, (Hardin) to Jane

He describes his arrest in Pensacola, Florida. Tells Jane "to be cautious in writing."

17. Oct. 14, 1877 21
From Mattie Hardin to Mrs. Jane Hardin
This letter says John was tried and the jury brought in a verdict of murder in the second degree. The penalty: Twenty-five years in the penitentiary.

18. Undated 22
From J. A. Lipscomb to (not indicated)
A lawyer speaks of getting John's case "Reversed."

19. Oct. 26, 1877 22
From Elizabeth Hardin to J. W. Hardin
She tells him that there was a plot made to kill him on the day of the Webb killing.

20. Oct. 26, 1877 25
From William and Mat Bowen to Jane Hardin
Mat Says Wes has taken an appeal to the higher court.

21. Undated 26
From E. Hardin to Johnnie
Says that the decision at Comanche was cruel.

22. Oct. 29, 1877 26
From M. Hardin to J. W. Hardin
Tells of Webb's possible motive for going to Comanche at the "Time of the difficulty."

23. Nov. 21, 1877 27
From Mattie Smith to J. W. Hardin
Mattie says her husband will give Jane all directions regarding how to come to their home.

24. Nov. 25, 1877 28
From Mattie Smith to Mrs. Jane Hardin
She tells Jane where they live, and that John did not get justice at Comanche.

25. Nov. 26, 1877 29
From M. Hardin to J. W. Hardin
Says he should have been cleared by the evidence, and that he will need a lawyer for the "Supreme Court."

26. Undated 30
From Elizabeth Hardin to John W. Hardin
She tells him that she has a true statement about an eyewitness to the killing of Deputy Webb.

PHASE 2

Year 1882

Year 1886

Year 1887

Year 1888

Year 1889

Year 1892

Year 1895

CPSIA information can be obtained
at www.ICGtesting.com
Printed in the USA
BVHW091956140122
626227BV00004B/63

9 781571 686220